THE ENIGMA OF MARY STUART

THE ENIGMA OF MARY STUART

Compiled and edited

by

IAN B. COWAN

LONDON
VICTOR GOLLANCZ LIMITED
1971

© Ian B. Cowan 1971

ISBN 0 575 00674 9

PRINTED IN GREAT BRITAIN
BY EBENEZER BAYLIS & SON LIMITED
THE TRINITY PRESS, WORCESTER, AND LONDON

To Anna

CONTENTS

ACKNOWLEDGEMENTS

For permission to reprint copyright matter the following acknowledgements are gratefully made:
B. T. Batsford Ltd., for extracts from *Scottish Kings* and *The First Trial of Mary Queen of Scots*, both by Gordon Donaldson; A. and C. Black Ltd., for extracts from *The Casket Letters* by T. F. Henderson; Cambridge University Press for extracts from *Mary Queen of Scots* and *The Tragedy of Kirk o'Field* both by R. H. Mahon, and extracts from *A History of Scotland* by C. S. Terry; Jonathan Cape Ltd., and the executors of the estate of Conyers Read for extracts from *Mr. Secretary Cecil and Queen Elizabeth* and *Lord Burghley and Queen Elizabeth*, both by Conyers Read; Jonathan Cape Ltd., and the author for extracts from *Queen Elizabeth* by Sir John Neale; Cassell and Co. Ltd., for extracts from *The Queen of Scots* by Stefan Zweig; Clarendon Press, Oxford, for extracts from *Mr. Secretary Walsingham and the policy of Queen Elizabeth* by Conyers Read, for extracts from *John Knox* by Jasper Ridley, and extracts from *The Reign of Elizabeth 1558–1603* by J. B. Black; Collins, Publishers for extracts from *Lord Bothwell* by R. Gore-Brown; Columbia University Press Ltd., for extracts from *James Stewart, earl of Moray* by Maurice Lee; Company of Scottish History for various extracts from articles in *The Scottish Historical Review*; Edinburgh University Press for extracts from *The Tyrannous Reign of Mary Stewart* by W. Gatherer; Hodder and Stoughton Ltd., for extracts from *Mary Queen of Scots* by D. Hay Fleming; Hutchinson Publishing Group for extracts from *Mary Queen of Scots* by T. F. Henderson; Robert Maclehose and Co. Ltd., for extracts from *Politics and Religion* by W. L. Mathieson; Scottish History Society for extracts from *Papal Negotiations with Mary Queen of Scots, Queen Mary's Letter to the Duke of Guise* and *Mary Queen of Scots and the Babington Plot* all three by J. H. Pollen; Scottish Text Society for extracts from *The Poems of Alexander*

1*

Scott, ed. by J. Cranston and *Satirical Poems of the Time of the Reformation,* ed. by J. Cranston; Weidenfeld and Nicolson Ltd., for extracts from *Mary Queen of Scots* by Lady Antonia Fraser; and Vision Press Ltd., for extracts from *The Casket Letters* by M. H. Armstrong Davison.

PREFACE

Theories as to the guilt or innocence of Mary, queen of Scots, have been as varied and multifarious as their authors, for if the basic evidence for and against the queen has little changed through-out the centuries, the attitude of writers towards that evidence has evolved from generation to generation. In the following pages an attempt has been made by means of an introductory analysis to sketch these changes of attitude, which are also illustrated by extracts from works on Mary written throughout the centuries. These extracts serve a two-fold purpose, for their interest is not only historiographical but also clearly illustrative of the enigma of Mary Stuart. (The Anglo-French form of the name as that most commonly adopted by Mary herself has been used throughout the introductory material, although the Scottish form 'Stewart' will be found in many of the citations. A similar disparity will be found with the title, the earl of Moray, the holder of which is frequently and inaccurately referred to as 'Murray'.) Every argument in favour of Mary's innocence can be countered by one against, and if in the introductory material which prefaces each of the controversial sections of Mary's life into which the contents are divided, the author unwittingly displays his own partiality, it is to be hoped that the reader will find the proper corrective, or rather the theory which satisfies his own particular inclination, in the extracts which follow. This much is certain, there can be no finality of judgement where Mary Stuart is concerned; and of this Elizabeth seems almost to have had foreknowledge when she dubbed her adversary 'The Daughter of Debate'.

For help in compiling this anthology I owe much to the assistance of the staffs of the National Library of Scotland, University of Glasgow Library and Baillies Institution, Glasgow. I am also indebted to Dr. W. Ferguson of the University of Edinburgh and Dr. T. I. Rae of the National Library of Scotland for their helpful criticism of my text.

University of Glasgow   IAN B. COWAN

INTRODUCTION

For over four centuries Mary, queen of Scots, has been the subject of countless works of literature and history, for her life has appealed as much to writers in a romantic genre as to those who see in it an opportunity for examining the religious conflict which was to split Europe for many generations. The element of religious propaganda was to be more to the fore in the centuries immediately following Mary's death, but even in later works in which the causation of her downfall comes to be examined in political rather than religious terms, bias of one kind or another is seldom absent and such accounts frequently display many of the traits and attitudes created in the sixteenth century.

Even before her death Mary attracted much attention from writers, but not until her marriage with Darnley in 1565 did the controversial issues begin to emerge which have ever since attracted authors and readers alike. Nevertheless, partisanship is not entirely absent even in the early eulogies: French poets such as Pierre de Ronsard in his royal panegyrics and Michel L'Hôpital in his epithalamium, *Carmen* (written on the occasion of Mary's marriage with the Dauphin in 1558) favoured a union between Scotland and France, but two Scots poets (George Buchanan in his *Epithalamium* and Sir Richard Maitland in his poem *Off the Queen's Maryage with the Dolphin of France*) looked with disfavour on the political implications of this alliance. On the political side Maitland, followed in 1562 by Alexander Scott in his *Ane New Yeir Gift to the Quene Mary when sche come first Hame*, also tendered political advice to their queen, urging her to choose upright advisers and to make a good marriage, husband and statesman alike evidently to be of Protestant persuasion. In the same year, however, Ninian Winzet in his *Certane Tractatis* made a plea for a pro-Catholic policy. Otherwise personal eulogy was the prime consideration and Mary's departure from France, following the

death of her husband Francis II in 1560, and the assumption of
her queenly duties in Scotland after her arrival there in 1561,
made little change in the romantic trifles proffered by the queen's
admirers.

But with Mary's marriage to Darnley, which reinforced the
Stuart claim to the English succession, new attitudes emerged and
these eulogies began to be tinged with echoes of political realities.
Thus a Scotsman, Sir Thomas Craig, in an *Epithalamium* was to
place his hopes in a possible union of England and Scotland,
whereas English writers reacted against the possibility by project-
ing several counter-arguments against that eventuality.

The question of Mary's marriage not only raised issues of international significance but also highlighted the important domestic
issue of religious affiliation. In the event, the Darnley marriage
alarmed Protestants, who feared a resurgence of Catholicism; but
this was seldom openly revealed as the reason for a new hostility
towards the queen. Instead she was attacked in works such as
Thomas Jeney's *Master Randolphes Phantasy* for allowing her immoderate passion to outstrip her reason in engaging in such a
union. On the other hand, Mary's co-religionists, like Peter
Frarin in *An Oration against the Unlawful Insurrections of the
Protestantes of our time under pretence to Refourme Religion* (Ant-
werp, 1566), saw in the marriage hope for Catholicism, and were
able to utilise the murder of Riccio by the protestant lords to
accuse them under the leadership of the queen's half-brother, the
earl of Moray, of launching an attack on an innocent queen.
Mary's innocence, however, even amongst her friends, was to be
much in doubt after the murder of Darnley and her marriage to
Bothwell in 1567. Thereafter contemporary supporters of the
queen were at a marked disadvantage in relation to their opponents, such as the ballad writer Robert Sempill, who were able to
attack Mary as an adulterous whore and thereby justify her
enforced abdication.

This line of attack was to be developed throughout the years of
Mary's imprisonment, and was assisted by Elizabeth's determination that the principle of inviolate sovereignty should not be under-
mined, a fact which led to the suppression of publication in London in 1587 of John Knox's *History of the Reformation in Scotland*.
For this reason, Mary's moral shortcomings were made the only

test of her right to rule, and her reputation besmirched in order that even Catholics would find it difficult to support her cause. But significantly in England works in this vein were only allowed to circulate unofficially lest sovereignty itself should fall into disrepute —a reminder of the precariousness of Elizabeth's position.

The most famous of such attacks was George Buchanan's *Ane detectioun of the doinges of Marie quene of Scottes* which was first published in Latin and Scots in 1571, with other editions including a French translation in the following year. This bitter attack on Mary became the standard work behind most contemporaneous works such as Thomas Wilson's *Actio contra Mariam*, which was published with the *Detectioun*, and in conjunction with Buchanan's later works *De Jure Regni apud Scotos* (Edinburgh, 1579) and his history of Scotland entitled *Rerum Scoticarum Historia* (Edinburgh, 1582), in which he expanded his case against Mary, was to provide the basis for many of the subsequent attacks upon the queen. If, however, immorality was an acceptable reason for deposition, Mary alive, even if imprisoned, constituted a threat to Protestantism through her claim to the English throne. Even in the eyes of her enemies, her Catholicism came to outweigh her moral shortcomings as her chief crime, and only a short time after her deposition works such as Nicholas Barnaud's *Dialogues* (Edinburgh, 1574) advocated her execution.

If Mary's Catholicism came to be her chief sin in the eyes of her enemies, it also came to constitute her chief virtue in the eyes of her defenders, who, once they were able to elude the matter of her apparent shortcomings, seized upon the political and religious factors in the queen's life as their chief form of defence. The most important of these was *A Defence of the honour of the right highe, mightye and noble Princesse Marie Quene of Scotland* (London, 1569) which was written by John Leslie, bishop of Ross. The author, a personal admirer of Mary, defended her character and career as queen of Scots and advocated the general right of women, including Elizabeth to rule, adding, however, Mary's particular claim to succeed Elizabeth on the throne of England, a point that was most strongly emphasised in a revised edition of the *Defence* printed at Liege in 1571 under the pseudonym of Philippes Morgan. These themes were taken up by others, notable among whom was David Chambers, a senator of the Scottish College of

Justice and an ardent supporter of Mary who in his *Discours de la legitime succession des femmes aux possessions de leurs parens* (Paris, 1579) relies heavily upon Leslie's *Defence*. In that work Mary's faith was not the central issue, but the final step in this direction was taken in 1578 when Leslie published in Rome his Latin History of Scotland—*De origine, moribus et rebus gestis Scotorum* (Rome, 1578) in the dedication of which, the theme of religious martyrdom and Mary's suffering for the faith had become predominant.

Even before her execution political rather than religious issues still remained uppermost as in Adam Blackwood's *Apologia pro Regibus* (Poitiers, 1581) in which he defended the queen's sovereignty and condemned her deposition by heretics; but others, such as Nicholas Sanders, whose *Rise and Growth of the Anglican Schism* was published posthumously in Latin (Rheims, 1585) and William Allen, in his tract *A True Sincere and Modest Defence of English Catholiques* (Ingolstadt, 1584), ably took up the religious theme which after the queen's execution was to become dominant.

With Mary's death, all hopes of a Catholic succession came to an end, as did the plots designed to replace Elizabeth on the throne. Leslie, whose work had always been politically motivated, retired from the fray to be succeeded by others no less valiant in her cause, whose purpose, like that of Saunders and Allen, was to utilise the queen's story as a means of promoting the cause of the counter-Reformation. In this cause Mary's execution was no less important than her imprisonment in England, while the actual events leading to her deposition in Scotland were pushed further and further into the background, seldom extending beyond the discussion of the right of subjects to depose their kings.

Mary's opponents quickly responded to claims based on the queen's Catholicism. Even before her execution the official case against her was being mounted, the indictment being carefully framed in order to avoid the charge that Mary's chief crime was her religion, this being all the more easily refuted after the execution solved this particular dilemma. Thus, while Mary's deposition and loss of sovereignty could still be attributed to her immorality, her treasonable activities in England described in works such as Richard Crompton's *A short declaration of the ende of traytors, and false conspirators against the state* (London, 1587) became the chief reason for her execution. Without impugning her Catholicism, Mary could thus be made to appear as a sinister political figure who had broken the laws of God and man, and it was in this guise Mary was to be presented to the world in numerous publications based on the official account of the execution prepared by Robert Wingfield.

The struggle thereafter largely centred around accounts of Mary's final hours, the Catholic supporters on their part seizing upon every word or phrase which might promote their case for religious martyrdom. Most successful in this attempt was Adam Blackwood, one of Mary's more reckless champions, who in his most important work *Martyre de la royne d'Escosse* (Edinburgh or Paris, 1587) recorded Mary's sufferings at the hands of the English from 1561 to her death, a theme to which he returned in his *La Mort de la Royne d'Escosse* (Paris, 1588). In both of these works, praise of Mary is unstinted while his castigation of the English government was skilfully brought about by a judicious selection of details favourable to his cause and a liberal smattering of mistruths such as the allegation that Riccio's murder was instigated on the advice of the English Privy Council. The importance of both volumes is incalculable: they immediately became, in conjunction with the works of John Leslie, the standard authorities for all pro-Marian writers, beginning with the poet Robert Southwell. To these basic works subsequent champions were not averse to adding details of their own invention.

But for the accession of Mary's son to the throne of England in 1603, as James I, the battle lines might have remained drawn with Mary's supporters on one side stressing her Catholicism and sufferings for the faith and her opponents on the other relying upon her immorality in Scotland and treasonable activities in England as the dual causes of her final downfall. The accession of a Protestant sovereign finally terminated the wider hopes of Catholicism which Mary had at one time personified, but equally inevitably it brought to an end the more vitriolic attacks on Mary herself, as with her son on the throne, the charges of immorality were necessarily forgotten and even treason was a dangerous line of pursuit as it might be held to question the Stuart claim to the throne of England. In these circumstances, Protestant writers turned to a more romantic genre of depicting an unfortunate queen whose downfall had been brought about by the caprice of fortune, while Mary's part in the various plots was reduced to a natural desire to escape rather than motivated by malice towards Elizabeth.

For these reasons, seventeenth century writers proved, on the whole, kindly towards Mary; Catholic writers continued in the Blackwood tradition while Protestants, as long as the Stuarts remained on the throne, tried to find a *via media* which would appease their sovereigns. Thus, although William Camden in his *Annals* (2 vols., London, 1615) selected material on Mary from both Protestant and Catholic sources, the latter on the whole was preferred as being more kindly disposed to the picture of Mary he was trying to present. Likewise William Udall, writing under the pseudonym of William Stranguage, in *The historie of the life and death of Marie Stuart, Queene of Scotland* (London, 1625) refuted Buchanan on the matter of Darnley's death, depicted Mary's marriage to Bothwell as one she was driven into by adverse circumstance and, in glossing over her execution, was more concerned in stressing that her condemnation in no way prejudiced James' right of succession than in assessing her guilt or innocence. If Camden and Udall prudently preferred Leslie's version of Mary's reign to that of Buchanan, Scottish historians were not so disposed, and even John Spottiswoode, who was commissioned by James VI to write his *History of the Church of Scotland* (London, 1655), if somewhat circumspect in associating Mary with Darnley's murder, follows Mary's sternest critic in ascribing her downfall to the 'violence of passion' for Bothwell, as did inevitably *The true history of the Church of Scotland* (Rotterdam, 1678) by David Calderwood, a staunch presbyterian to whom Leslie's arguments were 'but fretting and fooming . . . and impertinent harangs'. It is not without significance, however, that the latter was published at Rotterdam long after the author's death, while Spottiswoode's *History* appeared in the Cromwellian period, in which was also published *Cabala, sive scrinia sacra: mysteries of state and government in letters of illustrious persons* (London, 1654), which included certain information shedding new light on Mary's cause. Otherwise Protestant historians were either tactful or too much occupied with the disputes of the seventeenth century to re-examine the history of the Scottish queen.

This role instead was left to Mary's champions abroad. Prominent among those were G. Conn, *Vitae Mariae Stuartae* (Rome, 1624) and N. Caussin, *L'Histoire de l'incomparable Reyne Marie Stuart* (Paris, 1645). But the most successful was Pierre de Bourdeille, abbé de Brantôme, who died in 1614, though his work *Vies des Dames Illustries* was not published until 1665 (6 vols., Leyden, 1665–66). In many ways the work is derivative from Blackwood's but as a new romantic twist was frequently given to the events described, Brantôme's work, even more than his models to whose conclusions he imparted a new importance, has contributed more than any other similar work to the picture of a romantic and beautiful queen.

All in all, the seventeenth century saw a refurbishing of Mary's image. But in Britain this process was to be halted by the Popish plot of 1681 which inspired *A Brief History of the Life of Mary Queen of Scots and the occasions that brought her and Thomas Duke of Norfolk to their Tragical ends* . . . (T. Cockerill, London, 1681). A volume described by a pro-Marian as 'a folio containing a life of the Scottish queen, the old lampoons, the plots of the papists, the trials of Norfolk, and of Arundel, with similar types of party device'! While this may have been partially offset by the publication of Sir James Melville's *Memoirs of his own life, 1549–93* (London, 1683) edited by George Scott which was sympathetic to Mary and her cause, the Revolution of 1688 determined a marked change of attitude. This was heralded in 1689 by a reprinting of Buchanan's *Detectioun* which was soon followed by the first English translation of his *History*. Particular attacks on Mary ensued and in 1699 *A relation of the death of David Rizzi* (London, 1699), written by Patrick, lord Ruthven, one of the principals of the murder, was published with prefatory material from Buchanan concerning Riccio.

In the early eighteenth century Mary's detractors continued to further their cause but only against growing opposition. David Crawfurd, the Scottish historiographer royal, rose to Mary's defence in *Memoirs of the Affairs of Scotland* (London, 1706) and also in his anonymously published *A Vindication of Mary, queen of Scots, from the foul aspersions of Buchanan*, but his defence left much to be desired. Indeed, almost a century later, the publication by Malcolm Laing of *The Historie of James the Sext* (Edinburgh,

1804) proved that the *Memoirs*, which were supposedly based
upon the original manuscript of this work, had been manipulated
to support Crawfurd's case. Nevertheless, his preface has been
described as 'the first systematic pro-Marian answer to Buchanan's
libels'. This attack upon Buchanan was furthered in a more
scholarly fashion in Thomas Ruddiman's edition of Buchanan's
Opera Omnia (Edinburgh, 1715). In his attack upon Buchanan's
integrity, Ruddiman's scholarship was undoubted, but so too
were his Jacobite sympathies, and the controversies which ensued
were frequently dominated by political considerations. If this
controversy was somewhat arid, it led to further editions of the
Detectioun, and interest in the subject had undoubtedly been
rekindled. Further impetus was given to this revival by the publication in 1725 of Samuel Jebb's *De Vita et Rebus Gestis Mariae*
(2 vols., London, 1725). This was a collection of treatises relating
to Mary ranging from the anti-Marian *Detectioun* to pro-Marian
continental works such as Caussin's *L'Histoire* and Chambers'
Discours de la legitime succession des femmes. If anything Jebb's
collection tended to advance Mary's cause. A more balanced selection is to be found in James Anderson's *Collections relating to
Mary, queen of Scots* (4 vols., Edinburgh, 1727–28), which included Leslie's *Defence* and other pro-Marian pieces. Nevertheless, one of Mary's later apologists thought that Anderson's work
had been compiled to 'disgrace the queen for ever'. Irrespective of
the motive behind their compilation, both these works were to
become keystones in later Marian controversy, while in comparison
two lives of Mary, *The Secret History of Mary Stuart*—a series of
eulogies translated from French by Eliza Haywood (Edinburgh,
1725) and James Freebairn, *Life of Mary Stewart* (Edinburgh,
1725), both of which attempted to vindicate Mary, were to quickly
fade from public view.

On the other hand the publication of the first accurate edition
of Knox's *History* (Edinburgh, 1732), a work in which Mary is
not allowed any credit whatever, gave fresh impetus to the anti-
Marians. The balance was to be partially restored with the appearance of Robert Keith's *The history of the affairs of church and state
in Scotland from the beginning of the reformation . . . to the retreat of
Queen Mary into England, anno 1568* (Edinburgh, 1734). This
gave to scholars another massive compilation of documents from

which Bishop Keith wove the history of the reign of Mary. Her downfall he tended to ascribe to the turbulence of the Scottish nobility and the caprice of fortune, although he graciously acknowledged that Mary's acts may have contributed to the disasters which beset her.

Much of the interest aroused by Jebb's and Anderson's volumes revolved around the Casket Letters which came to be seen as central to the establishment of Mary's guilt or innocence. In 1754 Mary found a new champion in Walter Goodall who pronounced his interest in his title: *An examination of the letters said to be written by Mary, queen of Scots, to James, earl of Bothwell; shewing by intrinsick and extrinsick evidence that they are forgeries* (2 vols., Edinburgh, 1754). Goodall's evidence was largely philological and directed towards disproving that the French copies of the Casket Letters were copied verbatim from the lost originals. This he succeeded in doing, proving beyond doubt that the French copies had themselves been translated from versions in Scots, and as Goodall averred Mary would not have written in Scots, he could conclude the letters were fabricated. Unfortunately for the controversy while the first part of Goodall's thesis was incontrovertible for at least some of the letters, his arguments did not apply to all. Mary's detractors were able to argue in relation to the others that the Scot's versions were also translations from the original French, a re-conversion into French having taken place at a later date. The battle of the historians was thereafter enjoined in earnest and while David Hume, in spite of his Stuart bias, in his *History of England under the House of Tudor* (2 vols., London, 1759) and William Robertson in his *History of Scotland* (2 vols., London, 1759) contended on the ground that the writing had been recognised as Mary's that the letters were genuine, William Tytler in his *An historical and critical enquiry into the evidence against Mary, queen of Scots* (Edinburgh, 1760) rose to the queen's defence and refuted both Robertson and Hume. Tytler's position was not far removed from Goodall's, but Robertson refused to be drawn into controversy and while Hume attempted to parley with his opponent, Tytler undoubtedly had the best of the affray. Much ill-will had, however, been engendered in this contest and already by 1773, Sir David Dalrymple, Lord Hailes, could express the view in his *Annals of Scotland* (3 vols., London, 1797) that 'the Marian controversy has already become too angry and too voluminous'; but with battle joined it was inevitable that the struggle should continue, Dalrymple himself coming down on the side of the anti-Marian faction in his *Miscellaneous Remarks on 'The Enquiry into the evidence against Mary, queen of Scots'* (London, 1784). Three years later, however, John Whitaker, building upon Goodall and the apologist Gilbert Stuart's *History of Scotland* (London, 1782), published *Mary, queen of Scots Vindicated* (3 vols., London, 1787) his conclusions being followed by Thomas Crawford in *The History of Mary Queen of Scots* (Edinburgh, 1793). If anything the struggle had become more bitter and Whitaker's and Crawford's prejudices, which allowed no shadow of criticism to be levelled at Mary did little to abate the intensity of feeling on either side.

The early nineteenth century historians continued the feud in the same angry tone as their predecessors, some of whom they chose to ignore while others they slavishly copied. Thus Malcolm Laing in his *History of Scotland with a preliminary dissertation on the participation of Mary, Queen of Scots, in the Murder of Darnley* (4 vols., London, 1804), based most of his thesis upon Robertson's conclusions, little attention being paid to the criticisms of Whitaker. George Chalmers in his *Life of Mary Queen of Scots* (2 vols., London, 1818), a tedious and diffuse work which he believed would close the Marian controversy, reversed the process by uncritically following Whitaker's *Vindication*, inevitably coupling this with a further refutation of Hume and Robertson. Yet another resurrection followed. Hugh Campbell in *The love letters of Mary, Queen of Scots, with her love sonnets* (London, 1824), republished eleven letters previously printed in 1726 by Edward Simmonds as *The Genuine Letters of Mary Queen of Scots to James Earl of Bothwell* (Westminster, 1726). The spuriousness of these had never been doubted, but Chalmers had to expose them afresh in his *A detection of the love letters lately attributed to Mary* (London, 1825). The case for or against Mary had by this time become stereotyped, many of the combatants being content to repeat conjectures and opinions derived at second or third hand, and works such as Henry Glasford Bell's pro-Marian *Life of Mary, queen of Scots* (2 vols., Edinburgh, 1828) which contained chronological inaccuracies and self-contradictory evidence did little to advance the Marian controversy.

A significant change began about this date, however, as the discovery and publication of new source material opened up new horizons to the contestants on both sides. Among the more important of these was to be *Maitland's Narrative* (Ipswich, 1833); *Miscellaneous Papers principally illustrative of events in the reign of Queen Mary and James VI* (Maitland Club, 1834); A. Blackwood, *History of Mary Queen of Scots, a fragment* (Maitland Club, 1834); *Historical memoirs of the reign of Mary, queen of Scots* by Lord Herries (Abbotsford Club, 1836); and *Selection from Unpublished Manuscripts . . . illustrating the reign of Mary, queen of Scotland, 1543–68* (Maitland Club, 1837). Contributions from abroad were to be even more important. Of inestimable value to all future biographers were Alexandre Labanoff's *Lettres inedites de Marie Stuart* (Paris, 1839) and *Lettres, Instructions et Memoires de Marie Stuart* (7 vols., Paris, 1844), and Alexandre Teulet's *Papiers D'Etat, pieces et documents inedits ou peu connus relatif a l'histoire de l'Ecosse au 16ᵉ siecle* (Paris, 1852–60) and *Lettres de Marie Stuart* (Paris, 1859) which included the Casket Letters omitted by Labanoff. They became indispensable quarries for almost all subsequent biographies of the queen, especially after the translations of parts of Labanoff's work appeared in Agnes Strickland's *Letters of Mary Queen of Scots* (3 vols., London, 1842–43) and William Turnbull's *Letters of Mary Stuart* (London, 1845). Another important addition to this corpus of original material was the publication of the journal of Mary's physician, Bourgoing, by Regis Chantelauze *Marie Stuart, son proces et son execution d'apres le journal de Bourgoing, son medecin . . .* (Paris, 1876), although the editor's long and elaborate introduction is at times misleading. Documents from English repositories such as *Accounts and Papers relating to Mary, queen of Scots* by D. J. Crosby and John Bruce (Camden Society, 1867), the *Letter-Books of Sir Amias Poulet, Keeper of Mary queen of Scots* by John Morris (London, 1874), and *Claude Nau's History of Mary Stuart from the murder of Riccio to her flight to England,* an account of her affairs written by the man who became her secretary in 1575, edited by Joseph Stevenson (Edinburgh, 1883), all added to the fund of knowledge. Material was further augmented by the commencement of publication of various series of *Calendars of State Papers* (Foreign, Domestic, Spanish and Venetian) throughout the second half of the nineteenth century, to which were to be added in 1898 the *Calendar of State Papers relating to Scotland and Mary, queen of Scots.*

In the mid-nineteenth century, works in the older tradition inevitably continued to be written and amongst the most brilliant, but biased, of these was J. A. Froude's *History of England from the fall of Wolsey to the defeat of the Spanish Armada* (12 vols., London, 1856–70). Froude saw Mary as an ardent Romanist whose prime aim was the destruction of the Reformation, and although he drew upon material from English and continental archives, on this issue he allowed his prejudices to colour his judgments. Agnes Strickland, on the other hand, who also utilised original sources, was prejudiced in the other direction in her life of Mary Stuart, first published in her *Lives of the Queens of Scotland* (Edinburgh, 1850–59). Though there are occasional gleams of good sense, Miss Strickland, who has the honour of being the first to bring feminine intuition to bear on these all too human problems, introduced a fresh crop of myth and a romanticism which could describe Mary's writing in her water-stained inventory prepared before the birth of her son as 'now scarcely intelligible in consequence of the tears, which have apparently fallen upon it while the ink was wet'. Mary found a more scholarly champion in John Hossack, *Mary, queen of Scots, and her accusers* (Edinburgh, 1869; 2 vols., 1870–74). In printing the Book of Articles, submitted by her accusers at Westminster in 1568, he not only produced new documentary evidence but also used his legal training to good effect in analysing the Casket Letters. He emerged as Mary's ablest defender. But not all possessed Hossack's attributes, and some of Mary's apologists, such as Joseph Stevenson, the editor of Nau's *History of Mary Stuart* and author of *Mary Stuart* (Edinburgh, 1886), demonstrate the prejudice and bitterness of an earlier age. Likewise John Skelton, in works such as *Maitland of Lethington and the Scotland of Mary Stuart* (2 vols., Edinburgh, 1887–88), *The Impeachment of Mary Stuart* (Edinburgh, 1876), and *Mary Stuart* (London, 1893), if at times a brilliant apologist, is so careless in matters of factual accuracy and demonstrates such lack of judgment that little reliance can be placed on his statements or weight given to his opinions. But his plea that Mary's policy was one of moderation has much to commend it, even if her sincerity in pursuing such a policy must always remain in doubt.

If Mary's defenders in this era can be accused of partiality, so too can her accusers. Religious prejudice, as illustrated in Froude, was never far from the surface in nineteenth century controversy over Mary. This bias is also evident in David Hay Fleming's *Mary, queen of Scots from her birth to her flight into England* (London, 1897), but the changing climate of scholarship is marked by the outstanding citation by this author of notes and references which provide the reader with the opportunity of disagreeing with the evidence if he feels that it does not substantiate the hypotheses advanced. So too with T. F. Henderson's *The Casket Letters* (Edinburgh, 1889; 2nd edition with reply to objections, Edinburgh, 1890) which also added new evidence in the shape of the declaration which Morton made to the English commissioners at Westminster in 1568, and in which undoubtedly the best case for the genuineness of these letters is advanced.

As in the years following Mary's execution, interest in Mary's cause was not confined to English and Scottish writers and several notable contributions were to come from continental historians, although some exhibited the same weaknesses as their English and Scottish counterparts. Thus Alphonse de Lamartine in his *Mary Stuart* (Edinburgh, 1859), accepts too readily some of Buchanan's accusations against Mary, including her illicit love affair before Darnley's death. J. A. Petit in his *History of Mary Stuart, queen of Scots* (Edinburgh, 1873) emerged as a sentimental apologist for the queen's actions, as did Baron Kervyn de Lettenhove in *Maria Stuart 1585–1587* (2 vols., Paris, 1889) which has been described as a 'contribution to hagiology rather than history'. On the other hand, François Mignet produced a scholarly biography in his *Histoire de Marie Stuart* (2 vols., Paris, 1851), one of the features of this work resting in the full treatment accorded to the events following Mary's flight to England, a survey which the author continues beyond her execution to the Armada which he sees as directly involved in the saga. This view is in marked contrast to that of Martin Philippson who in the *Histoire du Regne de Marie Stuart* (3 vols., Paris, 1891–92) virtually concludes his analysis in 1568 on the ground that from that moment Mary 'lost all political importance'—an arbitrary and rather exceptional point of view. Otherwise, this work has much to commend it, for the author emerges, not as a partisan or a sentimentalist but as scholar who argues that Mary far from being a harmless innocent was a match for all her enemies with policies as far reaching as her opponents. If this much can be said to Mary's credit, however, Philippson also argues that the queen was subject to blind impulses; she had foreknowledge of Darnley's murder and passion eventually led to the undoing of years of constructive work. But if at the end the author appears to be an anti-Marian, his treatment of his subject is always fair.

Among German historians of this period, principal interest was aroused by the Casket Letters. In this field B. Sepp in his two works *Tagebuch der unglucklichen Schotten-Konigen zu Glasgow* (Munich, 1882) and *Maria Stuart und ihre Anklager zu York, Westminster und Hampton Court (1568–9)* (Munich, 1884), with the thesis that the main portions of the letters had been taken from a diary of Mary's, emerged as pro-Marian. So too did E. Bekker in Maria Stuart, Darnley, Bothwell [*Giessener Studien aus dem Gebiet der Geschichte*, no. 1 (1881)]. On the other hand, Harry Bresslau in Die Kassettenbriefe der Konigin Maria Stuart [*Historisches Taschenbuch*, 6 ser., i (1882)] analysed rather superficial arguments put forward by the pro-Marian French historian Baron Kervyn de Lettenhove in Marie Stuart d'apres les documents conserves au Chateau d'Hatfield (*Bulletin de l'academie royale de Belgique*, 2nd ser., xxxiv (1872), 80–111) and in revising Lettenhove's thesis by claiming that of the two letters published by the Frenchman as forgeries, one was genuine and the other part-genuine, also emerges as anti-Marian. This stand was adopted less successfully, however, by H. Forst in *Maria Stuart und der Tod Darnleys* (Bonn, 1894) who in examining the documentary evidence, other than the Casket Letters, which implicated Mary in the murder of her husband, displayed his superficial knowledge of the documents themselves and came off second best to Bekker and Breslau, whose opinions he had set out to refute.

It was on the controversial subject of the Casket Letters that Mary's historians entered the twentieth century, for in 1901 Andrew Lang published his *Mystery of Mary Stuart* (London, 1901) in which by skilful use of the Lennox Papers, he demonstrated how Mary's prosecutors prepared their case against her, and on the resultant evidence argued against the authenticity of the Casket Letters. This verdict, if somewhat hesitantly taken, initiated a running fight with T. F. Henderson, who had earlier argued the case for their authenticity and who with the publication of his major biography of *Mary, queen of Scots* (2 vols., London, 1905) took the opportunity of devoting an appendix to a direct attack upon Lang's hypothesis. The latter who had somewhat modified his views in a second edition of the *Mystery of Mary Stuart* in 1904 returned to the fray in an article entitled 'The Casket Letters' (*Scottish Historical Review*, vol. v, 1–12) which brought the inevitable reply from Henderson in 'Mr Lang and the Casket Letters' (*Scottish Historical Review*, vol. v, 161–174). Lang, allowing himself to be browbeaten and out-argued, slowly shifted his position and in the 1912 edition of *The Mystery of Mary Stuart* he eventually announced his conversion to Henderson's views, a concession which according to J. B. Black, *The Casket Letter Controversy* (Edinburgh, 1951), he should never have made. In contrast to the violent feelings engendered by the Lang-Henderson controversy, the account by T. G. Law in the *Cambridge Modern History* (vol. iii, 260–293, Cambridge, 1904), is careful and dispassionate, and without expressing any opinion of his own on the letters, he is content to state the difficulties over their acceptance or rejection.

Little by way of fresh source material has appeared in the twentieth century to illuminate this particular controversy but other periods and aspects of Mary's life have been more fortunate. In particular the portraits and possessions of Mary received definitive treatment in works such as Lionel H. Cust, *Notes on the authentic portraits of Mary, queen of Scots* (London, 1903) and Andrew Lang, *Portraits and Jewels of Mary Stuart* (Glasgow, 1906). On the record side a rich repository of source material was made available with the opening of the Vatican archives in 1881, documents from which were published in *Calendar of State Papers, Rome* ed. J. M. Rigg (2 vols., London, 1916–26). An earlier work which had drawn upon these archives was *Papal Negotiations with Mary queen of Scots during her reign in Scotland 1561–67* edited by J. H. Pollen (Scottish History Society, 1901), who also edited *Letter of Mary, queen of Scots to the duke of Guise* (Scottish History Society, 1904). Father Pollen in *Mary, queen of Scots and the Babington Plot* (Scottish History Society, 1922), in editing correspondence relative to that plot, also provided the most important addition to source material of recent times, although the introduction is no less valuable, and while the editor's sympathies undoubtedly lie with Mary, he freely admits to her complicity in the plot. The information revealed in these documents is in marked contrast to that in the earlier edition of the *Bardon Papers, documents relating to the imprisonment and trial of Mary, queen of Scots* by Conyers Read (Camden Society, 3rd series, xvii, 1909) which reveal nothing of cardinal importance and no fresh evidence on Mary's guilt or innocence. Likewise *The Trial of Mary, queen of Scots* by A. F. Stewart (Edinburgh, 1923) prints new detailed evidence brought against Mary, but throws no fresh light on the trial or proceedings while many of the texts are extremely inaccurate. On the other hand, if the latest edition of George Buchanan's writings on Mary in *The tyrannous reign of Mary Stuart* by W. A. Gatherer (Edinburgh, 1958) also produces no new evidence, by critically placing Buchanan against all other available sources the editor has set authors who relied upon Buchanan at a serious disadvantage.

These primary works are no less important for their valuable introductions, and likewise secondary works containing a large amount of primary material are often more important for the documents which they print than the commentary which accompanies them. Indeed in R. S. Rait, *Mary Queen of Scots, 1542–1587* (London, 1899), commentary is almost dispensed with completely and contemporary documents relating to Mary allowed to speak for themselves, and while this in itself cannot assure impartiality for the contemporaries themselves were not so, a fair and judicious balance has been achieved by the editor. Text and commentary normally go together, however, and in this category F. A. Mumby's two works *Elizabeth and Mary Stuart : The beginning of the feud* (Boston, 1914) and *The fall of Mary Stuart* (London, 1921), both of which use selected letters to illustrate their themes, and R. S. Rait and A. I. Cameron, *King James' Secret*, which deals with the attitude of James VI to the trial and execution of his mother, are useful contributions to the Marian saga.

By their very nature, works which are purely documentary tend to be more impartial than those of a secondary bent, and in this respect writers in the twentieth century have shown themselves more tolerant, if not less biased, than their counterparts in an earlier age. Total lack of bias is almost impossible and even T. F. Henderson in his two volume biography of *Mary, queen of Scots* (London, 1905), which has been described 'as sound, detailed and almost unbiased', cannot entirely escape this charge—in spite of his belief in the genuineness of the Casket Letters, his sympathy clearly lies with Mary rather than her accusers, a point of view which becomes more obvious in his later work, *The Royal Stuarts* (Edinburgh, 1914). A similar progression can be seen in the works of R. H. Mahon, which commenced with *The Indictment of Mary, queen of Scots* (Cambridge, 1923) in which he printed Buchanan's indictment, which the author argued was an early form of the Book of Articles and thus demonstrated how the case against the queen was strengthened as time went on. No opinion was, however, formulated on Mary's guilt or innocence. But in *Mary, queen of Scots* (Cambridge, 1924) Mahon graduated into the ranks of the Marians. His references are not always accurate, however, and as well, in his study of the Lennox narrative which had been used earlier by Lang in his *Mystery of Mary Stuart* and printed by Henderson as the Bill of Supplication, he supported the case for the falsity of the Casket Letters. He became more pronouncedly Marian in *The Tragedy of Kirk o' Field* (Cambridge, 1930) in which that plot had become one in which Darnley was planning to murder Mary. Side by side with this rather extraordinary theory that a convalescent concocted such a plot between his arrival in Edinburgh and his death ten days later without party or faction to support him, can be placed the equally ingenious suggestion of R. Gore Browne in his spirited *Lord Bothwell* (London, 1937) who following Mahon's theory that Darnley's agents introduced the powder adds a second and third band of murderers, Bothwell and his retainers who found the powder and lit the fuse to teach the king a lesson and Morton's men who happened to meet the fleeing Darnley. Bothwell is also exonerated by M. H. Armstrong Davison in *The Casket Letters* (London, 1965) in which the author also follows Mahon's thesis. The discussion of the Casket Letters themselves is somewhat more viable, but while the theory that manipulation and interpolation rather than outright forgery were the means by which the evidence against Mary was manufactured is attractive, the appearance of a mysterious 'other woman' by

whom it is suggested some of the letters to Bothwell were written
has less to commend it.

If little credence can be attached to this special pleading on
Bothwell's behalf, other biographies of figures central to the
Marian controversy are of considerable value. Thus, E. Russell in
Maitland of Lethington, the Minister of Mary Stuart (London,
1912), if anti-Marian insofar as the Casket Letters are accepted as
genuine, by carefully examining the career of Lethington does
much to illumine the earlier part of Mary's reign in Scotland.
Russell, however, accepts Moray as stainless, and in this judgment is closely followed by Maurice Lee in *James Stewart, Earl of
Moray* (London, 1953) who believes that the circumstantial evidence against Mary in the matter of Darnley's death is overwhelming. Other important biographies, which throw light on Mary and
her reign include Jasper Ridley's *John Knox* (Oxford, 1968) and
A. F. Steuart's *Signeur Davie, a sketch life of David Riccio* (London, 1922), an account of the conflicting evidence about Riccio and
detailing the few facts actually known about him.

If all these works leave the major controversies about Mary still
unsolved, the vituperation has abated, and the religious bias, for or
against Mary, has noticeably diminished in an era in which Catholic and Protestant are more tolerant of one another's views. Even
in the more popular works, toleration and moderation have become the keynotes in most biographies of Mary, many of which—
in the mode of Schiller's tragedy of *Maria Stuart*—disarm criticism by admitting Mary's complicity in Darnley's murder and her
passionate love for Bothwell, but still rise to the queen's defence.
Thus, Florence McCunn in *Mary Stuart* (London, 1905), a work
unencumbered by controversy and authorities, tries to ameliorate
the queen's guilt by attacking Knox, Moray and Morton, while
Roger Chavire in *Le Secret de Marie Stuart* (Paris, 1937), a work
also characterised by poor citation of sources, likewise emerges as
a moderate defender of the queen.

Defence is also a characteristic of works written in a romantic
style, the popularity of which has suffered no diminution, although
in this respect it should be noted that Martin Hume's *The Love
Affairs of Mary, queen of Scots* (London, 1903) is, in spite of its
title a serious political study based upon original sources, especially those in Spanish archives. In this work the thesis is advanced

that Mary's great objective was to become queen of England, and to bring back both countries to Roman Catholic obedience, both objectives which she hoped to achieve by her marriage intrigues. It has been observed that the weakness in this study lies in the fact that Mary's womanly qualities are not sufficiently stressed, but this certainly could not be said of romantic writers such as Marjorie Bowen in *Mary, queen of Scots, daughter of debate* (London, 1934), or Eric Linklater's *Mary, queen of Scots* (London, 1933) in which Mary's part in the mystery of Kirk o' Field is explained by 'a womanly zeal for nursing'. Likewise, feminine psychology played a large part in Stefan Zweig's interpretation of Mary's character which he found 'by no means abstruse' in his biography *The Queen of Scots* (London, 1935).

These works, and many others written in a similar vein, have little or nothing to add to the Marian controversy, and this is also true of other works with more serious pretensions. Samuel Cowan's *Mary Queen of Scots and Who wrote the Casket Letters?* (2 vols., London, 1901), which sets out to vindicate the queen, is lacking in scholarship and critical analysis, inaccurately printing documents which lack the originality claimed for them by the author, who in spite of his title has also little to say about the Casket Letters. More merit is to be found in A. H. Millar's *Mary Queen of Scots, her life Story* (Edinburgh, 1905), who, if somewhat prejudiced against Mary, is, however, content to weigh the opinions of her other biographers as does Sir Arthur Macnulty in *Mary, queen of Scots* (London, 1960), one of the more interesting of recent popular works, which include George M. Thomson's *The Crime of Mary Stuart* (London, 1967).

These more recent biographies have one feature in common with many of their earlier counterparts. Scant attention is paid to Mary's life before 1561 and frequently little more than epilogue suffices for the period of captivity from 1568. Jane Stoddart, following in the footsteps of J. E. A. de Ruble's *La Premiere Jeunesse de Marie Stuart* (Paris, 1891) attempted in *The Girlhood of Mary Queen of Scots* (London, 1908) to examine Mary's youth in France, but her volume, although useful as a corrective to other biographies which deal with Mary's stay in France in a perfunctory manner, is facile and strays far beyond the bounds of its subject matter.

A more serious omission in many biographies, however, is not the brief treatment accorded to Mary before 1561, but the almost equal disregard shown to her life after her flight from Scotland in 1568. Even T. F. Henderson in his comprehensive *Mary, queen of Scots* has little to say about the English side of Mary's career, and concurs with Philippson in stating that in 1568 'her political career was really over', a point of view which is highly debatable.

Works which have been written on this period have moreover tended to concentrate on Mary's trial and execution. Thus the nineteenth century writer Mrs. Maxwell Scott in *The Tragedy of Fotheringay* (London, 1895) and later Samuel Cowan in *The Last Days of Mary Stuart* (London, 1907) both relied for their information upon Chantelauze's edition of Mary's physician, Bourgoyne, but neither critically examined the journal or tried to assess Mary's complicity in the plot which led to her execution, a point which is fortunately dealt with in detail by Pollen in his introduction to *Mary, queen of Scots and the Babington Plot* and less satisfactorily by Alan G. Smith, *The Babington Plot* (London, 1936). The lack of importance attributed to the period of Mary's captivity by many of her biographers can profitably be supplemented by other works. Pre-eminent amongst these are the works of Conyers Read, *Mr. Secretary Walsingham and the policy of Queen Elizabeth* (3 vols., Oxford, 1925) in which occurs a detailed account of the Babington plot and a judicious evaluation of Mary's complicity; *Mr. Secretary Cecil and Queen Elizabeth* (London, 1955) with a shrewd assessment of the political repercussions of Mary's arrival in England, and *Lord Burghley and Queen Elizabeth* (London, 1960) in which the various plots centred around Mary are discussed in detail. Other works which place the Marian problem in its English perspective include J. E. Neale's *Queen Elizabeth* (London, 1934) and J. B. Black, *The Reign of Elizabeth, 1558–1603* (Oxford History of England, 1936), which in its original version is somewhat anti-Marian. This attitude is much less pronounced in the second edition (Oxford, 1959) as the preface to the volume demonstrates. Gordon Donaldson, *The First Trial of Mary queen of Scots* (London, 1969) also deals with Mary in England and in examining the enquiry held in 1568–69 to discover by what authority Mary's enemies had deprived her of her crown, reprints with critical interpolations the Book of Articles and attempts to place

the inquiry and the evidence therein in its proper historical perspective. The Casket Letters are rejected as forgeries, but while
the author admits this much in Mary's favour, he clearly indicates
that her detention in England was inevitable from the outset.

Professor Donaldson has also dealt with Mary's reign in Scotland in *Scotland: James V to James VII* (Edinburgh, 1965) and
Scottish Kings (London, 1967). His thesis is similar in both—a
successful policy of conciliation until 1565 when Mary's affairs
'began to be ruled not by the head, but by the heart', followed by
the downward path on which Mary is seen as at least having been
aware of schemes to murder Darnley, if not being party to them.
Her marriage to Bothwell, which encompassed her actual downfall, is explained by sexual passion, although it is admitted that
sound political advantages may also have influenced her decision.
If the author's sympathies lie anywhere they appear to be with
Mary, and yet on one point he does her an apparent injustice by
too readily assuming that Mary was already carrying Bothwell's
child before the murder of Darnley. Had she really been pregnant
in the months following the event, it seems unlikely that she could
have concealed her condition, and her miscarriage at Loch Leven
appears to have been the result of conception which occurred
after her abduction by Bothwell, rather than as an act of infidelity
before her husband's death.

This at least is the contention in the first major biography of
Mary since 1905, Lady Antonia Fraser's *Mary Queen of Scots*
(London, 1969), which effects a compromise between the romantic
and scholarly styles in which previous lives have often been written.
A sympathetic insight into Mary's character reveals the nervous
stress often leading to near breakdown at many critical junctures
in her career, but this analysis is not allowed to overshadow a discussion of Mary's political ambitions as the touchstone by which
she must be judged. Thus her early attempts to find a second husband are regarded as a matter of power politics, and even Darnley's
suitability as a candidate for Mary's hand first emerges through the
ties of blood and religion. Failure to await the necessary papal dispensation is seen, however, as an impetuous step compelled by
passion, rather than a matter of harsh political necessity stemming
from the fear that the nobility might prevent the marriage if further
delay was allowed. The Bothwell match, on the other hand, can be

2

described as a 'marriage of convenience' which could have been successful in solving the political difficulties in which Mary was enmeshed following the murder of Darnley, the queen's involvement in which is restricted to her known wish to be rid of her husband. This point of view will not satisfy everyone, and the refurbishing of the thesis that Mary's plotting during her captivity arose primarily from the wish to be free rather than from a desire to succeed Elizabeth evidently allows sympathy with Mary to obscure the political realities of the situation. If the hand of Buchanan can be discerned in Professor Donaldson's suggestion of Mary's adulterous affair with Bothwell, the influence of Leslie, Blackwood and Brantôme can be equally clearly seen in Lady Antonia Fraser's portrayal of Mary during her closing years. This gives credence to the thesis developed by J. E. Phillips in *Images of a Queen* (Los Angeles, 1964), in which he discussed in sixteenth century terms the growth of the dual legend of Mary, the innocent martyr or the adulterous murderess, that the enigma which was given manifestation at that time will persist until histories of the Queen of Scots no longer command attention. Historians will never agree to her character, and in these circumstances, it is perhaps inevitable that the picture of a romantic but ill-fated queen painted by Schiller and Swinburne, amongst others, is the one most likely to engage popular sympathy.

I

THE LEGEND

The enigma of Mary Stuart extends over every aspect of the queen's life. Even her legendary beauty has sometimes been disputed, and certainly her portraits aid this case. Friend and foe alike, however, attest to her charms, and this coupled to the tragic story of her downfall, captivity and the halo of martyrdom which accompanied her execution, has undoubtedly swayed the judgement of many historians who otherwise might have condemned her. And in the realms of literature, it has rendered her position impregnable.

Who is there, that, at the very mention of Mary Stewart's name, has not her countenance before him, familiar as that of the mistress of his youth, or the favourite daughter of his advanced age? Even those who feel themselves compelled to believe all, or much, of what her enemies laid to her charge, cannot think without a sigh upon a countenance expressive of any thing rather than the foul crimes with which she was charged when living, and which still continue to shade, if not to blacken, her memory. That brow, so truly open and regal—those eyebrows, so regularly graceful, which yet were saved from the charge of regular insipidity by the beautiful effect of the hazel eyes which they over-arched, and which seem to utter a thousand histories—the nose, with all its Grecian precision of outline—the mouth, so well proportioned, so sweetly formed, as if designed to speak nothing but what was delightful to hear—the dimpled chin—the stately swan-like neck, form a countenance, the like of which we know not to have existed in any other character moving in that high class of life, where the

actresses as well as the actors command general and undivided
attention.

Sir W. Scott, The Abbot, ii, 4.

Her portraits do her ill justice or her praises as the most beautiful
woman of her day malign her generation. Witchery of manner
rather than physical beauty must be accounted her charm. She
was tall, like her mother, but lacked her mother's regularity of
feature. Her face, somewhat long, was spoilt by a nose too prominent and a brow too high from which her russet hair was withdrawn. In no breast she inspired great passion, though she could
evoke loyal devotion from both sexes. On her husbands her hold
was ineffectual and weak. Yet Knox's ungracious eye observed
such 'craft' in her as he had not found in another of her age.

Terry, History of Scotland, 206.

One thing is historically certain: Mary was either beautiful, or she
bewitched people into thinking her beautiful. This is proved, not
by the eulogies of Ronsard and Brantome, a courtly poet, and a
courtly chronicler, but by the unanimous verdict of friend and
enemy. Even Knox calls her face 'pleasing'—which the authentic
portraits of her face hardly ever are; even Elizabeth recognised
something 'divine' in her hated rival; Sir James Melville styles her
'very loesome'; the populace of Edinburgh cried 'Heaven bless
that sweet face', says Knox, as she rode by, while English and
French ambassadors are in the same tale.

Lang, Portraits and Jewels of Mary Stuart, 13.

Mary Hamilton: For myself
        I cannot see which side of her that lurks
        Which snares in such wise all the sense of men;
        What special beauty, subtle as mans eye
        And tender as the inside of the eyelid is,
        There grows about her.

Mary Carmichael: I think her cunning speech—
    The soft and rapid shudder of her breath
    In talking—the rare tender little laugh—
    The pitiful sweet sound like a birds sigh
    When her voice breaks; her talking does it all.

Mary Seyton: I say, her eyes with those clear perfect brows
    It is the playing of those eyelashes,
    The lure of amorous looks as sad as love,
    Plucks all souls toward her like a net.
                    Swinburne, *Chastelard*, 14–15.

She was somewhat above the normal height for a woman, with a graceful and elegant, but well-developed, figure. Her neck was well-formed, but not unduly long or slim, and her shoulders were slightly sloped, leading to a vigorous and well-modelled bust. In later years her figure lost something of its grace and elegance through the stress of illness and confinement, but maintained its dignity up to the last hour at Fotheringhay. Her general appearance was that of a strong, clever, masterful woman, rather than a beautiful and delicate heroine of romance.
                Cust, *Portraits of Mary Queen of Scots*, 18.

2

QUEEN IN FRANCE

Born in December 1542 and queen of Scots within a week of her birth, Mary was sent to France for her own safety in August 1548. There she was to remain until August 1561, thirteen years which saw the shaping of her character at the French court then under the dominance of her mother's family of Guise. Largely through their influence she was betrothed to the Dauphin Francis, eldest son of the French King Henry II, the marriage taking place on 24th April 1558. Up to that point Mary's life in France had been a stereotyped courtly existence and while some writers have tried to attribute certain of Mary's later failings to her early upbringing, these attempts carry little weight. More apposite has been the criticism of Mary for signing, on the occasion of her marriage, not only the official promises to safeguard the liberties of Scotland, but also three secret documents whereby she assigned her Kingdom to the king of France in the event of her decease without heirs. Indeed, even without this eventuality Scotland during Mary's sojourn in France was becoming more and more an appendage of that kingdom. The realisation of this was to be one of the principal factors in the outbreak of the Reformation in Scotland, the success of which was to be aided by the death of Mary's mother, Mary of Guise-Lorraine, in June 1560. Mary's future at that date remained in the balance as she had become queen of France on the accession of her husband as Francis II in July 1559 and while she had earlier added to her titles by claiming at the instigation of the Guises the English crown on the death of Mary Tudor, she might have forfeited her Scottish throne had her husband not died in December 1560. The way was cleared for her return to Scotland, to which she brought among other legacies of her French upbringing, the conviction that succession to the English throne was hers by right.

The poets of the Court soon began to celebrate in their verses the marvels of her beauty and the treasures of her mind. . . . Ronsard, who was the Virgil of the age, expresses himself, whenever he speaks of her, in such images and with such delicacy and polish of accent, as prove that his praise sprang from his love—that his heart had subjugated his genius. . . .

In fullness of the springtide, from among the lilies fair,
Sprang forth that form of whiteness, fairer than the lilies there.
Though stained with Adonis' blood, the gentle summer rose
Lies vanquished by the ruby tint her cheeks and lips disclose.
Young Love himself, with arrows keen, hath armed her peerless eye,
The Graces too, those fairest three, bright daughters of the sky,
With all their richest, rarest gifts, my princess have endowed,
And evermore to serve her well have left their high abode.

Lamartine, Mary Stuart, 8–9.

'She is *brune*, with a clear complexion, and I think she will be a beautiful girl, for her complexion is fine and clear, the skin white, the lower part of the face very pretty, the eyes are small and rather deep set, the face rather long, she is graceful and not shy, on the whole we may well be contented with her.' [Duchesse de Guise.]

Cust, Portraits of Mary Queen of Scots, 20–21.

By general consent she was one of the most irresistible young women in France. In person she was tall and graceful, with dark brown eyes, chestnut hair, and a pale delicate complexion. It is hard to believe from her portraits that she was positively beautiful. No doubt a large part of her charm lay in the vivacity of her personality. Although she excelled in courtly accomplishments and conformed in the main to courtly conventions, she was at heart a free spirit with much of the freshness, simplicity, and abandon of a wild thing about her. Court life never tamed the primitive woman in her, a woman quick of wit and nimble of body, sensitive, proud, passionate; loyal to her friends, implacable to her enemies; courageous in action, indomitable in purpose.

Read, *Mr. Secretary Walsingham*, i, 42–3.

Mary's education was not neglected in France. After making due allowance for the flattery and exaggeration likely to be evoked in such a case, it is evident enough that she neither lacked brains nor assiduity. While her linguistic attainments were above the average, she apparently excelled in music, in needlework, in dancing and in horsemanship.

Fleming, *Mary Queen of Scots*, 17.

Her main course of study was directed towards the attainment of the best European languages. So graceful was her French that the judgment of the most learned men recognised her command of the language; nor did she neglect Spanish or Italian, although she aimed rather at a useful knowledge than at a pretentious fluency. She followed Latin more readily than she spoke it. The charms of her poetry owed nothing to art. Her penmanship was clear, and (what is rare in a woman) swift. Her excellence in singing arose from a natural, not an acquired, ability to modulate her voice: the instruments she played were the cittern, harp, and the harpsichord. Being very agile, she danced admirably to a musical accompaniment, yet with beauty and comeliness, for the silent and gentle movement of her limbs kept harmony of the chords. She devoted herself to learning to ride so far as it is necessary for travelling or for her favourite exercise of hunting, thinking anything further more fitted for a man than for a woman. . . . Several tapestries worked by her with wonderful skill are yet to be seen in France, dedicated to the altars of God, especially in the monastery in which she was nurtured on her first arrival in the kingdom.

Conn, *Vitae Mariae Stuartae* in Jebb, *De Vita et Rebus*, ii. 15.

Nature formed her for government. She was majestic, wise, generous and affable. Sincerity and uprightness were also among the
number of her virtues; and any occasional deviations from them
in the course of her life, may probably with justice be ascribed to
those slippery political principles which have characterised the
councils of France, instilled into her, not only at a period when she
could hardly think for herself, but inculcated by the authority of
her uncles, to whom she could not but listen with great deference.

The lessons of the Court of France, the most intriguing on
earth, and of the House of Lorrain, the most intriguing perhaps
that ever was in France, could not fail to make an impression upon
a young mind, however otherwise disposed by nature.

T. Robertson, *Mary Queen of Scots*, 5-6.

The court, in the midst of which Mary Stuart had grown up,
was then the most magnificent, the most elegant, the most joyous,
and we must add, one of the most lax, in Europe. . . . It was in this
school of elegance and depravity, which produced Kings so witty
and vicious, and princesses so amiable and dissipated, that Mary
Stuart received her education. During her childhood she only
derived benefit from it, although she could not fail to perceive
what was evil, and afterwards to imitate it; for what we see, is
sure eventually to influence what we do. But then she profited
simply by the charms and instruction diffused throughout this
agreeable and literary court, in which the King's daughters
devoted themselves to the study of languages and cultivated a taste
for the arts.

Mignet, *Mary, Queen of Scots*, i, 37-41.

Mary was in many respects the antithesis of her cousin the queen
of England. Brought up at the court of France, at that time the
most brilliant and gayest in christendom, she had enjoyed a comparatively sheltered existence, unharassed by the grim experiences
that had shaped and disciplined the character of Anne Boleyn's
daughter. True, the French court in the days of Henry II and

Catherine de Medicis was not the *vrai paradis du monde* depicted
by the poet Brantôme, but it was certainly not the 'school of depravity', described by the historian Mignet, where the *petite reine
d'Ecosse* 'could not fail to see what was evil and afterwards to
imitate it'. On the contrary, what evidence there is seems to point
in the opposite direction. France has always had the reputation of
looking well after her royal ladies, and Mary was, potentially at
least, one of them. She was educated along with the dauphin and
his sisters by the best schoolmasters in the Kingdom, Claude
Millot and Antoine Fouquelin, and her *gouvernantes* were chosen
with care. The dowager duchess of Guise, her grandmother, had a
trusteeship over her general up-bringing; and her uncle, the
Cardinal of Lorraine, albeit he was no saint, was too much concerned about his niece's dazzling future to permit irregularities
in the household.

Black, The Reign of Elizabeth, 63–64.

The diplomatic correspondence of the period proves but too
clearly that Foreign Powers regarded Scotland, during Mary's
minority, almost as a province of France. Soranzo reported to the
Doge and Senate on August 18, 1554, that 'Mary Queen of Scotland being now twelve years old, is out of her minority, during
which she was under the guardianship of the Earl of Arran, who
is also styled Duke of Chatelherault in right of a duchy given him
by the King of France. . . . The fortresses are all in the hands of
the French, and of the Queen Dowager, who being a French-
woman, it may be said that everything is in the power of his most
Christian Majesty, who keeps some thousand infantry there as
garrison, that force being sufficient, as in two days they can send
over as many troops as they please."

Stoddart, Girlhood of Mary Queen of Scots, 131.

Mary Stuart was now approaching the age of early womanhood,
and the interests of France required that the marriage which should
unite Scotland with that realm ought no longer to be delayed. The
necessary arrangements were hurried on accordingly. A letter

from King Henry to the Estates of Scotland was laid before them, in which he invited them to send deputies to Paris, there to witness the marriage of their Queen with his son, the Dauphin. The proposal was most cordially accepted by the Estates, which appointed a commission fully authorised to give the national consent to the union. When the Scottish envoys arrived in the French Court they were received with the most marked distinction, and the same respect was shown to them during the whole of their visit. These envoys took care that the legal instruments which were to secure to Scotland her laws, her liberties, and her privileges, should be executed with due legal precision. To all appearance the two nations were now welded together into one by a bond which could never be broken.

Stevenson, *Mary Stuart*, 146.

The marriage was marked by a transaction of deep duplicity. The Commissioners sent by the Scottish Parliament to France, 'for completing of the mariage of our Soverane Lady with my Lord Dolphin,' were charged with Instructions intended to protect Mary's interests on the one hand, and to safeguard the liberties of her country on the other. Accordingly, for the latter purpose, on the 15th April—nine days before the marriage—she acknowledged, over her own seal and signature, and over those of her curator, the Duke of Guise, that the Scottish Acts, Articles, and Instructions were for the evident advantage of herself and her kingdom; and she bound herself and her successors, by her 'royal word', faithfully to observe and keep the laws, liberties, and privileges of Scotland, to all the subjects of that kingdom, as they had been kept by their most illustrious kings. On the 30th of April—six days after the marriage—a similar document was signed by Francis and Mary as 'King and Queen of the Scots, Dauphin and Dauphiness of France.' On the 26th of June, Francis, as King of the Scots, declared that he not only wished to preserve their prerogatives, immunities, and ancient liberties intact and inviolate; but also to increase, amplify, and strengthen them. Over and above these documents, Henry and Francis promised, in their letters-patent of 19th April 1558, that they would maintain the liberties

of Scotland; and that, should Mary die without issue, the nearest
heir should succeed to the Scots crown without hindrance.

Nevertheless, Mary had been induced, on the 4th of April, to
sign secretly three documents of a very different kind. In the first
of these, in the event of her leaving no issue, she made over to the
King of France, by free gift, the kingdom of Scotland, and all right
which she had or might have to the kingdom of England. In the
second, with the advice of her uncles—the Cardinal of Lorraine
and the Duke of Guise—she made over to the French King, in the
like event, the kingdom of Scotland, until he was repaid a million
of money, or such other sum as should be found due for the defence of that country. In the third, she referred to the Scottish
intention of assigning her kingdom—in default of heirs of her
body—to certain lords of the country, as a depriving her of her
liberty of disposing of it; and protested that, whatever assent or
consent she had given or might give to the Articles and Instructions sent by the Estates of her Kingdom, she willed that the dis-
positions made by her in favour of the kings of France should be
valid, and have full effect. This last is signed by Francis as well as
by Mary. The young Queen—only in her sixteenth year—probably signed these deeds without fully realising their import. If so,
her heedlessness gives a rude shock to the panegyrics of those
apologists who speak of her precocity as phenomenal.

Fleming, *Mary Queen of Scots*, 22–24.

Cardinal de Lorraine and the princes of the house of Guise, though
not the governing party in France, at that time, were eager to co-
operate in any measure that tended to the aggrandizement of their
royal niece, and which, by sowing the seeds of a succession war in
England, might furnish Elizabeth with sufficient employment at
home. The first step taken by the rulers of Mary Stuart's councils
was to cause the royal arms of England and Scotland, surmounted
by the crown of France, to be engraved on her seal and plate, em-
broidered on her tapestry, and emblazoned on her carriages.

The grand display which was intended for a public assertion of
Mary's right to the crown of England was reserved for the day of
the tournament, July 6, 1559, held in the great square in front of

the palace of the Tournelles. . . . Mary was on that occasion borne to her place in the royal balcony in a sort of triumphal car, emblazoned with the royal escutcheon of England and Scotland, explained by a Latin distich, of which Strype has given this quaint version:

> 'The Armies of Marie Quene Dolphines of France,
> The nobillest lady in earth for till advance;
> Of Scotland Quene, of Ingland also,
> Of Ireland also God hath providit so.'

The car was preceded by the two heralds of her spouse the King-Dauphin, both Scots, apparelled with the arms of England and Scotland, and crying in the high voice 'Place, Place! pour la Reine d'Angleterre.' Little did the adoring crowd who responded to this announcement with shouts of 'Vive la Reine d'Angleterre!' imagine they were sounding the knell of their darling, for it was the assumption of this title that cost Mary Stuart her life.

Strickland, Mary Queen of Scots, i, 38–39.

Stanzas by Mary, queen of Scots, on death of her husband, King Francis II.

> What formerly was pleasant to my eyes
> Now gives me pain
> The brightest day,
> To me, seems dark and obscure night.
> For the most exquisite delights
> I now have neither relish or desire.
>
> As a relief for my singular misfortune
> I wander from place to place;
> But 'tis in vain to think of change,
> Which effaces not my grief;
> For scenes which formerly gave me delight
> Are now becoming frightful solitudes to me.

Campbell, Love Letters of Mary, Queen of Scots, 68–69.

3

RETURN TO SCOTLAND

Mary returned to Scotland on August 19th 1561 arriving at Leith in a thick fog which to Knox at least was a portent of bitter troubles ahead. Few of Mary's subjects saw the arrival of their queen at the age of nineteen in such a gloomy light and the festivities which welcomed her were sincere if tinged with reminders that Scotland was a kingdom in which the Protestants had gained ascendancy; a point which Mary had herself recognised by accepting the advice of her half-brother Lord James Stewart and landing at Leith rather than in the pro-Catholic north. This discretion was in accordance with the advice offered to Mary by poets and advisers alike, both of whom may have looked forward to a change of religious allegiance in the young queen. Nevertheless, while opinions may vary on Mary's political sagacity on her arrival in Scotland, most commentators, Knox and a few like-minded bigots excepted, have usually accepted and respected Mary's wish to have the Mass for herself and her household. Her ostensible policy of private Catholicism and public Protestantism was, however, a dangerous platform for even the most skilful politician, and had Mary not shown willingness to place herself in the hands of two Protestant advisers, Lord James Stewart and William Maitland of Lethington, her secretary of state, her personal reign might have been placed in jeopardy not long after her arrival.

The verray face of heavin, the time of hir arryvall, did manifestlie speak what confort was brought into this cuntrey with hir, to wit, sorow, dolour, darknes, and all impietie; for in the memorie of man, that day of the year, was never seyn a more dolorous face of the heavin, then was at hir arryvall, which two days after did so contineu; for besides the surfett weat, and corruptioun of the air, the myst was so thick and so dark, that skairse mycht any man espy ane other the lenth of two pair of buttis. The sun was not seyn to schyne two dayis befoir, nor two dayis after. That foir-warning gave God unto us; but allace, the most pairt war blynd.

Knox, *Works*, ii, 268–9.

Of the Quenis Arryvale in Scotland

Excellent Princes! potent, and preclair,
   Prudent, peerles in bontie and bewtie!
Maist nobil Quein of bluid under the air!
With all my hairt, and micht, I welcum thé
   Hame to thy native pepill, and cuntrie.
Beseikand God to gif thé grace to haive
   Of thy leigis the hairtis faythfullie,
And thame in luife, and favour to receave.

Now sen thow art arryvit in this land,
   Our native Princes, and illuster Queine!
I traist to God this regioune sall stand
Ane auld frie land, as it lang tyme has bein.
   Quhairin, richt schoone, thair sall be hard and seine
Grit joy, justice, gude peax, and policie:
   All cair, and cummer, baneist quyte and clein;
And ilk man leif in guid tranquillitie.

   .   .   .   .   .   .

Yet I exhort thé to be circumspect
   Of thy counsall in the electioune:
Cheis faythful men of prudence and effect,
Quha will for wrang make dew correctioune;
   And do justice, without exceptioune;
Men of knawledge, gude lyfe, and conscience,
   That will nocht failye for affectioune;
Bot of gude fame, and lang experience.

   .   .   .   .   .

And gif they Heines plesis for to marie,
   That thow haive help I pray the Trinitie

To cheis and tak ane husband without tarie,
To thy honour, and our utilitie;
   Quha will, and may, mantein our libertie;
Repleit of wisdome and of godlienes;
   Nobill, and full of constance and lawtie;
With guid successioune, to our quyetnes.

   .   .   .   .   .

And thoch that I so serve be nocht sa abill
   As I was wont, becaus I may not see;
Yet in my hairt I sall be firme and stabill
To thy Hienes, with all fidelitie;
   Ay prayand God for thy prosperitie;
And that I heir thy pepill, with hie voce,
   And joyful hairt, cryand continuallie
Vive Marie tres-nobill Royne d'Escoss.

Maitland, Poems, 16–18.

ANE NEW YEIR GIFT TO THE QUENE MARY, QUHEN SHE COME FIRST HAME, 1562

Welcum, illustrat Ladye, and oure Quene!
Welcum, oure lyone with the Floure-delyce!
Welcum, oure thrissill with the Lorane grene!
Welcum, oure rubent roiss vpoun the ryce!
Welcum, oure jem and joyfull genetryce!
Welcum, oure beill of Albion to beir!
Welcum, oure pleasand Princes maist of pryce!
God gif the grace aganis this guid new yeir.

This guid new yeir, we hoip, with grace of God,
Salbe of peax, trāquillitie, and rest;
This yeir sall rycht and ressone rewle the rod,
Quhilk sa lang seasoun hes bene soir supprest;
This yeir ferme fayth sall frelie be confest,
And all erronius questionis put areir;
To laboure that this lyfe amang ws lest
God gife the grace aganis this guid new yeir.

Heirfore addres the dewlie to decoir
And rewle they regne with hie magnificence;
Begin at God to gar sett furth his gloir,
And of his gospell gett experiēce;
Caus his trew Kirk be had in reuerēce;
So sall they name and fame spred far and neir:
Now, this thy dett to do with diligence,
God gif the grace aganis this guid new yeir.

Found on the first four vertewus cardinall,
On wisdome, justice, force, and temperās;
Applaud to prudent men, and principall
Off vertewus lyfe, thy wirschep till avance;
Waye justice, equale without discrepance;
Strenth thy estait with steidfastnes to steir;
To temper tyme with trew continuance
God gife the grace aganis this guid new yeir.

Cast thy consate be counsale of the sage,
And cleif to Christ hes kepit the in cure
Attingent now to twentye yeir of aige,
Preservand the fra all misaventure.
Wald thow be servit, and thy cuntre sure,
Still on the commoun weill haif e and eir;
Preiss ay to be protectrix of the pure;
So God sall gyde thy Grace this gude new yeir.

Gar stanche all stryiff, and stabill thy estaitis
In constance, concord, cherite, and lufe;
Be bissie now to banisch all debatis
Betuix kirkmen and temporall men dois mufe;
The pulling doun of policie reprufe,
And lat perversit prelettis leif perqueir;
To do the best, besekand God above
To gife the grace aganis this guid new yeir. . . .

A. Scott, *Poems*, 1--2.

Mary landed in Scotland with a mind full of anxiety and uncertainty. She came, alone and unprotected to assume the government of a country which had long been distinguished for its rebellious turbulence. The masculine spirit of her father had quailed before the storm. Her mother, whose intellectual energy she well knew, had in vain attempted to bring order out of confusion, and, harassed and fatigued, had at length surrendered her life in the struggle. For the last two years, it is true, the country had enjoyed not peace and tranquillity, but a cessation from an actual state of warfare. Nevertheless, the seeds of discontent, and of mutual distrust and hatred, were as abundant as ever. Mary's religion was well known; and her confirmed devotion to it was, by one party, magnified into bigotry, and pronounced criminal, whilst, by another, it was feared she would shew herself too lukewarm in revenging the insults which the ancient worship had sustained. Such being the state of things, how could a young, and comparatively inexperienced queen, just nineteen years of age, approach her Kingdom otherwise than with fear and trembling?

Bell, *Mary Queen of Scots*, i, 111-12.

The queen, conformably to the plan which had been concerted in France, committed the administration of affairs entirely to protestants. Her council was filled with the most eminent persons of that party; not a single papist was admitted into any degree of confidence. The prior of St. Andrew's and Maitland of Lethington seemed to hold the first place in the queen's affection, and possessed all the power as well as reputation of favourite ministers. Her choice could not have fallen upon persons more acceptable to her people, and, by their prudent advice, Mary conducted herself with so much moderation, and deference to the sentiments of the nation, as could not fail of gaining the affection of her subjects, the firmest foundation of a prince's power, and the only genuine source of his happiness and glory.

W. Robertson, *History*, ii. 62-63.

The affections of those of the Reformed Relligion (which was now by much the greater pairt of the commons of the Kingdome) was so averse from the Queen, that everie thing she did was constructed in the worst sense. If any thing was done that was not in favor of that pairtie, it was esteemed tirannie; that which was done to honor or satisffie them, it was called dissimulation. This honor of Leutenant of the kingdom, which the Queen confered upon Lord James (whoe was head of this pairtie) was by his owen procurment, yet was misconstructed by the people; for they said that the Queen had laid that charge upon him, not out of affection, but to hazard his lyffe.

Herries, *Memoirs*, 60.

With great diligence the Lordis repared unto hir from all quarters. And so was nothing understand but myrth and quyetness till the nixt Sunday, which was the xxiiij of August, when preparatioun began to be maid for that idoll the Messe to be said in the Chapell; which perced the hartis of all. The godlie began to bolden; and men began openlie to speak, "Shall that idoll be suffered agane to tack place within this Realm? It shall not." The Lord Lyndesay, (then but Maister,) with the gentilmen of Fyiff, and otheris, plainlie cryed in the close, "The idolater Preast should dye the death," according to Goddis law. One that caryed in the candell was evill effrayed; but then began flesche and blood to schaw the self. Thair durst no Papist, neathir yitt any that cam out of France whisper. But the Lord James (the man whom all the godlye did most reverence) took upoun him to keap the Chapell door. His best excuse was, that he wald stop all Scotishe men to enter in to the Messe. But it was, and is sufficientlie known, that the door was keapt, that nane should have entress to truble the Preast; who, after the Messe, was committed to the protectioun of Lord Johne of Coldinghame, and Lord Robert of Halyrudehouse, who then war boyth Protestantis, and had communicat at the Table of the Lord. Betwix thame two was the Preast conveyed to his chalmer.

Knox, *Works*, ii, 270–1.

4

CONCILIATION AND COMPROMISE

For four years after her return to Scotland, Mary's domestic policies were to enjoy outstanding success in both political and religious spheres. On the international scene, moreover, diplomatic communications were retained between Scotland and the continental Catholic powers, including the papacy. At the same time friendly relations were maintained with Elizabeth of England in the hope of persuading her to recognise Mary's claim to the English succession.

In Scotland, with the co-operation of Lord James Stewart (created earl of Moray in 1562) and Maitland of Lethington, the nobility was kept in check, a task more easily accomplished after the defeat of the earl of Huntly at Corrichie in October 1562. In this period, political realities appear to have mattered more to Mary than religious persuasion and, in spite of the fears of Knox, and the fair promises made to the Pope, Mary made little attempt, beyond occasional grants of personal protection, to aid her fellow Catholics. Nevertheless, if Mary did not actively seek to promote Catholicism, the door was always open to such change as she refused to officially countenance the Reformed church and the Treaty of Edinburgh with the acts of the Reformation parliament remained unratified. Mary, however, was to act on more than one occasion as though the statutes which she refused to ratify had the force of law. Thus, while the act forbidding the saying of the Mass lacked legal sanction, a proclamation of the Privy Council with similar intent was frequently acted upon. Under its terms several priests were punished for saying the mass and for a time the archbishop of St Andrews, John Hamilton, was also imprisoned. Likewise, in contradistinction to papal authority, Mary could declare in charters confirming the sale of church lands in 1565, that her assent was 'as lauchful and of als greit strenth and avale as from the Pope and sete of Rome'. This attitude is also to be seen in the fact that while she resolutely refused to recognise the Protestant church, she accepted, in 1562 some measure of financial compromise by which the Reformed

CONCILIATION AND COMPROMISE 53

church should be maintained from a general taxation of the benefices of the old church. By this arrangement two-thirds of their former revenues were left with the old incumbents, and the remaining one-third was to be collected by the government for allocation between itself and the reformed ministry. This scheme can be viewed in different ways. It left the structure of the old church intact and theoretically made it possible to envisage a successful counter-reformation—a plot which Knox always considered feasible. Nevertheless, it allowed the Reformed church some financial provision and was thus statesmanlike in reconciling varying interests. On the other hand Mary's concern appears to have been neither to hold out hope to the old church, or to give some unofficial recognition to the new, but to simply ensure adequate finance for her own administration.

In political terms all these policies had much to commend them. For the first four years of her personal reign Mary walked the political tightrope with the expertise of her mother, governing her Protestant kingdom and yet retaining her Catholicism as a passport to European importance and with it her claim to the English throne. Nevertheless, it is open to question how far these policies were personal, or rather those of Mary's two chief advisers. The queen is certainly to be found carrying through the traditional duties of the monarch by presiding at meetings of her council, attending the opening of parliament and holding justice ayres in various parts of her kingdom throughout which she traversed at regular intervals, but her critics aver that her real interest lay only in the pleasures of music, dancing and the chase. Mary's dependence upon Moray and Maitland may have made this inevitable, and in an age in which sovereignty was increasing in importance, she may have found this intolerable. Marriage alone could free her from this bondage. Darnley may have been seen, not only as an adjunct to her claim to the English throne (succession to which she had failed to secure) but also as the means of disposing with the advice of others. Mary may then have hoped to follow in conjunction with her husband policies which could really be called her own. It may have been for this reason that Mary eventually abandoned a system which had served her so well. She could not have foreseen that her policies, and the husband whom she had chosen to help her in her task, would both prove unequal to the occasion.

The Quenis Maieste . . . efter hir returnyng out of France to Scotland, behaved hir self sa princely, sa honorably and discretly, that
hir reputation spred in all contrees; and was determynit and also
inclynit to continow in that kynd of comelynes, unto the end of hir
lyf; desyring to hald nane in hir company bot sic as wer of the best
qualitez and conversation, abhorring all vices and vitious per-
sonnes, whither they wer men or wemen; and requested me to
assist hir in gevyng hir my gud consaill, how sche mycht use the
meatest meanis till advance hir honest intention; and incaice sche,
being yet yong, mycht forget hir self in any unseamly gestour or
misbehavour, that I wald warn hir therof, with my admonition to
forbear and refourm the sam. Quhilk commission I refused alto-
gither, saying that hir verteous actions, hir naturell jugement, and
gret experience sche had learnit in the company of sa many notable
princes in the court of France, had instructed her sa weill and maid
hir sa able as to be ane exemplar to all hir subjectis and servandis.
Bot sche wald not leave it sa . . . she maid me famylier till all hir
maist urgent affaires; bot cheifly in hir dealing with any forren
nation, sche schew unto me all her lettres, and them that sche
resauit fra uther princes: and willit me to wret unto sic princes
as I had acquaintance of, and to some ofther consellours; wherin I
forget not to set out hir vertus, and wald schaw hir again ther
answers, and sic occurences as posted for the tym betwen contrees,
to hir gret contentement. For sche was of a quyk spirit, and curious
to knaw and to get intelligence of the estait of uther contrees.

Melville, Memoirs, 130–1.

When on Mary's return Maitland became her minister, it is plain
that he was still firmly convinced that a close alliance with England, a perfect understanding with Elizabeth, was the one safe
practicable policy. Of this policy Mary appears entirely to have
approved. She put herself in his hands; he became 'the whole
guider of her affairs'. 'His advice is followed more than any others.'
We must remember, therefore, when we read the letters in which
he expresses the utmost confidence that were the Queens to meet
a religious accord might be brought about, that Lethington was at
the time the Queen's most intimate and trusted adviser. If anyone

in Scotland knew what Mary's real sentiments were, Maitland did.
Skelton, *Maitland of Lethington*, ii, 26-27.

Under the guidance of the Lord James (created Earl of Moray in
1562) and Lethington, Mary pursued a policy marked by high
political intelligence. The general design was to present her as all
things to all men—that is, to conciliate the Scottish Protestants
and commend her to Elizabeth for recognition as heir to the English
throne, but at the same time to keep alive the hopes of English
Roman Catholics who might prefer her to Elizabeth and to maintain communications with the pope and with continental Roman
Catholic powers. Thus, on the one hand, Mary reassured the pope
with fair words, she insisted on having mass in her own chapel, and
she did not ratify the acts of the Parliament of 1560 against the
mass and in favour of the reformed religion. On the other hand,
she several times issued a proclamation in virtue of which priests
were prosecuted and imprisoned for saying mass beyond the con-
fines of the court, she acquiesced in an arrangement whereby a
proportion of the wealth of the old Church was shared between the
crown and the Protestant ministers, and she consented to legislation
which implied the official recognition, though not the full establishment, of the Reformed Church.

While she pursued these policies, Mary was following the line of
conciliation, in the tradition of wiser Scottish monarchs. It was
also to her advantage that she was a young Queen who had peculiar
opportunities in a country where a royal court centred on a
sovereign of adult years had been unknown since 1542. She had an
attractive, possibly fascinating, personality, and her tall, athletic
figure, combined with her liking for open-air activities, must have
won her the affections of her people on her many progresses
through the country. Each year from 1562 to 1566 she was in Fife
in the spring, in 1562 and 1564 she was in Aberdeen and Inverness
in the summer, in the summer of 1563 she was in Argyll and Ayr-
shire, and in the autumns of 1565 and 1566 she was in the south-
west or south. Her principal residence was Holyrood, but she
spent some quite long periods at Stirling. There would seem to be
little doubt that both by policy and personality she made herself

acceptable to the great majority of her people. The leading irre-
concilable was John Knox, who made up his mind when he first
met her that she was 'indurate against God and his truth'. It was
caustically observed that he was as full of distrust of the Queen
as if he were 'of God's privy council' and knew her destiny. But
not even all the ministers, let alone the laymen, of his Church,
agreed with him, and many saw no fault in their Queen's policy.

Donaldson, *Scottish Kings*, 184–5.

Within her own borders the Government of Scotland adjusted
itself in a similar spirit of jealous compromise. In the circumstances in which she found herself Mary had hardly a choice of
alternatives as to her immediate policy. . . . she could count on no
effective support from France, and, at the date of her arrival, the
Protestant party, through the fervour of its convictions and the
ability of its leaders, was the prevailing power in the country.
From the first, therefore, Maitland and the Lord James were her
chief counsellors, and to them is due the policy of the country
during the early years of her reign. On the other hand, the Protestant leaders were in as precarious a position as Mary herself. The
course of events since the meeting of the Estates in August 1560
had shown that the triumph of Protestantism was by no means
assured. The majority of the nobles and the majority of the people
were still Catholic. But it was to the party of the old Church that
Mary by all her instincts was naturally drawn, and her very
presence served to consolidate its strength and to define its aims.
By the consenting testimony of the time, the return of their Queen,
with all the glamour of youth, beauty, and an interesting personal
history, went to the heart of the Scottish people. Skilfully used,
the charm of her youth, her sex, her grace and accomplishments,
should eventually have assured her the general support of the
country. Fortunately for the future of Protestantism, Mary possessed little of the steady prudence and personal dignity of her
mother. Yet, such as she was, her personal qualities materially
increased the difficulties of the Protestant leaders. Devoid of the
higher qualities of mind and character, she was clever, self-willed,
and ambitious. With such a character and schooled by her already

varied experience, Mary, in spite of her youth, was no passive instrument in the hands of her advisers. Through the weakness of
their respective positions, therefore, Mary on the one hand and
the Protestant Lords on the other, were driven to mutual concessions, which in their hearts they were equally bound to dis-
approve.

Mary's desire would have been to bring back the old religion,
and with the aid of France to place herself on the throne of England; but, as things now went, such a plan could be only a dream
of the future. Left to themselves, Maitland and the Lord James
would have maintained the late religious settlement at once out of
policy and honest conviction. In the interest of both countries
they desired their speedy union. As England had definitively broken
with Rome, it was in the nature of things that Scotland should show
the same front. Thus, what Mary desired mainly for personal
reasons, Maitland and the Lord James desired for the well-being
of the two countries; and it was this common object that supplied
the basis of mutual understanding and a common policy. Mary
gave herself to the Protestant leaders on the condition that they
secured to her the English throne; they, on their part, made com-
promises in religion and politics, which, during the next four years,
it was the burden of Knox to denounce as an ill-omened compact
between God and Antichrist. Even in the point of worldly wisdom
events were to prove that Knox had seen deeper into the possibilities of things than the politicians themselves.

Brown, *John Knox*, ii, 157-9.

This defeat of Huntly brought the north parts in a great obedience,
and mightily discouraged those of the popish faction throughout
the whole realm; for all that sort had placed their hopes on him
and his greatness both in the court and country. The eldest of his
sons, named George, after the loss of that field, fled to the duke his
father-in-law, and was delivered by him to the queen, who sent
him prisoner to Dunbar. In the end of January he was accused and
convicted of treason, his lands declared to be forfeited, and himself
committed to prison. Shortly after, John Hamilton, archbishop of
St Andrews, was committed in the castle of Edinburgh, for saying

and hearing of mass. The abbot of Crossraguel and prior of Whithern were used in the like sort, and divers priests and monks for the same cause censured. The severe proceeding against papists put many in hope that the queen should be brought to embrace the religion; which was farther assured by the countenance she gave unto the Church in the parliament kept at Edinburgh the May following, wherein divers statutes passed upon their petitions, as in the acts of that time may be seen.

Spottiswoode, *History*, ii, 23–24.

The Privy Council provided that two-thirds of the ecclesiastical revenues—or of what was left of them—should be secured to the clergy of the old Church for life, and that one-third should be divided between the Crown and the Protestant pastors. The provision thus made for the ministry may have been very inadequate—though many lords, it was said, had not so much to spend—but more than this the Church did not receive even after the deposition of Mary in 1567; and coming from a Catholic Queen, the concession was most valuable in itself as a recognition of the right of the new religion to be supported by the State. The Romanists, seeing the matter in this light, declared that there now wanted nothing but the meeting of the two Queens to overthrow the Mass and all.

Mathieson, *Politics and Religion*, i, 103–4.

In the stoole of Edinburgh, Johne Knox said, "Weill, yf the end of this ordour, pretended to be tacken for sustentatioun of the Ministeris, be happy, my judgement failleth me; for I am assured that the Spreit of God is nott the auctor of it; for, first, I see Twa partis freely gevin to the Devill, and the Thrid maun be devided betwix God and the Devill: Weill, bear witnes to me, that this day I say it, or it be long the Devill shall have Three partis of the Thrid; and judge you then, what Goddis portioun shalbe."

Knox, *Works*, ii, 310.

The Queen, who ... was at Stirling on the 28th June [1562], has returned to Edinburgh some short space thereafter, in which place her Majesty sits in the Privy Council on the 30th July. And on the 14th day of August thereafter, her Majesty was in the Council again at Stirling; and on the 25th of that month she holds a Council at Edzel, being then in a progress to the more northerly parts of her Kingdom.

Keith, *History*, ii, 157.

Mary sat daily in Council several hours, in deliberation with her ministers and advisers; but, while thus occupied, she employed her hands with her needle—a little table of sandal-wood, with her work-basket and implements of industry, being always placed by her chair of state. Every rightly constituted mind must appreciate this characteristic trait of feminine propriety in a young female Sovereign, whom duty compelled to take the presiding place in a male assembly. It was necessary for her to listen with profound attention to the opinions of every one, and to deliver her own; but, instead of allowing her native modesty to assume the awkward appearance of embarrassment or bashfulness, she took refuge from encountering the gaze of so many gentlemen by bending her eyes on her embroidery, or whatever work she was engaged in.

Strickland, *Mary Queen of Scots,* i, 96.

'I have often heard the most serene princess Mary, Queen of Scotland, discourse so appositely and rationally in all affairs which were brought before the privy council that she was admired by all. And when most of the councillors were silent, being astonished, they straight declared themselves to be of her opinion, she rebuked them sharply and exhorted them to speak freely, as becomes un-prejudiced councillors, against her opinion, that the best reasons only might overrule their determinations. And, truely, her reasonings were so strong and clear that she could turn their hearts to that side she pleased. She had not studied law; and yet, by the natural light of her judgment, when she reasoned matters of equity and justice, she ofttimes had the advantage of the ablest lawyers. Her other discourses and actions were suitable to her great judgment.' [Sir Thomas Craig.]

Stevenson, *History of Mary Stewart*, cxxiv.

In presence of the counsell she was grave; but when she, her fidlers, and other dauncing companiouns, gott the hous alone, there might be seene unseemelie scripping, notwithstanding that she was wearing the doole weid. Her commoun speeche in secreit was, she saw nothing in Scotland but gravitie, which she could not agree weill with, for she was brought up in joyousitie. So termed she dancing, and other things thereto belonging.

Calderwood, *History*, ii, 158–9.

The Parliament began 26th May [1563], on which day the Queen came to it in her robes, and crowned; the Duke carrying the Crown, Argill the Scepter and Moray the Sword. She made in English an oracion publiquely there, and was present at the condemnation of the two Earles, Huntley and Southerland.

Keith, *History*, ii. 199–200.

As the Queen was resolved not to tolerate such a public contempt and disowning of her authority, she intended now [1566] to pass in person towards the Borders, and hold Courts of Justice at the town of Jedburgh for the trial and punishment of all loose, disorderly and traiterous persons.

Keith, *History*, ii, 462–3.

She loved the hardy outdoor life with hawk and hound. During the four years preceding her marriage, passing . . . whole days in the saddle, she had ridden through every part of her Kingdom, except

the wild and inaccessible district between the Cromarty and Pent-
land Firths. Before she had been a month in Scotland she had
visited Linlithgow, Stirling, Perth and St Andrews. The spring of
1562 was spent in Fife; the autumn in the northern counties. She
was at Castle Campbell in January 1563, when the Lady Margaret
was married to Sir James Stewart of Doune. She went back for a
few weeks to Holyrood, but she left again in February, and did not
return until the end of May. . . . The spring of 1564 was spent in
Fife; then in July, Parliament having been dissolved, she went to
the great deer-hunt in Athol, where 'three hundred and sixty deer,
with five wolves, and some roes', were slain; crossed the 'Mounth'
to Inverness; visited the Chanonry of Ross; and returning leisurely
by the east coast reached Holyrood on the 26th of September.

Skelton, *Maitland of Lethington*, ii, 4–6.

Mary was no stateswoman. With so entirely feminine a mind as
hers, Maitland, when he came into contact with it in politics, could
have no real sympathy. She wished to be Queen of England, and
in that wish he cordially supported her; but, while Maitland regarded the Stewart succession as a means of healing the breach of
centuries in a manner most honourable to Scotland, with Mary
it was wholly a matter of personal ambition. . . . At the time of her
marriage with Darnley the love of power was still her predominant
passion. Indignant that she had gained so little by her policy of
conciliation at home and abroad, she resolved to break with Protestantism both in Scotland and in England, to defy Elizabeth, to
restore Catholicism, and to humble the power of the nobles.

Mathieson, *Politics and Religion*, i, 135–6.

5

HUNTLY AND CORRICHIE

Amongst the post-Reformation Scottish nobility one of the chief supporters of Catholicism, in spite of a momentary wavering towards the Reformed cause in 1560, was George Gordon, fourth earl of Huntly who was, however, to be crushed by Lord James Stewart, in the name of the queen at Corrichie in October 1562, the earl himself dying of apoplexy at the height of the battle.

Mary's part in the overthrow of Huntly has frequently been in dispute, her attitude in this matter being particularly perplexing to those who have sought to defend her innate Catholicism. Nevertheless, from the moment of her arrival in Scotland, Mary had shown herself unwilling to co-operate with the schemes of the earl who had attempted to persuade her to land at Aberdeen, and was later to boast he could raise three whole shires for the queen. Likewise, although Huntly was a member of her council, his advice was not always sought. Moreover his attractions as a co-religionist were counterbalanced by the threat which he constituted to the peace and well being of the kingdom through his powerful holdings throughout north-eastern Scotland, in addition to which he had held since 1549 the revenues of the earldom of Moray. If the wider purposes of the campaign of 1562 were not at first defined, a limited objective certainly lay in the repossession of these revenues, the title to which had been secretly conveyed to Lord James Stewart in January of that year. This fact has allowed some pro-Marian writers, in their anxiety to allay Mary's guilt in the crushing of this Catholic noble, to place all blame for the expedition on Lord James. In this they are joined by Knox who unwilling to give Mary any credit, even in the crushing of one of his adversaries, claimed that 'sche rejosed nott greatlie of the successe of that mater'. Most writers, however, have been content to recognise Mary's share in the venture and have either condemned her action as a political and religious blunder, or praised it as an act of necessity. Mary herself was not unaware of this duality for while she saw Huntly's defeat as a task well accomplished, she also knew that her Catholic friends in Europe might see matters in a different light. Thus, in writing to her uncle the Cardinal of Lorraine in January 1563, she asked him to 'make excuses if I have failed in any part of my duty towards religion'. Rather than signifying repentance, however, it has been observed that the tone of the letter 'can be more readily interpreted as an apologetic for something that had to be done'. Here as elsewhere political realities appear to have been of more significance to Mary than any phantom of religion.

Historically considered, it is no exaggeration to say that Huntly has been a target for the partisans of two contending factions. Calumniated upon one side by the Marian apologists, who have seen in him only a blot upon the memory of the object of their devotion, he has fared equally ill at the hands of the glorifiers of the Reformation, to whom he has presented himself merely in the light of the upholder of the doctrines of the 'Scarlet Woman' and the enemy of Murray.

Duncan, Mary Stuart and House of Huntly in *SHR,* iv, 365–6.

The Erle of Murray send message unto the Quene of the mervalouse victorye, and humblie prayed hir to schaw that obedience to God as publictlie to convene with thame, to geve thankis unto God for his notable deliverance. Sche glowmed boyth at the messenger and at the requeast, and skarselie wold geve a good worde or blyth countenance to any that sche knew earnest favoraris of the Erle of Murray, whose prosperitie was and yitt is, a verray vennoume to hyr boldened harte, against him for his godlynes and uprycht plainess. Of many dayes she bair no better countenance; whairby it myght have bene evidentlie espyed, that sche rejosed nott greatlie of the successe of that mater.

Knox, *Works,* ii, 358.

There can exist no doubt that the whole expedition was primarily
the work of Mary, and that outside instigation had little to do with
it. She entered upon the undertaking with the utmost zest, and
from first to last pursued Huntly with the ferocity of a tigress. In
the words of the English ambassador, Randolph, who accompanied
this royal progress and is the determining authority upon it, "She
is utterly determined to bring him to utter confusion".

Duncan, Mary Stuart and House of Huntly in *SHR*, iv, 368–9.

Some authors, guided by their prejudices rather than their re-
search, have imagined that the fate of this great baron may be
traced to a premeditated conspiracy of Moray, who carried the
queen north, and prevailed on her to provoke Huntly into rebellion
by her suspicions and neglect. This is mere conjecture, it is certain
that the northern progress was planned by the queen herself, and
that her council, of whom Moray was the chief, so far from exciting
Mary against Huntly urged her to visit him at Strathbogie . . . It was
natural that Moray should rejoice in the fall of so potent an enemy
to the Protestant party as Huntly. It is true that he availed himself
of his offences to strengthen his own power; but that prior to the
rebellion, he had laid a base design to entrap him into treason, is an
opinion founded on conjecture, and contradicted by fact.

P. F. Tytler, *History of Scotland*, iii, 167.

The exact nature of the understanding that existed between Mary
and Murray in regard to the uprooting of the house of Gordon, is
one of the problems of Scotch history which has remained unsolved. Bringing down as it did the tottering fabric of Roman
Catholicism in Scotland, the ruining of Huntly can only be
described, from the point of view of a Marian partizan, as a
political blunder of the first magnitude. The ardour, however,
with which the Queen flung herself into the campaign against her
co-religionists does not suggest any form of coercion and there is
no evidence that she required persuading in the matter. As to
Murray, who, according to Bishop Lesly, was the "sole favourite

and disposer of everything", at this period, his gain was immeasurable. Not only did he render secure his long coveted earldom, get quit of a dangerous adversary, and deal a staggering blow to Catholicism, but a favourable impression was made upon the mind of Elizabeth, and for the time being the English alliance was placed upon a footing of greater stability.

Duncan, Relations of Earl of Murray with Mary Stuart
in *SHR*, vi, 52–53.

Whatever the object of Mary's progress to the North may have been—whether it was planned by the Lord James for his own aggrandisement, as some Mariolaters affirm, or intended by Mary for his destruction as Knox suspected, or undertaken for her deliverance from his power and for her marriage to Sir John Gordon, as Huntly's grandson gravely records, or occasioned merely by Mary's desire to see the country and to establish good order—it had resulted in the disgrace, defeat, and death of the virtual ruler of the North, and in the utter ruin of his house for the time being. Huntly's overthrow and Sutherland's condemnation had, moreover, greatly weakened the influence of that Church, which she was assuring the Pope—alike by legate and by letter—was the object of her undying devotion; and she—the most fair rose among heretical thorns—had not scrupled to receive the rich ecclesiastical vestments seized at Strathbogie, some of which she was afterwards to hand over to the profligate Bothwell, and some to other profane purposes. If the most powerful of the Popish nobles had suffered on the one hand, the most prominent of the Protestants had, on the other, reaped substantial advantages. The Lord James had gone to the North as Earl of Mar, he returned to the South as Earl of Murray; and to him, too, there fell no mean share of the valuable spoils of Strathbogie.

Fleming, *Mary Queen of Scots*, 80–81.

3

6

A ZEALOUS CATHOLIC?

Mary's devotion to Catholicism has been frequently emphasised by friend and foe alike. The former has striven to describe the queen as a martyr for a religion to which she was always constant while the latter has seen in her devotion to her faith the principal cause of her downfall. Thus, Knox who firmly believed that Mary's sole concern was to restore the Catholic faith could write 'sche plainlie purposed to wrak the religioun within this Realme; to the Roman Antichrist sche hath maid her promeise: and from him sche hath takin money to uphold his pompe'.

At no time, however, did Mary provide the leadership which the forces of counter-reformation would have required. This attitude was apparent from the moment of her arrival in Scotland when she aligned herself with the party politically committed to the Protestant cause, and thereafter, Mary's attitude to religious issues was almost entirely guided by political considerations. Papal emissaries received little encouragement and although she informed the Pope in 1563 that 'we are now doing our best to make a number of prelates go to the Council [of Trent]', her real intention was quite the opposite. Indeed, far from being zealous for the propagation of her faith, Mary by her actions before 1564, showed such disinclination to aid her co-religionists that by 1565 communication between herself and the Papacy had almost come to an end.

It is in 1565 on the eve of her marriage to Darnley that the only real attempt to aid Catholicism comes to light. In February of that year, a Catholic evensong, which was later condoned by the queen, was held in Edinburgh and in March it was reported that as many attended mass in the capital as the Protestant service. Such evidence can be cited to show a more active policy on Mary's part to at least protect her fellow Catholics but whether it adds up to much more is extremely doubtful, and other evidence to the same end is less convincing. The provision of John Sinclair to the bishopric of Brechin in

September 1565 was not designed to aid the Catholic position in Scotland, and although following her marriage to Darnley, Mary informed the Pope that she would 'restore religion to splendour', and the Pope in turn congratulated Mary and Darnley in having 'restored the due worship of God throughout the realm', Mary appears to have been more interested in obtaining a papal subsidy at this time than promoting the faith. Her dealings with Philip of Spain appear to be of the same order, and information laid before that sovereign that she was following a Catholic policy also appears to have been financially motivated. It is impossible to be certain of Mary's designs at this juncture and a relaxation of the enforcement of the law against mass-mongering certainly seems to have been contemplated, but it is more than doubtful whether Mary ever thought much else was possible. She certainly never contemplated entering into a Catholic League and Mary's involvement in such a conspiracy, which some historians have insisted was initiated at Bayonne in July 1565, is a figment of their own imagination. As she was Catholicism's only hope of a revival in Scotland, however, she was able to play on that fact in her attempts to gain financial help. Whatever her motives, the possibility of further Catholic concessions never reappeared and as her political position grew more extreme, Mary revealed the extent to which her religious zeal was submersed in political reality when faced with the complete collapse of her policies she began in 1566 to make concessions to the Reformed church whereby succession to lesser benefices was assured and a degree of statutory recognition at last achieved.

In short, it is abundantly clear, whatever her Protestant detractors might aver, that in her public policy towards religion, political considerations came first with Mary, a fact which even her staunchest defenders are usually forced to admit. It was politic abroad to maintain Catholic promises, but even more politic at home to pursue political realities. That these considerations were in any way equally balanced undoubtedly stemmed from Mary's claim to the English throne, and but for that she would almost certainly have made concessions to the Reformed church at a much earlier date.

To impugn Mary's Catholicism in this way does not detract from the case of those writers who would maintain that Mary's personal devotion to her religious faith must be the prime consideration. Both to the Pope and his emissary De Gouda, Mary asserted that she would be 'prepared to die rather than to abandon her religion'. She resolutely refused to give up the Mass, and although a political con-struction can be placed even upon this action, her own words as re-ported in 1565 have a ring of truth when she exclaimed 'What? Wolde you that I sholde mayke marchandize of my religion, or frame myself to your menestors willes? It cane not be so.' Mary's personal beliefs have clearly a strong factual basis, but her marriage to Bothwell according to the Protestant form in 1567, poses even her most ardent eulogists with problems which are not easily answered especially since the Pope six weeks after the event himself declared that it was not his intention to have any further dealings with Mary 'unless in times to come he shall see some better sign of her life and religion than he has witnessed in the past'. At this stage it was believed that Mary was willing to become a Calvinist in order to salvage her political career. Mary's co-religionists were deeply shocked by her religious insincerity. They believed that she was apostatising from the basest of motives and not until her deposition and imprisonment in England did their interest in her religious constancy become alive again.

Nursed from her infancy in a blind attachment to the Roman Catholic religion, every means had been employed before she left France, to strengthen this prejudice, and to inspire her with aver-sion to the religion which had been embraced by her people. She was taught, that it would be to the glory of her reign to induce her Kingdom to the obedience of the Romish See, and to co-operate with the Popish Princes on the Continent in extirpating heresy. With these fixed prepossessions, Mary came into Scotland, and she adhered to this with singular pertinacy to the end of her life.

McCrie, *Knox*, ii, 22.

John Knox: Her soul
          Is as a flame of fire, insatiable,
          And subtle as thin water; with her craft
          Is passion mingled so inseparably

That each gets strength from other, her swift wit
By passion being enkindled and made hot,
And by her wit her keen and passionate heart
So tempered that it burn itself not out,
Consuming to no end. Never, I think,
Hath God brought up against the people of God
To try their force or feebleness of faith
A foe than this more dangerous, nor of mood
More resolute against him.

Swinburne, *Bothwell*, 46.

She saw her Church oppressed, but she could not help it, and
would not on that account break with those who governed in her
name. She could do nothing to remedy the evil and she did that
nothing gracefully, even felicitously.

Pollen, *Queen Mary's Letter to Guise*, xliv–xlv.

As Mary was a Catholic, and the party which opposed her was
mainly, though not entirely, Protestant, the success of the revolution brought with it the establishment of the Reformed Church.
This in itself was a very desirable result; but unfortunately it was
accomplished in a manner which detracted very greatly from its
value. Mary was more than a Catholic. Contrary to her own
wishes, she had become the embodiment of compromise in Scotland, the hope of all who believed that religion, however vitally
important, is not the sum and substance of a nation's life; and
her fall was a triumph of extreme principles, tempered only in
practice by the sagacity and the selfishness of their professed
adherents. It is true that Mary was by no means a martyr to her
faith, that she fell rather through her indifference than through her
devotion to Catholicism; but this consideration could have no
weight with men who regarded every evil that befell their adversaries as evidence of the divine displeasure.

Mathieson, *Politics and Religion*, i, 146.

The misapprehension which finally brought about the subversion of
Huntly, seems undoubtedly to have been his belief in the genuineness of Mary's Catholicism. In this, though doomed to be bitterly
deceived, he was just as much at sea as were the leaders of the
Calvinists. Of the fact that Mary had landed upon the shores of
Scotland indifferent to all scenes but that of the English succession, both factions were equally ignorant.

Duncan, Mary Stuart and House of Huntly in *SHR*, iv, 367–8.

Mary had every reason to congratulate herself in October 1565.
She had outwitted Elizabeth, married the one man who would
strengthen her claim to the English throne, and driven her rebels
across the frontier in ignominious flight. This she ultimately decided, was but the first step in the great Catholic design to which
she had committed herself. The next move was to restore the old
religion in Scotland; once this was accomplished she could come
to grips with her 'good sister' in London, with Spanish aid, and
reign over a united, Catholic Britain. If Mary had succeeded in
this grandiose scheme, the death knell of Protestantism would
have sounded all over Europe. It is not too much to say that the
course of events in Scotland in the winter of 1565–66, which culminated in the ruin of Mary's plots, was one of the decisive
factors in assuring the survival of British, and hence of European
Protestantism.

Lee, *James Stewart, earl of Moray*, 156–7.

At no time during Mary's reign in Scotland was there any secret
league or treaty made by the Catholic powers of Europe, in order
to uphold Catholicism and to suppress Protestantism. There was
not even a 'quasi-treaty' or a 'mutual understanding' to this effect.
On the other hand, there was a decided 'community of sentiment'
amongst Catholics on this subject, and it would appear that this
'community of sentiment' has been mistaken for a Papal League.

Pollen, *Papal Negotiations*, xxxviii.

Mary herself was deeply tinctured with all the prejudices of popery; a passionate attachment to that superstitition is visible in every part of her character, and runs through all the scenes of her life: she was devoted too with the utmost submission to the princes of Lorrain, her uncles; and had been accustomed from her infancy to listen to all their advices with a filial respect. The prospect of restoring the public exercise of her own religion, the pleasure of complying with her uncles, and the hopes of gratifying the French monarch, whom the present situation of her affairs in England made it necessary to court, counterbalanced all the prudent considerations which had formerly weighed with her. She instantly joined the confederacy, which had been formed for the destruction of the protestants, and altered the whole plan of her conduct with regard to Murray and his adherents.

To this fatal resolution may be imputed all the subsequent calamities of Mary's life. Ever since her return into Scotland, fortune may be said to have been propitious to her rather than adverse; and if her prosperity did not rise to any great height, it had, however, suffered no considerable interruption. A thick and settled cloud of adversity, with few gleams of hope, and none of real enjoyment, covers the remainder of her days.

W. Robertson, *History of Scotland,* ii, 143–4.

In 1566 there was got up a scheme of Pope Pius IV and the sovereigns of France and Spain to exterminate the Protestants over Christendom. It was called the Treaty of Bayonne. Mary never joined or subscribed to it, nor is there *bona fide* evidence that she was even asked to do so. The statement that she did comes from Robertson, and it would appear that he founds on a letter written by Mary to the Archbishop of Glasgow; but on reference to the original, it has been discovered that in Robertson's narrative the extract from Mary's letter has been garbled, and the meaning of her words reversed.

Cowan, *Mary Queen of Scots,* i, 95–96.

Nothing can be more unhappy for a people than to be governed by a sovereign attached to a religion different from the established; and it is scarcely possible that mutual confidence can ever, in such a situation, have place between the prince and his subjects. Mary's conduct had been hitherto, in every respect, unexceptionable, and even laudable; yet she had not made such progress in acquiring popularity as might have been expected from her gracious deportment and agreeable accomplishments. Suspicions every moment prevailed on account of her attachment to the catholic faith, and especially to her uncles, the open and avowed promoters of the scheme for exterminating the professors of the reformed religion throughout all Europe. She still refused to ratify the acts of parliament which had established the reformation; she made attempts for restoring to the catholic bishops some part of their civil jurisdiction; and she wrote a letter to the council of Trent, in which besides professing her attachment to the catholic faith, she took notice of her title to succeed to the crown of England, and expressed her hopes of being able, in some period, to bring back all her dominions to the bosom of the church. The zealots among the protestants were not wanting, in their turn, to exercise their insolence against her, which tended still more to alienate her from their faith.

Hume, *History of England*, 455.

Marriage to Bothwell

The mariage was maid in the palice of Halyrudhouse, at a preaching by Adam Bodowell bischop of Orkeney, in the gret hall for the consaill uses to sit, according to the ordour of the refourmed religion; and not in the chapell at the mess, as was the Kingis mariage.

Melville, *Memoirs*, 178–9.

Not only to dispense, in the case of what she was supposed to deem a holy sacrament, with the rites of a Church on behalf of which she had but lately been preparing a great crusade, but to submit for the first time in her life to Protestant rites, was evidence sufficient of how entirely she had now lost her bearings. She had almost ceased meanwhile to be a responsible being. The trials of her political situation, the miseries of her marriage to Darnley, from which his murder had come to be the only method of escape, and her passionate infatuation for Bothwell, had all contributed their share in effecting that mental and moral shock which, in the case of a woman, dissolves the conventional respectabilities that have been her main guidance, and lets loose the full flood of her emotional instincts.

Henderson, *Mary Queen of Scots*, ii, 461.

Mary's co-religionists were greatly shocked by the religious insincerity she displayed on this occasion. Her repeated promises of constancy before and after, and her constancy itself, which was never otherwise seriously shaken, bring her guilt in this matter into higher relief. To her friends abroad it seemed that she was actually apostatising from the basest of motives, and without the pretence of being convinced.

Pollen, *Papal Negotiations*, cxxxii.

THE CARDINAL OF ALESSANDRIA
TO THE BISHOP OF MONDOVI

Rome, 2 July 1567.

Most Reverend,—With your letter of the 18th of last month I received the five writings which you enumerated, and I have discussed all with our lord the Pope. In answer, he commissions me to write in the following manner, to wit, that whereas his Holiness has never hitherto dissembled about anything, he will not begin to do so now, especially in this all important matter of religion. Wherefore, with regard to the Queen of Scots in particular, it is not his intention to have any further communication with her, unless, indeed, in times to come he shall see some better sign of her life and religion than he has witnessed in the past. This is all

3*

the direction I have to give you for this affair, which your lordship will henceforth manage in conformity with the mind of his Holiness. Nothing more occurs to me at present except to offer you my continued service.

From Rome, on the 2nd of July 1567.

The Cardinal of Alessandria.

Pollen, *Papal Negotiations*, 397.

7

THE ENGLISH SUCCESSION

*At the age of seventeen, Mary who was queen of Scots in her own
right, and queen-dauphiness of France by marriage, laid claim to a
third Kingdom, that of England. The occasion followed the death of
Mary Tudor and the accession of her half-sister Elizabeth in November 1558, as the result of which Mary could claim, through descent
from Henry VII, to be heiress presumptive to the throne of England.
If, however, as many Catholics believed, Elizabeth was illegitimate
then Mary's claim was more immediate. The Guise faction in France
loath to miss any opportunity which might be turned to political advantage seized upon this, and persuaded Mary and Francis to assume the
royal arms of England, which they continued to do after Francis'
accession to the throne on 10 July 1559. A year later, however, by the
Treaty of Edinburgh (July 1560), it was agreed that in addition to
the withdrawal of foreign troops from Scotland that Francis and
Mary should abandon the use of the arms and style of sovereign of
England, thus recognising Elizabeth's title.*

*In its French context, Francis' death in December of that year
settled the issue, but while Mary apparently never used the style
'queen of England' after her husband's death, her refusal to ratify the
Treaty of Edinburgh after her return to Scotland constituted a perpetual irritant to Elizabeth. On several occasions Mary was urged
to accept the Treaty and with it Elizabeth's right to the English
throne. She always refused to do so, apparently seeing in her immediate claim to the English title, even though she no longer regarded
herself as queen, a weapon which might be used to wring from Elizabeth the concession that she was her heir. This Elizabeth was not
prepared to concede and so the situation remained unsolved in spite of
Maitland's valiant attempts to reach a compromise. Instead, after
four years of indecision in which Mary at least appears to have become more and more impatient, the queen of Scots took the impetuous
step of strengthening her claim by announcing her betrothal to Darnley*

*whereupon Elizabeth retaliated by announcing that she did not
intend to reveal her succession plans. The tumultuous events of the
following two years left Mary with little room to manœuvre on this
particular issue, but with her flight to England in May 1568 her claim
to the throne of that country and the fact that she had once borne the
title of its queen was to be a major factor in her imprisonment and,
after the numerous plots which her claims engendered, to be paramount
in leading finally to her execution.*

To be prepared for the course which this Princess would hold, and
to figure the extremes into which she might possibly run, we may
previously take, from the facts in her history, a view of the passions
which prevailed most in her mind.

Of all these, the earliest, the latest, and the strongest, was the
passion for power. In this, was she always absorbed. At all times,
she viewed herself as a Sovereign, and not only as the Queen of
Scotland, but about in her own person, or in that of her offspring,
to sit on the throne of England, and stretch forth a sceptre over the
whole British isles. The royal authority in her own Kingdom, she
would divide with no party, no minister, no husband.

                    T. Robertson, *Mary Queen of Scots*, 22–23.

The Quen being returnit in Scotland, was glaidly welcom unto the
haill subjectis. For folowing the consaill of hir frendis, sche behaved hir self humanly unto them all, bot committed the cheif
handling of hir affaires to hir brother the Pryour of St Androwes,
(whom efterwart sche maid Erle of Murray,) and to the secretaire
Liddington, as metest baith to hald the contre at hir devotion, and
also to pak up a strait frendschip betwen hir Majeste and the
Quen of England. For my L. of Murray had gret credit with my L.
Robert Dudly, wha was efterwart maid Erle of Leceister; and the
secretary Liddingtoun had gret credit with the secretaire Cicill. Sa
thir four pakit up a strait and sisterly frendschip betwen the twa

Quenis and ther contrees, as apperit outwartly na mair difference in langage, bot that the Quen of England wes the eldest sister, and the Quen of Scotland the yonger sister, whom the Quen of England promysed to declair second persone, with tym, according to hir gud behaviour; sa that lettres and intelligence past oukly [weekly] be post betwen them, and nathing mair desyred for the first then they mycht sea uther, be a meating at a convenient place, whereby they mycht also declair ther hartly and loving myndis till uther.

Melville, Memoirs, 91.

In the beginning of the next summer there was a great speech of the interview of the queens of England and Scotland, and messengers to and fro sent to agree upon the place, the time, and manner of the meeting. The motion came from the queen of Scots, who, as it was thought, greatly affected the same out of a desire she had to live in a firm peace with the queen of England, and make herself known to the subjects of that country. Neither was the meeting disliked of the better sort, as thinking it would serve, besides the preservation of the common peace, to bring her unto a liking of the reformed religion. But they who were popishly set, fearing greatly the conference, spake openly against it, saying, that of such interviews there was never seen any good fruit, and that it would not be safe for the queen of Scots to put herself in the power of her whose kingdom she had claimed. Not the less the treaty went on, and was concluded; York condescended to be the place of meeting, the numbers on either side agreed unto, and the time designed about the end of June. But whilst all things were in readiness for the journey, the queen of England excused herself by letters, desiring the interview should be put off till the next year; which the queen of Scots was not ill pleased to hear, for she feared if the same had held, that the French king and her uncles should have been much offended.

Spottiswoode, History, ii, 19.

William Matlane of Leithington, younger, being sent soone after
the arrivall of our queene to Queene Elizabeth, returned before
December. The effect of his negociation was to salute the queene
in his mistresse's name; to make knowne her good-will toward her,
and minde to interteane peace and unitie. He delivered also letters
directed from our nobilitie, wherein they remembred courteouslie
her former favour, requeisted her to provoke our queene to constant amitie by some tokins of her good affectioun; speciallie by
declaring her successour and heyre-apparent, in the nixt parliament: for that would be the most forcible meane to burie all former
rancour in oblivioun, and to exhaust the fountaine of discorde in
times to come. Queene Elizabeth answered, she expected another
ambassadge; that his mistresse according to her promise made, to
ratifie the treatie at Leith [Edinburgh], als soone as she returned
home, and might have the advice of her nobles. She had done so.
The other answered, that he was sent soone after her arrivall,
before she had medled with anie publick effaires: that she was
busseid in receaving courteous salutatiouns of her nobles, but
most of all in settling the estate of religioun: that manie of the
nobilitie, namelie, suche as dwelt in the remote parts, were not
then come to court, without whose advices she could not resolve
in suche a mater. The queene replyed, "What needeth new con-
sultatioun for that to which she had alreadie bound herself by seale
and subscriptioun?" The other rejoyned, he had no commissioun
for that bussinesse. In end, the queene said, "In regarde his mistresse hath not ratifeid the treatie, according to her promise, nor
deserved anie benefite at her hands, but rather had provoked her to
anger by usurping her armes, yitt she sould procure that nothing
be done in prejudice of her right, but leave it free to the estats to
decide betwixt her and her competitors. Successour she would
declare none. For unconstant people looke commounlie to the
sunne rysing, or designed successours, and forsake the sunne
setting; and designed and confirmed successours cannot conteane
themselves within bounds, but animated with their owne hopes, or
stirred up by malcontents, affected present governement. I will
not," quoth she, "be foolish as to hang a wynding-sheet before
myne owne eyes; or to make myself a funerall feast whill I am
alive." In end, the queene was drawin this farre, as to consent that
some commissioners sould meete for both sides, and reforme the

treatie after this manner; That the Queene of Scots absteane frome the armes of England, and the titles of England and Ireland, during her lyfe-time, and her childrein, if she had anie; and that neither she, nor anie of her posteritie, seeke to waiken or diminishe anie right our queene had to the crowne of England.

Calderwood, *History*, ii, 167–9.

Seeing no fruit of their action, Mary grew impatient of her Protestant advisers, and in the year 1564 she passed under new influences which eventually involved her ruin. Acting on other counsels than those of Moray and Maitland, she turned her thoughts to her cousin Darnley as the most suitable helpmate for all the ends she had at heart. As to what these ends were there can be no uncertainty; to unite the two crowns, to restore the old religion, to be in her realms what the French and Spanish monarchs were in theirs—were objects which by temper and upbringing she naturally desired to compass. To everybody it was apparent that her union with Darnley was admirably fitted to further these ends. After herself he had the best claim to the English crown, and as of her own religion he had the support of all the English Catholics. In Scotland his religion was a disadvantage; but, as events showed, not so serious as might have been anticipated.

Brown, *John Knox*, ii, 205–6.

8

MARRIAGE PROPOSITIONS

From almost the moment of her widowhood, the question of Mary's remarriage became the subject of discussion throughout Europe. Her brother-in-law, Charles IX of France, the kings of Denmark and Sweden, the heir to the Spanish throne—Don Carlos, the archduke Charles of Austria, and nearer home Lord Darnley and the earl of Arran were all reckoned as possible competitors for Mary's hand within a short space of time.

Mary's preference was undoubtedly for a continental marriage although such a union inevitably raised difficulties. The tying of Scotland to the coat-strings of a foreign power would not be popular among the nobility who had only recently raised the banner of revolt against the extension of French influence in Scotland, and even less to the liking of Elizabeth to whom such a match would constitute a personal danger. In the event, however, most of the foreign contenders for the queen's hand had too little to offer by way of return, for Mary was almost certainly seeking the necessary resources to help her implement her claim to the English succession. Only two of her foreign suitors, Charles IX and Don Carlos, could have done this, and as marriage to the former was never a practicable proposition, owing to opposition in France, the chief negotiations took place with the Spanish king, Philip II. Such a match would have allowed Mary to make a direct bid for the English throne, a point which Elizabeth saw only too clearly, and yet beyond certain negotiations of her own and the promise that if Mary married to please her, she would be made her heir, Elizabeth's hands were tied. The negotiations for the marriage on Mary's part, however, were not straightforward, and even without the insanity of Don Carlos in 1564 which brought the proposal to an end, it was by no means certain that marriage would have taken place. Nevertheless, the mere possibility had given Mary a strong bargaining point in her negotiations with Elizabeth over her rights of succession.

With the match at an end, this advantage passed to Elizabeth. No further continental suitors were to appear and with Arran, also insane, Mary's choice of future husbands had become extremely limited. Hence, perhaps, Elizabeth's disparaging offer of Robert Dudley and the permission granted to Henry, Lord Darnley, who was next in succession to the English throne after Mary herself, to return to Scotland. At this juncture Elizabeth had almost certainly predetermined to use the opportunity of a match between Mary and Darnley as an excuse for declaring that she would not name her heir, and at the same time such a marriage would end further continental speculation in Mary's future—both very positive points in Elizabeth's favour.

The two great objects which now filled Mary's mind, and employed the earnest deliberations of her ministers, were her right of succession to the English throne, and her marriage. On both points she was anxious, as indeed it was her interest, to consult the wishes of Elizabeth. She had now remained in a widowed state for three years: she was convinced that a speedy marriage was the best measure for herself and her kingdom; her opinion was fortified by that of Moray and Lethington, and her hand had been already sought by the king of Sweden, the Infant of Spain, and the Archduke Charles, second son of the emperor; yet Elizabeth, although ever ready to oppose every foreign match, continued to preserve much mystery in stating her own wishes on the subject. It was evident it could not long suit the dignity of an independent princess to listen to ingenious objections, and repress every royal suitor in submission to the wishes of a sister queen. About this time a report having reached the English court, that the successful candidate was one of the emperor's lineage, Cecil wrote in much alarm to Moray, who replied with firmness and good sense, that nothing serious had been yet concluded. But he added, that neither was it for her honour, nor could he advise her, to repress the suit of princes, however deeply interested in the continuance of the friendship between the two queens, and the mutual love and quietness of their subjects.

P. F. Tytler, *History of Scotland,* iii, 171.

The crowding drama of Elizabeth's reign changed, and interest began to centre on the personal relations between herself and Mary, two young Queens, cousins and neighbours. What was to be expected but relentless enmity? Elizabeth had as good as robbed Mary of the allegiance of her subjects, and set up a religious and political rule in Scotland that was obnoxious to her. Mary on her side had refused to ratify the Treaty of Edinburgh, and, given the will and power, could take a leaf out of her rival's book, stir up Catholic discontent in England, perhaps make a bid for the English throne. There was provocation and danger in her very widowhood, for she could challenge her cousin's attraction as the best marriage in Europe. Suitors who had spent money, time and temper on Elizabeth, were turning to woo a woman less virginal and elusive, and it was not many weeks before the names of Don Carlos of Spain, the Archduke Charles, the King of Sweden, and the King of Denmark, were on people's lips. With Elizabeth it was political necessity—perhaps also it was instinct—to begrudge another her half or wholly rejected suitors. Any one of these princes, if married to Mary, was likely to regard the English throne as a tempting morsel, and behind Don Carlos and the Archduke Charles there was powerful Catholic backing. The national boundary between England and Scotland might disappear, the two people be embroiled in religious war, and the greater part of the Continent be drawn in, setting Catholic against Protestant throughout Christendom. A nightmare these fears might be; but not an idle one. Europe was ripe for such folly. Knox and his like were Protestants first and Scotsmen, Frenchmen, or Germans afterwards, and it was the same with the growing number of ardent Catholics. Let the future, by happy fortune, escape the peril; still, the well-being of Christendom was linked with the relations of these two Queens.

Neale, *Queen Elizabeth*, 107–8.

Mary's matrimonial affairs occupied, at this time, the attention of her friends, foes, rivals, and kinsfolk. The desire of Philip II to accomplish a marriage between her and his heir, Don Carlos, had, from the first month of Mary's widowhood, caused equal uneasiness to the Queen of England and the Queen-regent of France. Cardinal Lorraine, preferring the interests of France to the aggrandizement of his niece, endeavoured to divert Mary from Carlos, by negotiating a matrimonial treaty, unsanctioned by her, with the Emperor, for a marriage between her and the Archduke Charles, the Emperor's third son, one of the rejected candidates for the hand of the Queen of England. The Archduke Charles was several years older than Mary, brave, prudent, and highly accomplished, and in all respects a more suitable consort for her than Carlos, who was three years her junior, and had already manifested strong symptoms of the fearful phrenal malady which had been inherited from his great-grandmother Joanna of Castile. He was, moreover, epileptic, and so intractable in temper that no one could exercise any beneficial influence over him, when plunged in his constitutional fits of gloom or irascibility, excepting his charming stepmother Elizabeth of France.

> Strickland, *Mary Queen of Scots*, i, 145.

In June [1563], Mary opened Parliament in great state, and was loudly cheered by the people on her way to the tolbooth of Edinburgh. Knox was angered by the pomp, and alarmed by the popular applause for the Queen, and he preached a sermon against what he later termed, in his *History*, the 'stinking pride of women'. Then, towards the end of the Parliamentary session, he preached another sermon in the presence of most of the nobility, in which he referred to the Queen's marriage.

'I hear of the Queen's marriage: dukes, brethren to emperors, and kings, strive all for the best game. But this, my Lords, will I say (note the day, and bear witness after) whensoever the nobility of Scotland, professing the Lord Jesus, consents that an infidel (and all Papists are infidels) shall be head to your sovereign, ye do so far as in ye lieth to banish Christ Jesus from this realm; ye bring God's vengeance upon the country, a plague upon yourself, and perchance ye shall do small comfort to your sovereign.'

This sermon angered many of the lords, the Protestants as well as the Catholics. The question of Mary's marriage was the subject of complicated intrigues in every court in Europe; the Archduke

Charles of Austria, Don Carlos of Spain, Eric XIV of Sweden, the Prince of Condé—for this Protestant leader was at one time the nominee of the Cardinal of Lorraine—and the Earl of Leicester, whom Elizabeth was urging her to marry, were all being considered as candidates for her hand. The marriage problem involved such considerations as the threat to English national security, the religious question, Mary's succession to the English crown, the relations between Philip II and the Emperor, and a possible alliance between the Guises and the Bourbons in France; and Lord James and Lethington were conducting elaborate and secret negotiations with most of the potential suitors. Knox's intervention exasperated them greatly. Events were soon to prove Knox right. As usual, while ignoring the diplomatic subtleties, Knox put his finger on the central political issue: the fate of the Reformation in Scotland depended chiefly upon whether Mary married a Catholic or a Protestant.

Ridley, *John Knox*, 425–6.

Where she should bestow her hand had fluttered European diplomacy since her return from France. Mary herself stood passive. Eager to win Elizabeth's recognition, she declared she would wed only with her cousin's goodwill. She could bestow her hand among so many suitors to Elizabeth disagreeable that her compliance deserved the return she was denied. She now resolved to force it by beckoning a husband from quarters Elizabeth disapproved. Her uncle the Cardinal of Lorraine introduced Archduke Charles of Austria. Mary refused him: his means were inadequate to assist her schemes. Catharine de' Medici, anxious lest Spain should usurp France's place in Scotland, proposed her son Charles IX, if Mary would wait till he was marriageable! The Guises scotched the proposal. Like Mary, their eyes were fixed on Don Carlos, son of Philip II of Spain, who hoped to add the British to the Spanish realms and secure tranquillity in the Netherlands through the friendship of the Guises. In the summer of 1563 the French were known to 'marvellously fear the marriage' and Elizabeth, greatly concerned, insisted that 'it will not be done.' Moray was not adverse to it. As Kirkcaldy of Grange wrote to

Randolph in April 1564, the proposal was entertained 'to cause England grant our desyris.' If the marriage took place, it promised Moray supremacy in Scotland in his sister's absence and the triumph of Calvinism. Knox thundered against the union, Elizabeth threatened that it would be held an act of hostility, the Cardinal of Lorraine, preferring his Austrian candidate, captured the Pope's opposition to it, and in August 1564 Philip abandoned the project. His son was not sane.

Perturbed by the stir of Catholic suitors round Mary, Elizabeth, after long hesitation, suggested her favourite Dudley. The descent from the heir of Spain and the New World to an English earl was considerable and to Mary disagreeable. Dudley, who professed to be a Protestant, was acceptable on that ground to Knox, who welcomed the unlooked-for prospect of a Protestant Consort. Maitland, Moray, and Mary herself entertained the proposal only as a lever to secure recognition by Elizabeth. In September 1564, Sir James Melville went into England to probe Elizabeth's purpose, whether she proposed to acknowledge Mary if the marriage took place? Elizabeth's coquettish arts vainly assaulted Melville's defences. He brought back a positive verdict: 'In my judgment there was neither plain dealing nor upright meaning, but great dissimulation, emulation, and fear' in the English queen. In November 1564, Moray and Maitland met Elizabeth's representatives at Berwick. Mary's recognition was refused. Dudley joined the lengthening procession of rejected suitors and the 'lusty youth' Darnley comes upon the scene.

Terry, History of Scotland, 214–5.

It is perhaps too much to say that Mary was dragged upon the dangerous slope solely by her fervent love for the youth she married; for she was desirous with a similar object of wedding the deformed lunatic Don Carlos whom she had never seen; but, putting aside her possible adoption—real or feigned—of the other alternative, political submission to England, the Catholic conspiracy, which was her principal aim, was not served in any important degree by her hurry to marry Darnley, whilst it consolidated and brought to a head all the Protestant distrust against her, both in Scotland and England. If she had not been precipitated blindly by her love she would have seen, as Elizabeth always did, the enormous advantage of keeping herself free, and shifting the balance as required by circumstances. Murray, Argyle, and the Protestants might have been made to counteract Athol, Glencairn, the Gordons, and the Catholics. The Hamiltons and the Lennoxes might, by hatred of each other, all have been made humble servants of the Queen; and, following the example of Elizabeth, Mary might have attracted or repelled one suitor after another, whilst the plan for the capture of England by the Catholics with the aid of Spain was fully matured, and all the parties pledged, the trump card in Mary's hand, her own marriage, being kept unplayed until everything was ready for decisive action.

Hume, *Love Affairs of Mary Queen of Scots*, 269–70.

9

MARRIAGE TO DARNLEY

After the failure of the continental negotiations to find Mary a husband, suitors were to appear somewhat nearer home. Elizabeth proposed that Mary should marry Robert Dudley, earl of Leicester, but the sincerity of the offer, or Mary's own attitude to the offer, were never put to the test, for the return of the queen's first cousin, Henry Stewart, Lord Darnley, to Scotland in February 1565, presented her with a new and more pleasing suitor to whom she was married in July of that year.

Several problems surround Mary's marriage. The reaction of Elizabeth was one of indignation, but many writers have considered this to be feigned as Elizabeth herself was instrumental in allowing Darnley to return to Scotland. Likewise, a simultaneous pronouncement that she did not intend to reveal her own succession plans had the effect of encouraging Mary to disregard Elizabeth's wishes, and at the same time commended Darnley, with his own claims to the English succession even more warmly.

Mary's reasons in marrying have also been open to debate. Thomas Jeney's contemporary poem Master Randolphes Phantasey *advanced passion and lust as the principal motivation for this match, and many writers since have followed this line of thought. There is little doubt that Mary did take an instant liking to Darnley, but without the greater recommendations which the marriage possessed, it is doubtful whether the affair would have prospered. As had been mooted long before Mary ever set eyes on him, marriage to Darnley would strengthen her claim to the English throne while as his mother, Lady Lennox, if not Darnley himself, was a staunch Catholic, such a match would be to the liking of continental Catholic powers and the Pope. Marriage, moreover, would not only provide affection and an additional claim to the English throne, but with Darnley as king, for the crown matrimonial was to be conferred upon him, an extension of the personal power which she had hitherto lacked. Nevertheless, although there were sound political reasons for marriage, these had to be balanced against the inherent disadvantages of defying Elizabeth and of arousing the opposition of Moray in particular and her Protestant subjects in general. As a result the intrigues leading to the marriage were more protracted than is sometimes imagined and for some time after his arrival Mary was wavering on political grounds on the wisdom of allying herself with Darnley. This indecision can be seen in a letter of Randolph to Cecil on 27th March 1565 in which he wrote 'What to do or wherein to resolve she is marvelously in doubt'. If the awareness of the political realities of such a match were evenly balanced, the growing affection for Darnley which blossomed as she nursed him through an attack of measles in early April, made up her mind.*

Even then mad infatuation did not take control, and only on 15th May after Darnley's recovery did Mary set in motion the negotiations for the marriage which required a papal dispensation as the suitors were related within the prohibited degrees of matrimony. However, before these negotiations could be finalised and the indult granted, the banns were proclaimed on 22nd July and the marriage solemnised a week later. On grounds of passion it has been suggested that Mary was 'so anxious for the marriage of her choice that she could not wait for the dispensation'. Others have argued that she acted on the principle that permission had already been granted. Neither proposition is entirely convincing and the real reason for speed may have been political. The forces of opposition to the marriage were massing under Moray, and it was undoubtedly deemed politically expedient to marry in order to crush the incipient revolt, a result which was quickly achieved by the Chase-about-raid in which Mary demonstrated her new found authority by making Moray and his accomplices take refuge in England.

Lord Darnley . . . at his first commyng fand the Quen in the Wemes, makand hir progress throw Fyfe. Hir Maieste tok weill with him, and said that he was the lustiest and best proportionit lang man that sche had sean; for he was of heich stature, lang and small, even and brent up; weill instructed from his youth in all honest and comely exercyses. And eftir he had hanted a quhill in court, he proponit mariage to hir Maieste; quilk sche tok in ane evell part at the first, as sche told me that same day hir self; and how sche had refused the ring quhilk he then offerit unto hir. Where I tok occasion, as I had begun, to speak in his favour, that ther mariage wald put out of dout ther title to the succession.

Melville, Memoirs, 134.

History and tradition have both asserted that the first interview between Mary and Darnley took place in the wave-beaten towers of Wemyss, on the coast of Fifeshire, in 1565; but documentary evidence proves that these ill-fated cousins met four years earlier, in the ominous gloom of Mary's *deuil* chamber, in the French King's palace at Orleans. The presentation of Darnley was easily effected through the agency of his uncle, the Lord D'Aubigny, who was in the service of the young French monarch; and, having been in that of the late Queen-regent of Scotland, was on confidential terms with Mary herself, to whom his relationship afforded him easy access, even during her seclusion from the rest of the world.

Strickland, Mary Queen of Scots, i, 56.

Mary and Darnley first met on February 17th, 1565. Their marriage had indeed been talked of by gossips since the death of Mary's first husband; but Mary had certainly not hitherto been inclined to the match, and when they did meet there was nothing at all like love at first sight. The chances of their marrying are first treated as a practical question by Randolph, on the 15th of April. On the 15th of May, Darnley, who had been ill in bed, was able to leave his room, and was thereupon declared Earl of Ross. This act as far as we know, was Mary's public declaration that they were engaged.

Pollen, Dispensation for Marriage of Mary Stuart
in SHR, iv, 241.

The Queen of Scots being now resolved to bestow her hand on Darnley, sent her Secretary, Maitland, to London, to intimate her intentions, and to obtain Elizabeth's approbation. This was the very last thing Elizabeth meant to give. The matter had now arrived exactly at the point to which all along she had wished to bring it. She had prevailed upon Mary to abandon the idea of a foreign alliance; she had induced her to throw away some valuable time in ridiculous negotiations concerning the Earl of Leicester; she had consented, first that the Earl of Lennox, and then that his son, Darnley, should go into Scotland; and she did not say a single syllable against the proposed alliance, till she had allowed Mary to be persuaded that no marriage in Christendom could be more prudent. It was now that the cloven foot was to betray itself. . . . She assembled her Privy Council, and, at the instigation of Cecil, they gave it as their unanimous opinion, that 'this marriage with my Lord Darnley appeared to be unmeet, unprofitable, and directly prejudicial to the sincere amity between both the Queens.'

Bell, *Mary Queen of Scots*, i, 220–2.

It is agreed by all historians, that, at last, the unceasing and virulent opposition of Elizabeth, Murray and their partizans, drove her with precipitation to the marriage-bed. That, immediately after this, she acted with rapidity and vehemence . . . ; three days only after the marriage, resumed her measures of vengeance against Murray; in less than a month, took the field in person; rode with loaded pistols; pursued him and his faction before her; would hearken to no accommodation; accept of no submission; forced them out of the Kingdom; . . . she was in the meridian of her prosperity.

T. Robertson, *Mary Queen of Scots*, 44–45.

Both Buchanan and Knox acknowledge that this marriage was very generally believed not to be contrary to the Queen of England's liking, whatever grimace she might put on. And I have thought fit here to set down the French agent, Mons. Castelnau de Mauvissiere's sentiments of this matter. This gentleman, speaking of our Queen's marriage with foreign Princes, saith—'But all these great alliances were equally disagreeable to the Queen of England, who never dreaded a sharper thorn in her foot than some potent foreign alliance to be made by the Queen of Scotland, whose Kingdom lyes so close upon hers, that they are only separated by a fordable river; and so she might be easily annoyed from thence by a bad neighbour.—This the Queen of England foreseeing, cast her eyes on the young Lord Darnly, to make a present of him to the Scottish Queen—and found means to persuade the Queen of Scots, by several powerful considerations, that there was not a marriage in Christendom which could bring her more certain advantages, together with the eventual succession to the throne of England, which she (the Queen of Scots) pretended to be lodged in her person, than this with the Lord Darnly; because they two being joined in matrimony, with the consent of the Queen of England and the wisest men in both Kingdoms, would fortify each other's title, and so take out of the way many scruples which in the event of time might come to disturb these two neighbouring States. . . .' Then after he has told how fond our Queen became of this marriage, and that she sent *him* into France to obtain that King and the Queen-mother's consent to the marriage, he adds— 'On my road I met the Queen of England, who had been travelling into some parts of her Kingdom; but her Majesty did not outwardly show the joy and pleasure which was in her heart, when I told her that this marriage was advancing apace; on the contrary she affected not to approve it: which thing, however, did rather hasten than retard it.' After he had been in France and obtained their Majesties' consent to the marriage, he returns through England, and then says—'I found the Queen of England much colder towards the Queen of Scots than formerly, complaining that she had subtracted her relation and subject, and that she was intending to marry him against her consent and approbation. And yet I am assured that these words were very far from her heart; for she used all her efforts, and spared nothing to get this marriage a-going.'

Keith, History, ii, 280–1.

One of the sterotyped traditions that surround the Queen of Scots is that she was *amante passionée*; that she was 'struck with the dart of love', as Lennox puts it, for Darnley; . . . Nothing could in fact be less probable. To suppose a princess of her upbringing capable of arranging her matrimonial affairs on the basis of personal inclination is to forget all the *convenances* which hedged royal ladies of the time with impenetrable closeness. Royal alliances were first and last matters of political negotiation and national advantage; there was not a princess alive with a greater appreciation of her duty than Mary: 'She will never yield to any marriage, how fit or profitable soever it be for her, unless she see that her reputation (that is her princely dignity) shall not diminish by the match'. Thus wrote her secretary in December 1564, and he had opportunity of knowing her mind. Princely dignity was with her a fetish; nurtured by the nation that as Queen, crowned of Scotland and presumptive of France, she was as one set apart by divine will. Not healthy ideas for a young woman, but tending to keep her from disposing of herself by that mere human frailty, that we call 'falling in love'.

Mahon, Mary Queen of Scots, 30–31.

Nowe ryffe report dothe brute all abroode,
that I am a Gwyssian by the sewrer syde,
rather given whollie to weld with the sworde,
than work that wisdome have firmlie affied,
or use advise with reason alyed,
that peace propoundeth to purchase me praise,
than to persever in theis Rigorus wayes.

But, ledd with affection affyed with trust,
first I begonne to wedd as I wold
suche one as I demed wold serve my Lust,
rather than might my weale well upholde,
whose tender yeres of counsaile was colde,
for, prowde of the pray of princelie estate,
where I gave the cheke was redye to mate.

Thomas Jeney, Master Randolphes Phantasey
in Satirical Poems, i, 17.

It was not, probably, till she married him that Mary plumbed the depths of Darnley's inanity; but, with her clever wits sharpened by her experience in such a school of human nature as the French court, can it be credited that she fell blindly in love with this raw and conceited boy? Or is any such theory needed to account for her eager determination to marry him at all hazards! Since what the pious would term the 'leadings of Providence' had apparently decided that, if her political aims were to be accomplished, her choice of suitors was now restricted to the 'fayre jollye yong man,' she was naturally disposed to take the most favourable view of him she could; and she may well have thought—as women are apt to think—that she would be able to fashion him into something much better than he was.

Henderson, Mary Queen of Scots, i, 307.

She certainly was not without reasons for hoping that the dispensation might have been granted and on its way to her before the marriage was celebrated. At all events she was sure that it would be granted soon. If they did not cohabit until the dispensation arrived, the fault will, after all, not have been so very grave. The advantages that could be derived from immediate action would, to a politician, have seemed invaluable.

Yet, when we have allowed as much as we like on these scores, there will always remain the fault, unpardonable especially in a woman, of want of principle regarding the sacredness of marriage, a sacredness which should have been dearer to her than life. She was deliberately risking an invalid union, and according to the law of the Church she achieved one. It makes one augur ill for her constancy in the time of temptation, soon to come, when nothing short of heroic adherance to principle would be able to save her.

Pollen, Dispensation for Marriage of Mary Stuart
in SHR, iv, 247–8.

A revolution was undoubtedly in process of formation in order to hinder the match, and if a revolution broke out, there might be an end to Catholicism altogether. On the other hand, if she could marry at once, the rebels would be deprived of their pretext for recourse to arms, and she would acquire a very much stronger position, partly because marriage would settle many things which now hung doubtful, partly because she and many others were still under the impression that Darnley was a real hero, who would be the salvation of Scotland.

Pollen, Papal Negotiations, xciii–xciv.

The disaffected Lords, how soon they heard of the solemnization of the Queen's marriage, and her Proclamation thereupon, appointing to her husband the dignity and title of King, and that all publick letters should pass and be directed in the King's name as well as in her own, did immediately send forth their complaints into all parts, as if the Kingdom was openly wronged, and the liberties thereof oppressed, and a King imposed upon the people without advice and consent of the States (a thing they alledged was contrary to the laws and received custom of the country); desiring, therefore, all good subjects to lay the matter to heart, and join with them in resisting these beginnings of tyranny. But though the faction was busy in thus fomenting a rebellion in the nation, yet they had the mortification to see but very little ear given to their wicked insinuations; and even Mr Knox acknowledgeth—'There were diverse bruits among the people, some alledging that the cause of this alteration (in the discontented Lords) was not for religion, but rather for hatred, envy of sudden promotion or dignity, or such worldly causes.' The Lords had already taken themselves to arms, and the Queen had likewise taken proper measures to disappoint their enterprizes; and now their Majesties were resolved to crush them before they had time to spread the poison into the minds of their loyal subjects.

Keith, History, ii, 348–9.

The marriage of the queen of Scots had kindled afresh the zeal of

the reformers, because the family of Lenox was believed to adhere
to the catholic faith; and though Darnley, who now bore the
name of King Henry, went often to the established church, he
could not, by this exterior compliance, gain the confidence and
regard of the ecclesiastics. They rather laid hold of the opportunity to insult him to his face; and Knox scrupled not to tell him
from the pulpit, that God, for punishment of the offences and in-
gratitude of the people, was wont to commit the rule over them to
boys and women. The populace of Edinburgh, instigated by such
doctrines, began to meet and to associate themselves against the
government. But what threatened more immediate danger to
Mary's authority, were the discontents which prevailed among
some of the principal nobility.

The duke of Chatelrault was displeased with the restoration,
and still more with the aggrandizement, of the family of Lenox,
his hereditary enemies; and entertained fears lest his eventual
succession to the crown of Scotland should be excluded by his
rival, who had formerly advanced some pretensions to it. The earl
of Murray found his credit at court much diminished by the interest
of Lenox and his son; and began to apprehend the revocation of
some considerable grants, which he had obtained from Mary's
bounty. The earls of Argyle, Rothes and Glencairn, the lords
Boyde and Ochiltry, Kirkcaldy of Grange, Pittarow, were instigated by like motives; and as these were the persons who had most
zealously promoted the reformation, they were disgusted to find
that the queen's favour was entirely engrossed by a new cabal, the
earls of Bothwel, Athole, Sutherland and Huntley; men who were
esteemed either lukewarm in religious controversy, or inclined to
the catholic party.

Hume, *History of England,* 455.

Mary Stuart had never before occupied so powerful a position.
She possessed the obedience of her subjects, and commanded the
respect of foreign powers. It now behoved her to employ her skill
in consolidating the power which she had obtained by her courage.

Mignet, *Mary Queen of Scots,* i, 198.

The new sovereigns began their reign with measures of successful vigour, which seemed to promise a strong and orderly government under the old religion and the old regal authority. A portion of the Protestant barons, including Murray, Glencairn, Rothes, and Kirkcaldy of Grange, resolved to combine against the new order of things. They stated that the laws against idolatry were not enforced, and that the mass and other abominations were tolerated. They stated, further, that the true religion was oppressed; and though this was not according to strict fact, unless the countenance given to Popery were to be set down as oppression, yet it is plain that Protestantism was in imminent danger; for the queen and her supporters were as fully determined to suppress Heresy whenever they were able, as Knox and his party were to suppress Idolatry. But there were other grounds for opposition of a constitutional character. The queen had not ventured to face a Parliament, and ask their sanction to her late doings. She had not only taken to herself a husband without consulting the great Council of the nation— an indecorous and ungracious thing—but she had proclaimed her husband as King of the Scots. It was maintained that this was illegal, since the monarch reigned by the assent of the Estates of the realm, and could not transfer any portion of the sovereign power to another without the intervention of these Estates.

Burton, *History of Scotland*, iv, 123.

10

RICCIO

Mary's triumph in the Chase-about-raid which followed her marriage to Darnley was short lived. The political advantages which the match had seemed to offer proved transitory and the element of infatuation which may have been present was equally quickly dispelled. The alliance between crown and nobility which had characterised the years 1561–65 was shattered and the hostility of the majority of the nobility was only too evident. Mary, moreover, no longer had a friendly Moray to rely upon and Maitland who had been pushed into the background by the marriage was not well disposed to the queen's interests. This situation may have been as Mary had intended, but if so, much depended upon the character of her husband who unfortunately for the queen's policies soon revealed himself to be a man of straw.

In this situation, it is hardly surprising that Mary sought new advisers. Among these were the earl of Bothwell who was firmly committed to the queen's cause, and outside the ranks of the nobility David Riccio who had first entered her service in 1561 as a bass singer. His musical talents and charm appear to have allowed him to overcome the natural handicap of being ugly and in 1564 he was made French secretary by Mary. In the emergency of 1565, he appears to have shared Mary's confidence to the resentment of her natural councillors who were not slow to show their displeasure by spreading rumours that Riccio was both a papal agent and the queen's lover. Neither of these two assertions appear to have had the slightest basis of truth, although they have been frequently repeated by Mary's detractors, and even the part which Riccio played in policy making has been grossly over stated, as his position was possibly no more than that of a confidant.

Nevertheless, Darnley was easily persuaded by some of the disaffected nobility of the truth of all these assertions, and on a promise of the crown matrimonial, which Mary had withheld, he joined the

4

band who on 9th March 1566 brutally killed Riccio in the presence
of the pregnant queen. Mary never forgave Darnley for this threat to
her unborn child, but for a time was forced to effect a reconciliation
with her husband whom she had detached from her captors in order to
escape. Darnley henceforward was equally hated by his wife and the
nobility, and this coupled to the fact that Mary thereafter was forced
to pardon Moray and others who had opposed her marriage, makes
the murder of Riccio one of the turning points in her reign.

Maitland was not easily discouraged; but he was ill at ease after
the Lennox marriage. He was not misled by Mary's rapid progress
and brilliant peremptoriness. She had spoken with the spirit of a
Queen; neither France nor England, she had declared, should
come between her and her revolted subjects; and he could not but
admire the force and independence of her bearing. But it was not
diplomacy. He knew that on these lines no solid or permanent
success was to be looked for. Mary could not afford the luxury of
humiliating her formidable rival; had she been discreet she would
have held her tongue, and preserved, while she went her own way,
a show of amity with England. But she was a woman—an angry
woman—with weak and evil counsellors at her side.

Skelton, *Maitland of Lethington*, ii, 155.

Within also ludged the Queenes Secretarie, David Rizio, a Ped-
montane, a man of greate and longe experience, and understoode
best of anie ther the afaires of the state, weele respected of his
mistres for his singular witte, now beinge olde. He was a man of
no beautie or outwarde shape, for he was mishapen, evil favoured,
and in visage werie blacke; but for his fidelitie, wisdome, prudence,
wertue and his other goode partes and qualities of minde he was
richlie adorned.

Blackwood, *History of Mary Queen of Scots*, 9–10.

The Queen's *musicians,* as objects of amusement, and still more, as essentials, in her religious worship, engaged much of her attention. In 1561 and 1562, she had five violars, or players on the viol, who seem to have been all Scotsmen: John Feldie, Moreis Dow, William Hoy, John Dow, a name consecrated to music, and John Ray. The Queen had three players on the *lute,* at the same time. The Queen played on the lute, and virginals, as we learn, from Melvill. In 1564, when Melvill, was sent, from Mary, to Elizabeth, she asked him, if his mistress played well, to which he answered, *reasonably,* as a queen. Mary had also a schalmer, which was a sort of pipe, or fluted instrument, but not a bagpipe: ... The Queen had, also, a small establishment of *singers.* Melvill informs us, that the Queen had three valets of her chamber, who sung three parts, and wanted a bass, to sing the fourth part: And Rizzio being recommend to the Queen, as a person fit to make the fourth, in concert, was drawn in, sometimes, to sing with the other valets.

Chalmers, Mary Queen of Scots, i, 72–73.

Mary had, after a few days of marriage, abandoned her transient fondness for the youth she imagined she had loved, conceived a coolness for Darnley, and became again prodigal of everything towards Rizzio, on whom she lavished power and honours, violating the almost sacred etiquette of the times, by admitting him to her table in her private apartments, and, suppressing the name of the King in public papers, substituted that of Rizzio. Scotland found she had two Kings, or, rather, the nominal King disappeared to give place to the favourite.

Lamartine, Mary Stuart, 38.

Side by side with Darnley's apparent loss of credit with the Queen, the influence wielded by Riccio became more marked. Buchanan affirms that Riccio's equipages and the rank of his attendants exceeded those of the king: and although Buchanan is a better rhetorician than historian, Riccio was not only well paid for his services by the Queen, but received large sums by way of

bribes from those requiring special favours. If we are to hold that
Mary's partiality for him was a mere caprice, then it was a very
infatuated one; and unless she required of him political services,
the performance of which could not safely be entrusted to others,
then the lover theory becomes at least by far the most probable.

Henderson, *Mary Queen of Scots*, ii, 364–5.

Buchanan is the only contemporary author who has ventured to
commit to writing the scandalous tale of an amour between the
Queen and Rizzio, which, when examined into, hath not the shadow
of truth, or even probability, to support it. Yet such is the malign-
ity of party-prejudice, that with many this story passes current.
Had there been the least ground for such calumny, we are pretty
certain, that the Queen's accusers, Murray and Morton, would not
have omitted so important an article in the black accusation which
they afterwards published against her, and, what seems pretty
remarkable, even Buchanan, in his libel called the *Detection*, has
not the smallest insinuation of any such amour.

W. Tytler, *Historical and Critical Enquiry*, ii, 4.

The queen was not content with raising Rizzio out of obscurity,
and to show him to the people, but she devised another way to
clothe him with domestic honour; for whereas she had, for some
months before, permitted more company than was usual to sit at
her table, that so in the crowd his place might be less envied; by
this face of popularity she thought such an unusual sight would be
in some measure rendered more familiar through the multitude of
guests, and daily usage, and so men's high minds be gradually
inured to bear anything. At last it came to this, that none but he,
and one or two more, sat at a table with her. ... sometimes at
Rizzio's own lodgings. But the way she thus took to abate did but
multiply the general reflections, for it nourished suspicions, and
gave occasion to strange discourses. Men's thoughts were now inclined to the worst, and what served to inflame them was, that he
exceeded even the King himself in household furniture, apparel

and the number of noble and stately horses, so that the matter looked the worse for this, because all this ornament, instead of doing him credit, made him odious and ridiculous. . . .

These things were spoken openly, but in private men went further in their mutterings, as is commonly the case in matters not very credible; yet the King would never be persuaded to believe it, unless he saw it with his own eyes; so that, one time hearing that Rizzio was gone into the queen's bed-chamber, he came to a little door, the key of which he always carried about him, and found it bolted in the inside, which it never used to be. He knocked, but no one answered; upon which, conceiving great wrath and indignation in his heart, he could hardly sleep a wink that night.

Buchanan, *History of Scotland,* 436.

The character of Riccio, as created by Buchanan, requires some examination. Buchanan's picture of him, as a low-born schemer who wormed his way into the graces of the Queen and became the unofficial ruler of the court, to the exclusion of the King, has been generally accepted, and is undoubtedly the portrait drawn of him in the popular imagination. In fact, however, little is known of him beyond what Buchanan says. The three contemporary sources from which most of our knowledge of the man is drawn agree only in the following points: that he came to Scotland in 1561, along with Morette, the Savoyard ambassador; that he came from Piedmont; that he was first employed by Mary as a singer; that he became one of the Queen's secretaries; that he became friendly with Darnley; that he acted as a principal in the marriage. These are facts. Apart from this meagre information, we are left with Buchanan's libel. And much of what Buchanan says of him may be discounted. In the first place, it is extremely doubtful that Riccio was as low-born as Buchanan states. A lay secretary, and a musician, was a highly educated person in the sixteenth century. Mary was herself moderately skilled in languages, and would have had no use for an incompetent secretary. If Riccio took Raulet's place, as Randolph says, he is bound to have been efficient enough. It is interesting to note, too, that the name of Riccio occurs earlier in Italian diplomatic records. It may well be that David Riccio

sprang from a class of cultured Italian bourgeoisie which played
so great a role in European history at this time. If this is the case—
and it is certain that Riccio was cultured—it is not surprising that
Mary, herself so fond of the arts and graces of the European court,
so sadly lacking in Scotland should have had a special place in her
regard for the polished Italian.

Gatherer, *The Tyrannous Reign of Mary Stewart*, 22–3.

'I have good reason for me, for since yonder fellow David came in
credit and familiarity with your Majesty, you neither regarded me,
entertained me, nor trusted me after your wonted fashion; for
every day before dinner you were wont to come to my chamber,
and past the time with me, and this long time you have not done
so; and when I came to your Majesty's chamber, you bare me little
company except David had been the third person; and after sup-
per your Majesty used to sit up at cards with the said David till
one or two after midnight. And this is the entertainment I have
had of you this long time.' Her Majesty answered, that it was not a
gentlewoman's duty to come to her husband's chamber, but rather
the husband to come to the wife's. The King answered: How
came you to my chamber in the beginning, and ever till within
these six months, that David fell into familiarity with you? Or am
I failed in any sort in my body?

Ruthven's Relation in Keith, *History*, iii, 268.

Darnley: I saw it, I first—I knew her—who knew her but I,
That swore—at least I swore to mine own soul,
Would not for shame's sake swear out wide to the world,
But in myself swore with my heart to hear—
There was more in it, in all their commerce, more
Than the mere music—he is warped, worn through,
Bow-bent, uncomely in wholesome eyes that see
Straight, seeing him crooked—but she seeing awry
Sees the man straight enough for paramour.
This I saw, this I swore to—silently,

Not loud but sure, till time should be to speak
Sword's language, no fools' jargon like his tongue,
But plain broad steel speech and intelligible,
Though not to the ear, Italian's be it or Scot's,
But to the very life intelligible,
To the loosed soul, to the shed blood—for blood
There must be—one must slay him—you are sure—
 as I am?
For, I was sure of it always—while you said,
All you, 'twas council-stuff, state-handicraft,
Cunning of card-play between here and there,
I knew 'twas this and more, sir, I kept sight,
Kept heed of her, what thing she was, what wife,
What manner of stateswoman and governess—
More than all you saw.

      Swinburne, *Bothwell*, 9–10.

The said Lord Ruthven at his entring in, said unto the Queen's Majesty, let it please your Majesty that yonder man David come forth of your privy-chamber, where he hath been over-long. The Queen answered, what offence hath he done? Ruthven answered, that he made a greater and more hainous offence to her Majesty's honour, the King her husband, the Nobility and Commonwealth. And how? said she. If it would please your Majesty, said the Lord Ruthven, he hath offended your honour, which I dare not be so bold as to speak of. As to the King your husband's honour, he hath hindered him of the Crown-Matrimonial which your grace promised him, besides many other things which are not necessary to be expressed; and hath caused your Majesty to banish a great part of the Nobility, and to forfeit them, that he might be made a Lord. And to your Commonweal he hath been a common destroyer, hindring your Majesty to grant or give anything but what passed through his hands, by taking of bribes for the same.

    Ruthven's Relation in Keith, *History*, iii, 266.

The murder of Riccio marks the turning point in Mary's career, both personally and politically. The character of her husband had been laid bare; henceforth she could feel for him nothing but contempt and loathing. Bothwell she could not but regard as the prop of her throne: coming events were casting their shadows. Far more important, the murder of Riccio demonstrated that the Catholic policy that Mary had been pursuing for the past year was utterly bankrupt. Even with many of the Protestant nobility in exile, those who remained had been sufficiently strong to invade her palace, carry off her trusted servant from her side, and cruelly murder him almost under her eyes. True, the murderers were now fugitives, but this had been accomplished only at the price of compounding with the rebels of 1565. The marriage on which she had based her hopes of Catholicizing both England and Scotland had turned out to be the means of ruining her hopes. Mary abandoned the Catholic policy, and never revived it while she was on the Scottish throne. In fact, in the remaining fifteen months of her reign, she followed no well thought-out foreign policy at all, and her conduct of domestic business hinged mainly on questions of personality. The murder of Riccio spelled the ruin of the old religion in Scotland, and that meant England too was safe. It was a decisive event in British history.

Lee, *James Stewart, earl of Moray*, 170.

I I

THE MURDER OF DARNLEY

After the death of Riccio, Mary's sense of political isolation must have grown greater. Her reconciliation with Darnley was no more than an expedient designed to foil the murderers, and while this end was further achieved by pardoning Moray and some of his associates in the Chase-about-raid, as distinct from those who had plotted against Riccio, the opposition to the queen's policies, if divided, was nonetheless real. In these circumstances the earl of Bothwell must have commended himself more and more as the strong man to replace the ineffectual Darnley and revive the policies to which Mary was politically committed. Bothwell's political utility to Mary at this juncture can hardly be doubted, but much more debate has been occasioned by the extent to which Mary allowed infatuation for the earl to play a decisive part in her choice of ally. From Buchanan onwards writers, including Spenser in The Faerie Queene, *have asserted that Mary was Bothwell's lover before Darnley's death, some averring that the queen's reconciliation with her husband shortly before his murder stemmed from the fact that she was carrying Bothwell's child. This suggestion has been equally vigorously denied, and the evidence does appear to bear out this conclusion.*

If Mary's relationship with Bothwell must remain somewhat uncertain, it is equally clear that her estrangement from Darnley grew more complete after the birth of her child, the future James VI in June 1566. That event in itself, however, made it more difficult to annul the marriage as James' legitimacy would consequently have been threatened. Mary certainly made no secret of the fact that she wished to be rid of her husband, and while she may not have contemplated violent means, the many members of the nobility who hated Darnley possessed no such scruples. Mary must have known this only too well when she made her wishes known. Some writers have, however, tried to make her wholly blameless while others have made her an accomplice in the actual deed. The issue on which the latter viewpoint

4*

usually hinges is that of Mary's motive in bringing her sick husband from Glasgow to Kirk o' Field, Edinburgh. Was the reconciliation genuine, whether prompted by pregnancy or not, or was it a device to place Darnley in the hands of his enemies? The circumstantial evidence against Mary is strong, but the truth can never be ascertained as even greater mystery surrounds the personage of the murderer or murderers who on 10th February 1567 blew up Darnley's lodging and left the King strangled in the garden. Multifarious theories have been advanced: a plot against both King and Queen, a scheme by Darnley to murder Mary which somehow misfired have both been mooted as possibilities. Attempts to incriminate members of the nobility have added the Hamiltons, the Douglases, associates of Moray (who was prudently absent from Edinburgh at the time of the crime), and of course the prime suspect James Hepburn, earl of Bothwell. Even Bothwell has had his champions, but it is difficult to believe that he was not implicated in the plot, even if the actual murder was carried out by another group of conspirators, of whom the Douglases representing the earl of Morton are chief suspects. In the confusion which surrounds the mysterious affair of Kirk o' Field, and the various solutions which have been proposed as to who killed Darnley, the essential point which must not be overlooked is the nature of the deed itself. The murder of Darnley was a political assassination, the murderer was commonly believed to be Bothwell, and while Mary's collusion in the deed cannot be proved, her actions subsequent to the crime inevitably aroused suspicion.

It was only the accident of her birth that had made a politician of Mary Stewart. A strong, fearless, generous, revengeful, high-spirited woman, she felt too keenly the joy of living to care much for distant and impalpable results; and as politics proved more and more disappointing to her love of power, the flood of passion within her overflowed into another channel. From the time, when she resolved to marry Darnley—from motives of policy indeed, but in a very impolitic spirit—she was no longer the patient schemer of her early days in Scotland; and the assassination of

THE MURDER OF DARNLEY

Riccio in March, 1566, which dissipated her dreams of absolutism, and added hatred to contempt for a brutal and imbecile husband, cut her finally adrift on the downward course.

Mathieson, *Politics and Religion*, i, 137.

In proportion as her husband sunk, the Earl of Bothwell rose in her confidence and esteem. He had adhered, though a protestant, to her mother, the queen regent, against the congregation, and continued abroad in the service of Mary, before her return to Scotland, from whence he was soon expelled for a supposed plot against Murray's life. On the disgrace and banishment of that nobleman, he was recalled and received into immediate favour; and on the assassination of Rizio, he acquired by his successful services, the most unbounded influence over the mind of the queen. In addition to the wardenship of the three marches, till then conferred upon separate persons, he was rewarded with the office of lord high admiral, the abbeys of Melrose and Hadding-ton, and the castle and lordship of Dunbar; together with an ex-tensive grant of the crown demesnes. Huntly, whose sister he had lately married, was appointed chancellor by his interest, and all favours and preferment passed through his hands. His opinion was consulted upon every occasion, and his interposition was employed in every transaction at court. His extensive possessions had rendered him powerful; his birth and personal advantages vain and ambitious; his embarrassments desperate; and when the queen's attachment to Darnley was converted into a cold mistrust, or a rooted aversion, his faithful services, insinuating address, and unremitted assiduity, are supposed to have made a deep im-pression upon her susceptible heart.

Laing, *History of Scotland*, i, 13–14.

James Hepburn Earl Bothwell, hereditarie heigh Admirall of Scotland, had been all his lifetime a faithfull serwant of the crowne, a man valiant, and for magnanimouse prowesse, abowe all others; but, as touching other thinges, audacious, proude,

inconstant, changable, and easie to be perswaded, readie to under-
take, and more readie to put in execution.

Blackwood, History of Mary Queen of Scots, 24.

Scho ane zoung Woman suddanely advancit to the heist Degre of
Authoritie, quhen scho had never sene with hir Eyes, hard with
hir Eirs, nor considderit in hir Hart ye forme of ane Kingdome
governit be Law; and thairto was furnischit with the untemperate
Counsellis of hir Kinnismen, quha thameselfis practisit to set up
ane tyrannous Reule in *France*, indevourit to draw richt Equitie,
Lawis and Customes of Ancesteris to hir awin only Beck and
Plesure.

Of this immoderate Desyre thair brist out from hir mony tymes
mony Wordes discloising it. This scho studyit Day and Nicht.
Bot aganis this Desyre thair withstude the Custome of the Coun-
trie, the Lawes and Statutis, and principally the Consent of the
Nobilitie, quha remaning saif scho culd never attene it. To the
end thairfoir, that scho micht be abill violentlie to atcheve it, scho
determinit be Force to remufe all that stude in hir Way, bot scho
wist not weill be quhat Meane, or be quhais Help to attempt it.

Fraude was the Way to wirk it, for yat utherwise it was not
possibill to be obtenit. For this Purpois thairfoir, *Bothwell* onely
semit the fittest Man, a Man in extreme Povertie, doutfull
quhidder he wer mair vyle, or mair wickit, and quha, betwene
Factiounis of sindrie Religiounis, despying baith Sydes, counter-
futit ane Lufe of thame baith.

Buchanan, Detectioun, 57-58.

In an age when many gentlemen and ladies could not sign their
names, Bothwell wrote, and wrote French, in a firm, yet delicate
Italic hand, of singular grace and clearness. His enemies accused
him of studying none but books of Art Magic in his youth, and he
may have shared the taste of the great contemporary mathema-
tician, Napier of Merchistoun, the inventor of Logarithms. . . Quite
possibly Bothwell may really have studied the Black Art in Cor-

nelius Agrippa and similar authors. In any case it is plain that, as
regards culture, the author of *Les Affaires du Conte de Boduel*, the
man familiar with the court of France, where he had held command in the Scots Guards, and had probably known Ronsard
and Brantôme, must have been a *rara avis* of culture among the
nobles at Holyrood.

Lang, *Mystery of Mary Stuart*, 17–18.

Some time after this, the queen appointed to go to Jedburgh, to
hold a convention; and, about the beginning of October, Bothwell
prepared an expedition into Liddesdale; where he conducted himself, neither according to the place which he held, nor the dignity
of his family, nor the expectation of any man. While there, a
wretched highwayman, whom he had taken and almost despatched
with a leaden bullet unawares, wounded him, and so he was
carried to Hermitage castle, in great danger of his life. When
the news of this came to the queen at Borthwick, though the
winter was very sharp, she flew in haste, first to Melrose, and next
to Jedburgh. There, though she received certain intelligence that
Bothwell was alive, yet, being impatient of delay, and not able to
forbear, notwithstanding the severity of the season, the difficulty
of the way, and the danger of robbers, she hastened her journey,
accompanied by such attendants as hardly any honest person, even
of a mean condition, would have trusted with his life and fortune.

Buchanan, *History of Scotland*, 440.

On the day on which Mary left Edinburgh [8th October 1566]
Bothwell was severely wounded by one of the clan of the Elliots,
whom he had attempted to capture, and for some time his life was
in danger. The intelligence must have reached Mary immediately
upon her arrival in Jedburgh, yet there she remained, intent upon
the duties which had brought her thither. It was not until the 16th,
when the assizes had closed, that she took her famous ride to sympathise and condole with the nobleman who had been wounded in
the discharge of his duty as her servant.

Stevenson, *History of Mary Stuart*, cxxix.

Queen: You are my soldier; but these silk-soft words
         Become your lips as well as mine, when love
         Rekindles them; how good it is to have
         A man to love you! here is a man indeed,
         Not fool or boy, to make love's face ashamed,
         To abash love's heart and turn to bitterness
         The sweet blood current in it. O my fair lord!
         How fairer is this warrior face, and eyes
         With the iron light of battle in them left
         As the after fire of sunset left in heaven
         When the sun sinks, than any fool's face made
         Of smiles and courtly colour! Now I feel
         As I were a man too, and had part myself
         In your great strength; being one with you as I,
         How should I not be strong?

                        Swinburne, *Bothwell*, 151–2.

A little before winter, when the ambassadors from France and
England came to be present at the baptism of the infant prince,
the queen strove, as far as money or industry could, to make
Bothwell appear the most magnificent personage amongst all her
subjects and guests at the entertainment; while her lawful husband
was not allowed necessaries for the ceremony, and was even forbid
to come in sight of the ambassadors; his servants also, that were
appointed to be his daily attendants, were taken from him, and
the nobility received an intimation not to take any notice of him.
But thus her implacable carriage towards him, which the nobles
noted both now as they had before, moved them to have the
greater compassion upon him, when they saw one so young and
harmless used after this reproachful manner; and not only to bear
it patiently, but even endeavour to appease the rage of his wife, by
the most servile offices he could perform, in order, if possible, to
gain some degree of favour. As for the poverty of his dress, she
laid the fault upon the embroiderers, goldsmiths and other trades-
men, though it was a false and scandalous excuse, for everyone
knew that she herself was the occasion of it; and that, for fear Bothwell should not have ornaments enough, she wrought many of them

with her own hands. Besides all this, the foreign ambassadors were desired not to enter into any discourse with the King, though they were in the same castle together the most part of the day.

Buchanan, *History of Scotland*, 441.

The speculative suggestion—though it can be nothing more—may be advanced that at this stage Mary was suddenly struck by the fear that she was pregnant; and there is some evidence that, if she was not pregnant at this time, she became pregnant shortly afterwards, for it was said in June that she was 'five months gone with child'. Now everyone knew that any child of Mary's could not have been fathered by Darnley, who had now been completely estranged from her for at least three months. Mary might well have concluded that she must at all costs resume marital relations with her husband, at least for a time. On this view, her purpose in bringing him to Edinburgh was not to encompass his death but to preserve his life from the dangers which she knew threatened it. The idea that her aims were purely political, or even that she was bringing him to a place easy of access for his enemies, is hard to reconcile with the fact that she went out of her way to play the part of a loving wife, visiting him daily, twice spending the night in the room below his, giving him a ring and promising to sleep with him as soon as his convalescence was completed—which it would have been on the day after he was killed.

Donaldson, *The First Trial of Mary Queen of Scots*, 40–41.

What is virtually impossible is the suggestion, sometimes made since by historians, that the queen could have conceived twins by Bothwell in January before Darnley's death, and carried them in complete secrecy, without the faintest contemporary report of her pregnancy, throughout the vital months following the Kirk o'Field tragedy. It was mid-June before Bedford heard that the queen was pregnant; although Guzman, the Spanish ambassador in London, wrote to Philip II on 21 June, saying that the Scottish queen was five *months* pregnant, he probably mistook five months for five weeks, since there is no reference of any sort through March, April and May to the royal pregnancy, which would have been becoming rapidly more apparent as the queen's figure changed. This was an age in which such facts were speedily known by the accurate news service of servants' gossip; as a girl queen in France, Mary's prospects of becoming a mother had been intimately assessed by the ambassadors at the court. Randolph's extraordinarily early reports of Mary's pregnancy with James in the autumn of 1565 will be recalled—he heard the first rumours of her condition about five weeks after conception, giving as his reference such 'tokens . . . annexed to the kind of them that are in that case'. The spring months following the Kirk o'Field tragedy were among the most critical of Mary's existence, in which her every word and action were watched, checked and reported; how inconceivable is it then that an event of such moment as her growing pregnancy outside the bonds of marriage should have passed quite unnoticed until the sixth month, by observers who would certainly have grasped joyfully at such a convenient weapon to destroy, if not Mary, at least Bothwell, the child's father.

Fraser, Mary Queen of Scots, 343–4.

In January, 1567, she was well aware that something was intended against Darnley by Bothwell, Lethington and others. Yet her next step was to seek Darnley in Glasgow, where he was safe among the retainers of Lennox, and thence to bring him back to Edinburgh, where his deadly foes awaited him.

Now this act of Mary's cannot be regarded as merely indiscreet, or as a half-measure, or as a measure of passive acquiescence. Had she not brought Darnley from Glasgow to Edinburgh, under a semblance of a cordial reconciliation, he might, in one way or another, have escaped from his enemies. The one measure which made his destruction certain was the measure that Mary executed, though she was well aware that a conspiracy had been framed against the unhappy lad. Even if he wished to come to Edinburgh, uninvited by her, she ought to have refused to bring him.

Lang, Mystery of Mary Stuart, 118–19.

THE MURDER OF DARNLEY

Mary went to Glasgow with nothing but the most loving devotion
to her husband, and from that time, till his death, any other con-
struction of her actions would be inconsistent with the best historical narratives of her life. She nursed him day and night during
her visit, after which he proposed that she should take him with
her to Edinburgh, to which she agreed. She suggested Craigmillar
for an abode, as it was situated on rising ground and was very
healthy. Curiously enough, he refused to go there; and as for
Holyrood, its recent history put it out of the question. Mary in these
circumstances wrote to Maitland to provide a house. Maitland,
who recommended the Kirk of Field, is alleged to have shown this
letter to Bothwell. This we think is very improbable. Bothwell was
in Liddesdale, seventy miles distant. It is evident . . . that Maitland
was the mouthpiece of the faction who, for purposes of their own,
wished Darnley put into the Kirk of Field.

Cowan, Mary Queen of Scots, i, 152–3.

Mary's conduct towards Darnley after Craigmillar, and before
his murder, and her behaviour later as regards his murder, and her
behaviour later as regards Bothwell, are always capable of being
covered by one or other special and specious excuse. On this occasion she brings Darnley to Edinburgh that a tender mother may be
near her child, that a loving wife may attend a repentant husband,
who cannot be so safe anywhere as under the aegis of her royal
presence. In each and every case there is a special and not an in-
credible explanation. But one cause, if it existed, would explain
every item of her conduct throughout, from Craigmillar to Kirk o'
Field: she hated Darnley.

Lang, Mystery of Mary Stuart, 120.

The illness which had brought him almost face to face with death,
and more than all, the Queen's devotedness, had been powerful
lessons to Darnley. One day Mary came to his side as he was
closing a letter to his family. Darnley handed it to her. She saw in it
very sincere and beautiful words in praise of her tenderness and

attentions to him: she read too of his regrets for the past, and the vow registered as to the future. Though that letter was not meant for the Queen, yet it touched her heart; she again and again kissed Darnley, and for a long time held him folded in her arms. Health was returning and they were congratulating each other on the happy life before them. They never dreamed that their love was to have an end so sudden and so cruel.

Petit, *Mary Stuart*, i, 135.

Thus died in a barbarous and wicked manner King Henry, formerly Lord Darnly, in the twenty-first year of his age, and just two years from his coming into Scotland, within which such short space he had experience both of the smiles and frowns of fortune in a very eminent degree. He is said to have been one of the tallest and handsomest young men of the age, that he had a comely face and pleasant countenance, that he was a most dextrous horseman, and exceedingly well skilled in all genteel exercises, prompt and ready for all games and sports, much given to the diversions of hawking and hunting, to horse-racing and musick, especially playing on the lute. He could speak and write well, and was bountiful and liberal enough. But then to balance these good natural qualifications, he was much addicted to intemperance, to base and unmanly pleasures; he was haughty and proud, and so very weak in mind, as to be a prey to all that came about him; he was inconstant, credulous and facile, unable to abide by any resolutions, capable to be imposed upon by designing men, and could conceal no secret, let it tend ever so much either to his own welfare or detriment.

Keith, *History*, ii, 506–9.

Mary's behaviour before and after Darnley's murder is, in the opinion of many, quite sufficient to establish her guilt. It is not easy to get over the incontrovertible outstanding facts, that she was on bad terms with him until the suspicious reconcilation, which was so quickly followed by his tragic death; that the favour which she had been showing to Bothwell continued to increase,

although he was commonly and justly regarded as the chief murderer; and that, in spite of the remonstrances of her outspoken
friends, she married him so soon after the murder. Around these
central facts are grouped multitudes of details, almost every one
of which has been the subject of keen controversy. To one set of
writers, the general drift of these details only shows more clearly
Mary's infatuated love for Bothwell, and her determination to have
him in spite of all obstacles. To another set, they furnish convincing proof that she was the unfortunate, if not helpless, victim of
a huge conspiracy to hurl her from her throne.

Fleming, Mary Queen of Scots, 160.

Then brought he forth with griesly grim aspect
Abhorred Murder, who with bloudie knyfe
Yet dropping fresh in hand did her detect,
And there with guiltie bloudshed charged ryfe:
Then brought he forth Sedition, breeding stryfe
In troublous wits and mutinous uprore:
Then brought he forth Incontinence of lyfe,
Even foule Adulterie her face before,
And lewd Impietie, that her accused sore.

Spenser, The Fairie Queene, 622.

The whole City was startled with the Crack, which was in the
Night Time, but more with the News of the King's Death, whilst
the Manner of it was no less various censured than reported. Some
thought it merely accidental, others, (and they of the first Rank in
the Nation) firmly believed *Murray* and *Morton* the Authors.
Many accused *Bothwel*, as one who had of late shown more than
the common Affection of a Subject for the Queen's Interest, and
who, by removing *Henry*, made Way for himself: But the more
prevailing Opinion was, that the Queen herself, resenting too
deeply the Murder of her Servant, and her injured Reputation,
had an Hand in the Matter; and that by her Contrivance, or, at
least, Connivance, the King and his Servant had been first

strangled as they lay asleep and a Bed, and their Bodies carried
to that Place where they were found after the House was blown
up. This Story, tho' of all the rest the least likely to be true, was
carefully and industriously spread abroad, and maintained under
Hand by *Murray* and others, her secret Enemies, and Authors of
the Fact; her preceding Coldness to the King, and her constant
Friendship for *Bothwel*, favouring their Endeavours to defame
her. Few were at the Pains to examine the Matter narrowly, or to
object that the *Queen*, who had been so often pressed by the
Council to consent to a Divorce, lay under no Necessity of pursuing such a violent Method, attended with so much Sin and
Danger, even tho' she had truly hated her Husband. It was not
considered that it had been easier to have done it at *Stirling* or
Glasgow, or in any Place less populous than in *Edinburgh*; that it
was not consistent with common Prudence, to have strangled him
first, since that Force, which threw Stones ten Feet long and four
Feet in Breadth, a vast Way into the adjacent Gardens, was
enough to have dispatched him; or that she was not so weak as not
to have feigned at least a more perfect Agreement with the King,
to render herself less suspected: I say, no Man was at the Pains to
consider these Things, or to remember that she was naturally mild
and religious; but as if a general Tendency to promote her Ruin
had seized all Mankind, this barefaced Story, true or false, was
swallowed down untouched.

Crawfurd, *Memoirs,* 11–12.

Even were we not furnished with the most unquestionable proofs
of her complicity by the confessions contained in her letters, the
authenticity of which we have established elsewhere, as well as by
the declarations made in presence of their judges and upon the
scaffold, by the subaltern actors in this tragic drama, her conduct
both before and after the murder would suffice to convince us that
she was a party to the crime. Her journey to Glasgow, at a time
when she was loudest in her expressions of distrust and hatred of
Darnley; the marks of tenderness and hopes of reconciliation
which she had displayed towards him, in order to induce him to
come with her to Edinburgh: the selection of Balfour's house,

which was convenient only for the commission of a crime, and wherein she consented to reside that he might not refuse to reside in it; the care with which, on the evening before the murder she removed from it all the furniture of any value which it contained; the conveyance of the powder and introduction of the two principal assassins into her own room, whether neither the powder could have been strewn nor the murderers concealed without her connivance, as she might otherwise have come downstairs and discovered all; and finally her departure from Balfour's house where she had promised to pass the night, a few hours before Darnley was killed and the house blown into the air—prove only too conclusively that she was acquainted with the whole plot.

Mignet, *Mary Queen of Scots*, i, 271–2.

The question naturally arises, whether, when we find that so many of the leading men in Scotland were concerned in the murder of Darnley, it was possible for the Queen to have remained in ignorance of the plot? But to this it may be answered, that the Scottish nobles had in that age brought the art of secret plotting to the highest degree of perfection, and that the Queen had been kept entirely in the dark respecting the conspiracy against Riccio in which a still greater number of persons, including her own husband were engaged. Not the slightest intimation of the plot reached her ears until the assassins of her secretary stood before her. Assuming that she was innocent, the enemies of Darnley had still stronger motives for secrecy; for the crime they contemplated was of a still more heinous kind, and in the case of miscarriage they could count upon no external aid.

Hossack, *Mary Queen of Scots*, i, 267–8.

Heir followis the testament and tragedie of umquhile
King Henry Stewart of gude memorie. . . .
Into the tyme of this my extasie,
Quhen I was in this fearfull fantasie,
With *feinzeit* fair and *wylie* wordis discreit
Scho come to me with greit humilitie,

Lamentand sair my greit calamitie,
My langsum lyfe and sair tormentit Spirite,
Promittand, with ane faithfull hart contreit,
In tyme to cum, with reuerence me treit
To my degre, in honoure, luife, and peace.
Traistand into hir *wylie* wordis sweit
My hart and lyfe into hir handis compleit
I put, and past vnto the Sacrifice.

Quhat sall I wryte how I was tourblit thair?
I wat it wald mak ony haill hairt sair
For to reuolue my tristsum tragidie.
How that thay bucheouris blew me in the air
And stranglit me, I shame for to declair,
Nouther to God nor honoure hauand Ee.
I houpit weill to haue na ennymie
Into this Realme; fra my natiuitie
Thair was na man quhome to I did offend.
Dissauit far I fand the contrarie:
Off Tygeris quholpis, fosterit in tyrannie,
Ane treuthles troup hes drewin me to this end.
Sempill Ballates in *Satirical Poems*, i, 41.

Certane serwantis of Boithwellis, guiltie of the heinous crime, wer executed to death, after they had beene extraordinarielie racked, to drawe some one woorde, if they could be driwen therto throwe the paine of the torment, althought not true in the selff, against ther Mistres, after ewerie blowe and stroake of the bitle or hammer, askinge whether ewer her Maistie had spoken to them of the facte, or commaunded the murder of her husband. . . . But notwithstandinge anie torment they could uise, to bringe foorth so much as one woorde against her Maiestie to her preiudice, they wold newer accuse her, saying often, fie upon such crueltie, they wold not speake against her to condemne themselwes to the devil, do what they wold against ther bodie, ther soules was Godis.
Blackwood, *History of Mary Queen of Scots*, 51–52.

No unprejudiced investigator can fail to recognise Mary's complicity in her husband's murder. However, if this complicity was a crime, it was a 'crime passionel'—one of those terrible actions for which not the individual but his passion is responsible, at a time when passion has full sway.

One who wishes to plead extenuating circumstances, can only do so on the ground of 'diminished responsibility' through passion, and not on the ground that she knew nothing of the matter. She was not acting boldly, joyfully, in full awareness, and under the promptings of her own will, but at the instigation of an alien will. I do not think it can be justly said that Mary went to Glasgow in a spirit of cold calculation in order to bring Darnley back into the danger zone; for in the decisive hour (as the Casket Letters prove), she was filled with repulsion and horror at the thought of the role which was imposed on her. Doubtless, she had beforehand talked over with Bothwell the plan of removing Darnley to Edinburgh, but one of her Letters shows with remarkable clearness how, as soon as she was a day's journey away from her controller, and thus partially freed from the hypnotic influence he exercised upon her, the slumbering conscience of this magna peccatrix began to stir. We must draw a clear distinction between her, as one of those who are driven into crime by mysterious forces, and those who are criminals through and through; for at the moment when Mary began the actual carrying out of the plan, when she found herself face to face with the victim she was to lead to the slaughter, she was no longer inspired by hatred or by vengeful sentiments, and her innate humanity struggled desperately against the inhumanity of her commission. At the moment of the crime, and even when she was engaged in removing Darnley to the place of assassination, the true womanliness of her nature surged up. But this revulsion of feeling came too late. In the Kirk o' Field affair, Mary was not only the huntress cunningly seeking her prey; she herself was also the quarry. Behind her she could hear the crack of the huntsman's whip. She trembled at the thought of the bullying wrath of her lover Bothwell should she fail to lead the victim to the sacrifice; and she trembled, likewise, lest, through weakness, she should forfeit the Earl's love. Only on the ground that Mary was suffering from a paralysis of the will, and did not at the bottom of her soul will her own deed, only when we recognise that she was inwardly in revolt against the actions that were forced upon her, can we at least sympathetically understand a deed which, from the outlook of abstract justice was unpardonable.

Zweig, *The Queen of Scots*, 176–7.

We find that, for more than two years after that event [the death of Darnley], no one was publicly charged with the murder except Bothwell and the queen; and we know that it was the interest of the ruling faction in Scotland at the time to confine the accusation to these two persons. We find that, after the leaders of that faction commenced to quarrel among themselves, they began to accuse each other of the crime; and eventually that it was laid to the charge, upon evidence more or less trustworthy, of nearly all the principal nobility of Scotland. The murder was at first represented as one of a purely domestic character, arising from the queen's hatred of her husband and her violent passion for Bothwell; and the Glasgow letters were obviously fabricated to give this aspect to the case, for they implicate only her and her supposed paramour. But this view is inconsistent with the undoubted guilt of the leading nobility, who, from motives either of interest or revenge, nearly all desired Darnley's death. An impartial examination of the facts cannot fail to lead us to the conclusion that the mysterious assassination of the King was not a domestic, but a political, crime; and it was one which for many a day secured political power to that faction which from the first had opposed his marriage, and had never ceased from the time of his arrival in Scotland to lay plots for his destruction.

Hossack, *Mary Queen of Scots*, i, 264–5.

Bot quhairto gadder we Argumentis as in a doutfull cace, quhen scho hirself will not suffer us to dout at all? Scho, the Quene hirself, I say, oppinly protestit, not to hir Luifer in Bed, not amang hir Confederatis in secreit Chalmer, not befoir few and meane Persones of Estate, apt to Flatterie, constranit be Povertie, or of Purpois affectionit: Scho hirself, I say, oppinlie confessit, that scho culd not live ane gude Day, gif scho wer not red of the King; and that not anis, nor unadvisitly, bot in Presence of yai Person-ages quhome scho usit to call to Counsell in the wechtiest Affairs.

Buchanan, Detectioun, 47.

Albeit he was her Head in Wedlocke, yet was he otherwise but a member of her Commonweale, subject to her, as to his principal and supreme Governesse, and to her Lawes, by the due and ordinary Processe and Course whereof, he might justly have been convicted, condemned and executed, aswel for the Murther committed upon *David* her Secretarie, in whose Body his Dagger was found stabbed, as for the imprisoning of the Queene, and for the attempting to remove her from civil Government, to intrude himself thereto, and for divers others the like Pageants by him plaid.

Who can nowe reasonably thinke, that where she, by Lawe and Justice, might have fully satisfied this her falsely surmised Will and Desire, that she would not take the opportunities in this Sort offered, but omitting them al, seeke unlawful Meanes to his Destruction? This vehement Presumption of her Innocency is much holpen, for that she would not consent to a Divorce betwene her and the Lord Darnley . . . though she were moved thereto by a great Number of her Nobilitie, and by such as be now her greatest Adversaries.

Leslie, Defence, 7–8.

Mary: King Darnley's bloody ghost
          Threat'ningly rises from his grave before me,
          And he will never be at peace with me
          Until my cup of misery is full.

          .   .   .   .

Kennedy: Not yours the deed; you did not murder him.

Mary: I knew it; I suffer'd it; and smiling,
          Beckon'd him to the death snare.

          .   .   .   .

> And bloody vengeance will come on me for it!
> Thou seek'st to comfort me, and speak'st my doom.

Kennedy: Because thou hinderdst not, thou didst it not.
            Passion's blind frenzy had laid hold of thee,
            And bound to the yoke of the seducer Bothwell.
            Ah, not alone the villain ruled thy bosom
            With man's supremacy of power and will;
            But with foul spells, and charms, and hellish potions.
            All evil arts——

Mary: His evil arts were none
            But his determined purpose and my weakness.
                            Schiller, *Maria Stuart*, 221-3.

What becomes of all their boasting of evidence against *Bothwell*?
Murray began the accusation of his Sovereign in these words: 'As
James Earl of *Bothwell* was the chief executer of that horrible and
unworthy murder; so was the Queen in the foreknowledge, counsel, device, persuader and commander of that murder' A man
would almost be tempted to grant the whole of this, to wit, that the
first part of the sentence was equally true with the last; because, for
aught appears, there is no truth in either. And one might venture,
I think, to advance the contrary, 'that as *James* Earl of *Bothwell*
was not the executer; so neither was the Queen the commander
of that murder.' At least it might well be inverted thus: That as the
Queen was not the commander of that murder, and did not write
the letters to *Bothwell* for that purpose; so neither is there any
probability or reason to think that he was the executer, or even
knew anything of the matter.
                            Goodall, *Examination of the Letters*, i, 391.

The murder seems to have been carefully planned so as to indicate,
if possible, that it could not have been the work of her and Bothwell. The impression meant to be conveyed was that the murder of

the Queen, as well as that of her husband, was intended—that the Queen's escape was a mere accident, caused by her absence that night at the marriage of Bastian. But for the desire to convey this impression, it would have been enough to have killed Darnley in the Queen's absence—without the sensational accompaniment of an explosion. The explosion was a mere ruse; its aim was not to destroy Darnley, but to conceal the method of murder. As a method of assassination it lacked sufficient certainty: the victim might not even be mortally injured by it; and, besides, the mere noise was an objection unless there was a corresponding advantage. To make sure of the victim's death it would be necessary to effect it before blowing up the house; and in order to convey the impression that he was killed by the explosion, no weapon was used against him: he was strangled or suffocated. But, for some reason, the work was bungled. We must suppose it was intended to leave the bodies of Darnley and his servant, Taylor, in the house for the explosion to work its will on them: but they appear to have been caught in the grounds in the act of escaping. Mr Lang is inclined to think that the actual assassination was the work of Huntly and the Douglases; but although the fact of the suppression of evidence against others than Bothwell has to be remembered, as well as the general unreliability of the subordinate agents' statements, the chances are that Bothwell would see to the assassination himself. Whatever, also, may have been the case with Huntly, we cannot suppose that the Douglases had much to do with the assassination.

Henderson, Mary Queen of Scots, ii, 431–3.

Mary was not entirely unaware of the measures which were being taken by the nobility to secure in one way or other the removal of Darnley, that if she did not expressly sanction the enterprise, she failed, firmly and promptly, to forbid its execution.

Skelton, Maitland of Lethington, ii, 205.

Kirk o' Field was deliberately chosen as the place to which Darnley should return, by conspirators led by Sir James Balfour, instigated as to the object, but not necessarily as to details, by Father Edmund Hay. The Earl of Lennox and his son, Darnley, were both aware of, and conniving in, the attempt, which was only one of several which had, so far, failed. The object was to destroy the Queen, who had refused to adopt the measures put before her to effect the Counter-Reformation; the Regency, possibly the Kingship, would then be assumed by Darnley.

The *modus operandi* was to mine the large reception room . . .; in it the Queen and many of the nobles were expected to assemble on her return from Holyrood after the wedding party. The match was to be fired, and Darnley to escape, on the approach of the returning party. The plot, however, had leaked out. The Queen was warned not to return; but a large party did approach the place, and the conspirators carried out the programme in the belief that the moment had arrived. Darnley was met in the south garden, escaping, and was there strangled, a consent to his capture having been wrung from the Queen when the plot was opened to her.

Neither Bothwell, nor Moray, nor the Douglases were responsible for the explosion, but all were represented at the execution of the real culprit, the first perhaps in person, though I doubt if he reached the scene until the deed was done. If he had, it would have made no difference, for not one of them would raise a finger to save Darnley.

Mahon, *Tragedy of Kirk o' Field*, xiii–xiv.

From the first throughout Europe, it was universally held that Bothwell had been the murderer-in-chief and that Mary had been his confidant. Even the Pope and the papal legate denounced the unhappy woman in the strongest terms. But what chiefly disturbed the minds of foreign princes was not so much the murder itself. The sixteenth century was not greatly troubled about moral questions, or likely to be squeamish about a bagatelle such as political assassination. It was but a couple of generations since Machievelli had published *The Prince*, and ever since (as indeed before!) murder for 'reasons of State' had been regarded as a trifling matter, or at most venial sin. There was scarcely a royal house in Europe without some such skeleton in its cupboard. Henry VIII had made no bones about the execution of wives he wanted to get rid of. Philip II would not have liked to be pressed with questions about the murder of his son Don Carlos. The Borgias (Pope Alexander VI and his son Cesare) have an evil reputation as poisoners. Still there is a distinction to be drawn. The aforesaid princes did their deeds by proxy, and liked to keep their own hands 'clean'. What her fellow sovereigns expected from Mary Stuart was a strenuous and personable attempt at self-exculpation; and what they took amiss was her ostentatious indifference. Coldly, at first, and then with rising indignation, they watched their imprudent sister, who did nothing to avert suspicion; who refrained from having a few commoners hanged and quartered; who went on amusing herself by playing pall-mall, and had as her chosen companion the man who was unquestionably the chief instigator of the murder. With honest anger, Mary's trusty ambassador in Paris reported that her impassivity was making a very bad impression. 'You yourself have become the object of calumny here, being regarded as having planned and commanded this crime.' With a frankness which will ever redound to the credit of this churchman, he told the Queen unless she atoned for the murder in the most explicit and uncompromising manner, it would be better for her to have lost life and her all.

Zweig, The Queen of Scots, 195–6.

It was not her own subjects alone who suspected Mary of having been accessary to this unnatural crime; nor did an opinion, so dishonourable to her character, owe its rise and progress to the jealousy and malice of her factious nobles. The report of the manner and circumstances of the King's murder spread quickly all over Europe, and, even in that age, which was accustomed to deeds of violence, it excited universal horror. As her unhappy breach with her husband had long been matter of public discourse, the first conjectures which were formed with regard to his death, were extremely to her disadvantage. Her friends, at a loss what apology to offer for her conduct, called on her to prosecute the murderers with utmost diligence, and expected that the rigour of her proceedings would prove the best and fullest vindication of her innocence.

W. Robertson, *History of Scotland*, ii, 196–7.

If Mary's behaviour before the murder of Darnley lends color to the belief that she was guilty of foreknowledge of the crime, her conduct afterwards . . . absolutely confirms it. She made no serious attempt to punish the criminals. When the man whom all Scotland knew to be guilty was brought to trial, she so arranged matters that the trial became a farce, heaped honors on him, and finally married him. Each one of her actions, from the restoration of Archbishop Hamilton's court to the marriage with Bothwell, is susceptible of an explanation which is consistent with innocence, and Mary has not lacked apologists who have exercised their ingenuity to explain them away. But, taken all together, these explanations simply do not ring true. The evidence for guilt is too overwhelming, even without the Casket Letters. . . . When to all this is added the fact that virtually all her contemporaries who knew the facts—not only partisans, such as Morton and Knox, but men who wished her well, such as Moretta and Du Croc—thought her guilty, it becomes next to impossible to believe in her innocence. Alas for the romantics—it must be concluded that Mary was by no means the helpless victim of circumstances.

Lee, *James Stewart, earl of Moray*, 198.

12

MARRIAGE TO BOTHWELL

If Mary's relationship with Bothwell before the murder of Darnley must occasion some doubt, there is less room for conjecture following that event. Mary's state of mind after her husband's death has been variously interpreted, but clearly the steps which she took to ascertain the truth were exceedingly half-hearted. The trial of Bothwell which was fixed for 12 April 1567 was manifestly collusive as Bothwell's accuser, Darnley's father, the earl of Lennox, could not safely appear and the earl was consequently acquitted. Mary's motives in pursuing this course are not entirely clear. Her detractors have seen her deeds as a manifest sign of her inordinate passion for Bothwell, but her defenders have urged her innocence on the grounds that she believed in the justice of his acquittal. The latter theory has little to commend it, but passion should not be too readily accepted as the only reason for her actions. Three months separated the murder and her subsequent marriage and this period saw several sound political moves by means of which Mary attempted to reconcile church and nobility to her side. Bothwell likewise canvassed for political support and on 19 April 1567 obtained such help in the 'Ainslie's Tavern Bond' signed by eight bishops and twenty-one lords, many of whom may have hoped Bothwell could restore the situation. Even this has been interpreted as part of a wider plot devised by the nobility to encompass the downfall of both Mary and Bothwell and as such has frequently appealed to defenders of Mary. Nevertheless, this suggestion overlooks the fact that by mid-April 1567, the earl had become her only means of political survival, and that her abduction by Bothwell on 24 April appears to have been an acknowledgement of this fact. The case for forcible abduction is not strong and Mary was to stress thereafter that she had not married under duress. Before marriage could take place, however, the arrangements for Bothwell's divorce from his wife, Lady Jane Gordon, had to be expedited, and the explanation of Mary's part in this taxes the ingenuity of her most devoted admirers. Finally on the

*occasion of her marriage to Bothwell on 15 May 1567, Mary pre-
sented her supporters with their greatest problem as the ceremony of
marriage was conducted by Adam Bothwell, the reformed bishop of
Orkney, according to the protestant form. Nevertheless, even at this
juncture passion or love may not have been the central factor in a
union which had become for both parties an act of political necessity.
Following the marriage Mary continued to bargain for support, but
her calculations had failed. Her lords might have countenanced her
adulterous affair with Bothwell, but the permanent triumph of Bothwell through this marriage they could not stomach. The Edinburgh
mob might play on Mary's moral shortcomings when they decried her
as a whore, but it was her political alignment with Bothwell which
caused the nobility to take to arms. Lack of morality might in retro-
spect be sufficient grounds for deposing a queen, but it required a
political opposition to effect it. Nevertheless, if there is no doubt that
it was Mary's marriage which caused her downfall, and led a month
later to her defeat at Carberry on 15 June 1567, care must be taken in
following Buchanan and his imitators in combining cause and effect
and concluding that it was passion alone which led to her marriage
and thus encompassed her downfall. Bothwell's interest in the union
was almost certainly political and the reverse may be equally true.
Marriage for both was the last desperate political gamble, and while
Mary may have retained some affection for Bothwell, there are indi-
cations following their marriage of convenience that the queen was not
wildly enamoured with her new husband. These feelings must have
been inevitably quickened by the realisation that the political tide had
turned against her.*

The Queen, according to the ancient custom should have keeped
herself 40 days within, and the doores and windowes should have
been closed in token of mourning: but the windowes were opened,
to let in light, the fourth day. Before the twelfth day, she went out
to Seatoun, Bothwell never parting from her side. There she went
out to the fields to behold games and pastimes. The King's armour,
horse, and household stuffe, were bestowed upon the murtherers.

A certain taylour, when he was to reforme the King's apparel to Bothwell, said jestingly, He acknowledged here the custom of the country, by which the clothes of the dead fall to the hangman.

Knox, *Works*, ii, 550.

Nor can it be disputed that many of the allegations against Mary which were at one time urged with what appeared overwhelming force, have been deprived by more recent investigation and keener criticism of not a little of their weight. That the criminal relations between Mary and Bothwell were notorious for months before the murder (the fact being that there is no suggestion in any contemporary document of improper or unusual intimacy, and that, on the contrary, the prudence and wisdom of her conduct up to the day of the murder are warmly commended by those who were nearest to her at the time); that immediately on her recovery from her confinement she went to Alloa with a crew of 'pirates' of whom Bothwell was the Captain (the fact being that she was accompanied by her brother and the chief nobles of her Court); that whenever she heard of Bothwell's wound she flew to Hermitage Castle like a distracted mistress (the fact being that she did not visit Hermitage, again in the company of her brother, until she had held the assizes at Jedburgh, and until Bothwell was out of danger—ten or twelve days after she had first heard of the accident); that whenever Darnley was murdered, casting aside all decent restraint, she went to Seton to amuse herself at the butts with her lover (the fact being that she went to Seton by the advice of her physician for change of air,—leaving Bothwell and Huntly in Edinburgh to keep the Prince till her return); that she was eager for the marriage and hurried it on with unseemly haste (the fact being that on the very day of the ceremony she was found weeping bitterly and praying only for death):—these and similar calumnies have been conclusively and finally silenced.

Skelton, *Maitland of Lethington*, ii, 208–10.

She knew sufficiently well that the almost universal opinion of the
5

people pointed to Bothwell as the main conspirator, and yet from the first her attitude to him remained to say the least, as friendly as before; he did not become in any degree a less favoured companion, nor did his influence in her counsels suffer any diminution. Her best friends, when they mentioned to her with hesitation the rumours that she intended to marry Bothwell, warned her against taking such a fatal step, but her answer was that matters were not yet 'that far agaitwait'. The excuses that have been made on the score of broken or uncertain health can scarcely be regarded seriously, for Mary, notwithstanding a very dangerous illness in October, had made her journey to Glasgow in midwinter, and also remained late at a ball on the very eve of the murder. If she was engaged in such a conspiracy, no doubt anxiety, and perhaps remorse, might affect to some extent her health and spirits. That spells of perhaps somewhat artificial gaiety should be succeeded by fits of depression, or even of hysterics, was at least as consistent with guilt as with innocence. There is no evidence of anything approaching mental prostration, and no symptom that her presence of mind had deserted her. Severe mental conflict there probably was, and, it may be, some halting between two opinions, but all through the crisis her mental faculties were alert and keen. Her letters addressed to the Archbishop of Glasgow and to Lennox, are all remarkable specimens of feminine tact, and their skilful fencing is wholly directed towards one purpose—that of parrying awkward suggestions as to the means which should be employed to avenge the murder. The question as to whether Mary was really in love with Bothwell is a comparatively minor one, for she could scarcely have been blind to the main motive which actuated Bothwell in carrying out the plot. Undoubtedly the evidence—apart even from the Casket Letters—favours the supposition that she was in love with him, rather than the supposition that she married him unwillingly. At any rate, he claimed his reward, and she granted him the reward he claimed. The fatal weakness, indeed, of all such arguments as are used to establish either Mary's absolute or partial innocence of the murder is, that they do not harmonize with the leading traits of her disposition. She was possessed of altogether exceptional decision and force of will; she was remarkably wary and acute; and she was a match for almost any of her contemporaries in the art of diplomacy. She was not one to be concussed into a

course of action to which she had any strong aversion, and in all
matters vitally affecting herself was in the habit of using her own
independent judgment.

Henderson, *Casket Letters*, 6–8.

The queen's supine inattention to the murder of her husband, after
the promise of such rigorous vengeance, can neither be imputed to
excess of grief, nor to the imbecility incident to a female reign. She
was neither a minor nor susceptible to tutelage. Her real character
was displayed at her marriage, in the quick apprehension, the
spirit, vigour, and resolution with which she anticipated and
quelled an insurrection; and at the assassination of Rizio, by the
most consummate dexterity, art and address. If innocent herself,
she must of course have suspected some desperate party or leader
then at court; nor could she possibly believe that her husband was
murdered, without the least surmise of the real author, or the
cause of his death. Her suspicions must have fastened either upon
Murray and his adherents among the reformers, or on the Hamiltons, the hereditary enemies of Lennox, or on Bothwell and his
associates; the three parties that prevailed at court. The first
might justly allege, that he had neither procured the house, nor
conducted the King thither; the second, that they were all absent
except the archbishop. But if the queen suspected Murray, the
Hamiltons were ready to join with Bothwell and Huntly, either to
imprison him, or, if he fled from justice, to attaint him in parliament: if she suspected the Hamiltons, Bothwell, Lennox and
Murray were prepared to reduce a potent family that had aspired
to the crown. If, on the contrary, she had suspected Bothwell, but
had rendered him too formidable to be arrested at court, the conduct proper to be pursued was obviously the same as at the murder
of Rizio; to retire to the castle of Edinburgh, or to Stirling castle,
and under the direction of Murray, Mar, or Lennox, to summon
her nobility and subjects to her aid. If innocent, she must have
suspected somebody, and the means of detection were evidently
in her hands. The persons who provided, or furnished the lodging,
the man to whom the house belonged, the servants of the queen
who were entrusted with the keys, the King's servants who had

previously withdrawn, or were preserved at his death, his brother
Lord Robert, who had apprized him of his danger, were the first
objects for suspicion or inquiry, and their evidence would have
afforded the most ample detection. Had she consulted either the
preservation of her character or the gratification of a just revenge,
the path lay open before her, and a small portion of the spirit,
vigour and address which she had formerly exerted on the assassination of Rizio would have sufficed to discover the real conspirators, and, by adequate vengeance, to rescue her own reputation from censure. But if accessary, or in the least privy to the
murder of her husband, she must have acted precisely as she did.
After a slight or specious inquiry, she would omit all further investigation of the crime of which she was conscious; and retire
from the keen observation and reports of her capital, in order that
the memory of her husband during her absence, and the silence of
government, might gradually be effaced from the mind of the
people.

Laing, *History of Scotland,* i, 53–55.

Urged by these repeated appeals, she at last resolved that Bothwell
should be brought to a public trial; but the circumstances which
attended this tardy exhibition of justice were little calculated to
justify her in the opinion of her people. He had now become so
powerful by the favour of the crown, and the many offices conferred upon him, that it was evident, as long as he remained at
large and ruled everything at court, no person dared be so hardy
as accuse him. His trial accordingly was little else than a mock
ceremonial, directed by himself, and completely overruled by his
creatures. The Earl of Lennox, who at an earlier period had in vain
implored the queen to investigate the murder, and to collect,
whilst it was attainable, such evidence as might bring the guilt
home to its authors, now as earnestly and justly pleaded the
necessity of delay. He had been summoned to appear and make
good his accusation against Bothwell; but he declared that it was
in vain to expect him to come singly, opposed to a powerful adversary, who enjoyed the royal favour, and commanded the town and
the castle. He conjured the queen to grant him some time, that he

might assemble his friends; he observed, that when the suspected persons were still at liberty, powerful at court, and about her majesty's person, no fair trial could take place; and, when all was in vain, he applied to Elizabeth, who wrote to Mary in the strongest terms, and besought her, as she hoped to save herself from the worst suspicions, to listen to so just a request. It was forcibly urged by the English queen, that Lennox was well assured of a combination to acquit Bothwell, and to accomplish by force, what could never be attained by law; and she advised her, in the management of a cause which touched her so nearly, to use that sincerity and prudence which might convince the whole world that she was guiltless.

It is not certain that the Scottish queen received this letter in time to stay the proceedings, for it was written only four days previous to the trial; and the Provost-marshal of Berwick, to whom its delivery was intrusted, arrived at the capital early in the morning of the twelfth of April, the very day on which the trial took place. The state in which he found the city soon convinced him that his message would be fruitless. When he entered the palace, the friends of the Earl of Bothwell were assembled. They and their followers mustered four thousand men, besides a guard of two hundred hagbutters. This formidable force kept possession of the streets, and filled the outer court of the palace; and as the castle was at his devotion, it was evident that Bothwell completely commanded the town.

It was scarcely to be expected that a messenger whose errand was suspected to be a request for delay should be welcome; and although he announced himself to be bearer of a letter from Elizabeth, he was rudely treated, reproached as an English villain, who had come to stay the "assize," and assured that the queen was too busy with the matters of the day to attend to other business. At that moment Bothwell himself, with the Secretary Lethington, came out of the palace, and the provost-marshal delivered the Queen of England's letters to the secretary, who, accompanied by Bothwell, carried them to Mary. No answer, however, was brought back; and after a short interval, the earl and the secretary again came out, and mounted their horses, when he eagerly pressed forward for his answer. Lethington then assured him that his royal mistress was asleep, and could not receive the letter; but the excuse was hardly uttered before it was proved to be false, for at this moment, a servant of De Croc, the French ambassador, who stood beside the English envoy, looking up, saw, and pointed out the queen and Mary Fleming, wife of the secretary, standing at a window of the palace; nor did it escape their notice that, as Bothwell rode past, Mary gave him a friendly greeting for a farewell. The cavalcade then left the court and proceeded to the Tolbooth, where the trial was to take place, Bothwell's hagbutters surrounding the door, and permitting none to enter who were suspected of being unfavourable to the accused.

From the previous preparations, the result of such a trial might have been anticipated with certainty. The whole proceedings had already been arranged in a council, held some little time before, in which Bothwell had taken his seat, and given directions regarding his own arraignment. The jury consisted principally, if not wholly, of the favourers of the earl; the law officers of the crown were either in his interest, or overawed into silence; no witnesses were summoned; the indictment was framed with a flaw too manifest to be accidental; and his accuser, the Earl of Lennox, who was on his road to the city, surrounded by a large force of his friends, had received an order not to enter the town with more than six in his company. All this showed too manifestly what was intended; and Lennox, as might have been anticipated, declined to come forward in person. When summoned to make good his accusation, a gentleman named Cunningham appeared, and stated that he had been sent by the earl his master to reiterate the charge of murder, but to request delay, as his friends, who had intended to have accompanied him, both for his honour and security, had changed their resolution. On this being refused to Lennox's envoy, he publicly protested against the validity of any sentence of acquittal and withdrew. The jury were then chosen: the earl pleaded not guilty; and, in the absence of all evidence, a unanimous verdict of acquittal was pronounced.

P. F. Tytler, *History of Scotland*, iii, 242–4.

Never was there any thing more ridiculous, than to accuse a man upon the credit of such pasquils, set up secretly in the night-time, by one who would not appear or acknowledge them. Yet *Lenox* insisted by his letters to have the manner brought to a trial, and even would not have it delayed till parliament should meet, which was to be on the xiv day of April. The Queen complied with his desire, and, by her letter directed to him the xxiv of March, requested him to come to her to *Edinburgh* before hand: But he would not. Being therefore warned in the legal manner, and conscious that he had nothing to justify his accusation, he changed his mind, and would needs have the trial delayed.

Goodall, *Examination of the Letters,* i, 351–2.

It was evident to all the world that this famous trial was collusive; nor could it well be otherwise. Argyle, Morton, Huntly, and Lethington were all more or less participant in the king's murder, they were the sworn and leagued friends of Bothwell, and they conducted the whole proceedings. It has been argued by Mary's advocates, that she was a passive instrument in the hands of this faction, and could not, even if willing, have insisted on a fair trial. But, however anxious to lean to every presumption in favour of innocence, I have discovered no proofs of this servitude; and such imbecility appears to me inconsistent with the vigour, decision, and courage, which were striking features in her character.

P. F. Tytler, *History of Scotland*, iii, 244.

All that wer provided to go upon this triale, wer of Murraies factioune and faworites: they onlie ar charged to take instruction and judgment of the processe; if they did cleare and absolwe him, it is ther faulte, if they knew him culpablie guiltie, they did against her commission giwen them; and not takinge notice of the thinge accordinglie, be them selwes guiltie, and maie be supposed to be of councell and knawledge of the facte. Shee can not iustlie be blamed (shee being in such anguish of minde as shee was in for the death of her husband), for the miscareinge of the triale of that, which, by the lawes of the landes, shee trusted them with. Shee did not thinke, that they, whome shee put in truste to trie the mater,

had subscribed with ther handes the write and instrument of agre-
ment to do this wicked parricide, and sealed the same approwinge
it. . . . But because they them selves who wer of that factioun wer
guiltie, none of ther associates and complices wer punished, and
so Boithwell ther copartner, against ther consciences, was absolwed,
not for anie goode which they did beare him, they being ever his
mortall ennemie, but to make ther mistres her selff to be suspected
thereoff.

Blackwood, History of Mary Queen of Scots, 32–33.

The Earle *Bothwel* was acquited by his Peeres, according to the
common and ordinarie Trade and Maner, in suche cases usually
observed. These unnatural and disloyal Subjects, these most
shameful craftie Colluders, her Adversaries and Accusers, I meane
the Earle *Morton*, the Lord *Simple*, the Lord *Lindzay*, with their
Adherents and Affinitie, especially procured, and with al Diligence
laboured his Purgation and Acquital; which was afterwards confirmed by the Three Estates, by Acte of Parliament.

These, these, I say, whereof some are now the vehement and
hotte Fault-finders, and most earnest Reprovers and Blamers of
the said pretended Mariage, were then the principal Inventers,
Practisers, Persuaders and Compassers of the same. They procured a great part of the Nobilitie to solicite the Queene to couple
hirselfe in Marriage with the said Earle, as with a man most fitte,
apt and mete for her present Estate and Case.

First, alleaging the dangerous Worlde, and oft inculcating into
her Minde and Remembrance, the present perilous Time and
Dealinges of Menne, whiche, the better to prevent, and more
surely to withstande, by their Counsel and Persuadings induced
her, and by other their crafty Doinges, as it were, enforced and
constrained her to take a Husband to be her Comforter, her
Assister, her Buckler and hir Shilde, to defend hir against al her
whatsoever Adversaries.

If she would be contented so to doe, they promised him Service,
and to the Queene loyal Obedience. Yea, many of them bound
themselves to the said Earle by their owne Hande-writing to assist,
mainteine and defende him against al Men that would then after

challenge or pursue him, as guiltie of the said Crime. The which their Doings the Queene considering and fearing Dangers imminent, and withal calling to Mind the sundry and divers Uprours and Seditions already made against her, the wretched and most cruel Murther of her Secretarie in her own Presence, the late strange and miserable Murther of her Husband, the Distresse, the Discomforte and Desolation, wherein she was presently bewrapped, the Earles Activitie in martial Feates, and the good and faithful Service done by him to her Mother and to herself, fearing some new and fresh Sturre and Calamitie, if she should refuse her Nobilities Request (though very circumspect and naturally prudent in al her other Doinges) yet neverthelesse a Woman, and especially never to that Houre ones admonished, either openly or privately after the Earles Acquital, that he was guiltie of the said Fact, nor suspecting any Thing therof, yelded to that, to the whiche these craftie, colluding, seditious Heads, and the Necessitie of the Time, as then to her seemed, did in a Maner enforce her.

Leslie, *Defence*, 26–28.

Bothwell being a lewd minded man, blinded with ambition, and therefore venturous to attempt, quickly laid hold on the hope offered unto him, and villainously committed the murther. But Murrey had secretly gone home a prettie way off, fifteene houres before, that he might no way be suspected; and that hee might from thence give aid unto the conspirators, when any need was, and all the suspition might light upone the Queene. As soone as hee returned unto the Court, both he and the Conspirators commended her unto *Bothwell*, as most worthy of her love, for the Nobilitie of his familie, his valour shewed against the English, and his approved fidelitie. They put in her head, that she being alone and solitarie, was not able to repress the tumults that were raised, prevent secret plots, and uphold the burthen and heavie weight of the Kingdome. Therefore she might doe well to take as a Companion of her bed, counsell, and danger, the man that could, would and durst oppose himself against all trouble. And they drove and enforced her so farre, that the fearfull woman, daunted with two tragicall murthers, and remembring the fidelitie

5*

and constancie of *Bothwell* towards her and her mother and having
no other friend unto whom to resort, but unto her brother's
fidelitie, gave her consent: Yet upon these conditions, that above
all this, provision might be made for the safetie of her little sonne;
and then, that *Bothwell* as well might be cleered from the murther
of the King, as also from the bond of his former mariage.

Stranguage, *Life and death of Marie Stuart*, 34–35.

AINSLIES TAVERN BOND

In caice heireftir anie Maner of Person or Persones in quhat-
sumevir Manner sall happin to insist farder to the Sklander and
Calumniatioun of the said Erle of *Bothwell*, as participant, Airt or
Pairt of the said hyneous Murthor, quhairof ordinarie Justice hes
acquite him, and for the quhilk he hes offerit to do his Devoire be
the Law of Armes, . . . wee, and everie ane of us, be our selffes, our
Kyn, Friendis, Assistaris, Partakeris, and all that will doe for us,
sall take trew, essauld, plane and upricht Pairt with him, to the
Defence and Mantenance of his Quarrell, with our Bodies, Here-
tage and Guids, agains his privie or publick Calumnyatoris, bypast
or to cum, or onie utheris presumeand onie Thing in word or deid
to his Reproach, Dishonor or Infamie. MAIROVIR, weying and
considdering the Tyme present, and how our Soverane the Quenes
Majestie is now destitute of a Husband, in the quilk solitarie State
the Commonweall of this Realme may not permit her Heines to
continew and indure, but at sum Tyme her Hienes in Appearance
may be inclynit to yield unto a Mariage; and thairfore in caice the
former affectionate and hartlie Service of the said Erle done to
her Majestie from tyme to tyme, and his uther gude Qualities and
Behaviour, may move her Majestie so farr to humble her selff, as
preferring ane of her native born Subjectis unto all forrane Princis,
to tak to Husband the said Erle, wee and everie ane of us under-
subscryveand upon our Honors and Fidelitie, oblies us, and pro-
mitts . . . to forder, advaunce and set fordwart the Mariage, to be
solemnizat and compleitit betwix her Hienes and the said noble
Lord.

Anderson, *Collections*, i, 109–10.

Among the subscribers of this paper we find some who were the Queen's chief confidants, others who were strangers to her councils, and obnoxious to her displeasure; some who faithfully adhered to her through all the vicissitudes of her fortune, and others who became the principal authors of her sufferings; some passionately attached to the Romish superstition, and other zealous advocates for the Protestant faith. No common interest can be supposed to have united men of such opposite principles and parties, in recommending to their sovereign a step so injurious to her honour, and so fatal to her peace. This strange coalition was the effect of much artifice, and must be considered as the boldest and most masterly stroke of Bothwell's address.

W. Robertson, *History of Scotland*, ii, 211-12.

Although these proceedings of the Earl of *Bothwell*, and his behaviour towards the Queen were most arrogant and presumptuous; yet much might be said in excuse, as to his case in particular, which every man's own mind will readily suggest to him: For certainly these persons who subscribed the band for advancing him to that marriage, and defending him and assisting him in these attempts, were far more to be blamed than he: But the party who first joined in that band, and stood by till the marriage was over, and then rose up against him, were altogether inexcuseable.

Goodall, *Examination of the Letters*, i, 372-3.

Thair remanit ane Thing, quhilk na les vexit the Quene then offendit the Pepill; that is to say, hir companying with *Bothwell*, not altogidder sa oppinly as scho wald fane have had it, and yit not sa secreitly bot the pepill persauit it, for that all Mennis Eyis wer gasing upon thame. For quhairas *Bothwell* had ane Wyfe of his awin, and to tary for ane Divorce was thocht ane over lang Delay, and in the meane tyme, the Quene culd nouther oppinly avow to have him, nor secreitly enjoy him, and yit in na wise culd be without him, sum Schift, thocht not ane honest ane, yit ane Schift forsuith must be devysit; and quhen they culd not think upon ane better, it

seemit thame ane mervellous fyne Inventioun, God wait, that
Bothwell suld ravische and tak away the Quene be Force, and sa saif
hir Honour. Sa within a few Dayis efter, as the Quene was returning from Striviling, *Bothwell*, forceabillie tuke hir be the Way, and
caryit hir to *Dunbar*, quhidder with hir Will, or aganis hir Will,
everie Man may esilie persaif be hir awin Letteris that scho wrait
to him be the Way as scho was in hir journay.

Buchanan, Detectioun, 33–34.

Bothwell had gained over and drawn to his side all the lords of the
council, with a view to this special object. Some helped him
honestly, from friendship; others from fear, being in dread of
their lives; others dissembled, meaning through him to carry out
their own secret ends and private designs. Having thus secured
their help and advice, and seeing the difficulties which would arise
from the delay to which he was subjected, Bothwell resolved, by
some means or other, to seize the person of the Queen, and then
(having already gained the consent of all the lords) to compel her
to give hers, in order to bring the negociation to a conclusion.
Different plans were proposed, varying according to the varying
intentions of the proposers; but in the end, it was carried out in
the following way.

As the queen was on the road from Stirling (where she had been
to visit her son, the prince) to Linlithgow, she was met by the Earl
of Bothwell at the head of fifteen hundred horsemen, armed
according to the custom of the country. The earl of Huntley was in
attendance upon her, but at that time he was a warm partizan of
Bothwell. Bothwell carried her to Dunbar castle, which belongs to
her Majesty, of which the Keeper was Whitlaw. In answer to
complaints which she made, she was reminded that she was in one
of her own houses, that all her domestics were around her, that
she could remain there in perfect liberty and freely exercise her
lawful authority. Practically, however, all happened very dif-
ferently, for the greater part of her train was removed, nor had she
full liberty until she had consented to the marriage which had
been proposed by the said lords of the council. Shortly afterwards,
it was publicly celebrated in Holyrood Palace in Edinburgh, by the

Bishop of Orkney. All the people were admitted, and the chief of the nobility were present, who gave proof that they looked on the union with great satisfaction, as greatly tending to the advantage of the kingdom.

Nau, *Memorials of the Reign of Mary Stewart*, 39–40.

No anxiety on a biographer's part to relieve his subject of the guilt of abusing Mary's trust and forcing on her the marriage that proved her ruin can provide her with a motive for a fake kidnapping. What would Mary gain? Marriage with her captor can be the only answer. But if from passion or policy she wanted to marry Bothwell, why should she resort to this trick? Everywhere was plain sailing. The dignitaries of her Church had signed their approval; so had her lords temporal; if the gentry and populace might murmur at so hasty a union, how could a simulated rapine placate them? Would it not make them more indignant with the kidnapper and less inclined to accept him as a bridegroom? The disadvantages to Mary were so manifest, the gains so non-existent, that it is difficult to believe that her brain, often injudicious but never cretinous, conceived or consented to the plan!

Bothwell would see the question in another light. Here was he, an ideal bridegroom, the favourite of women, whitewashed by the courts, guaranteed by the peerage and the bench of bishops! One thing stood between him and the safety he desired so desperately —a woman's fancy. He liked women, without thinking much of them. He did not mean to let Mary's ill-considered refusal upset his plans. She would, he felt sure, come to appreciate him and she would be the better for a husband who knew his mind. Once married, his influence would rule her, as her uncles had ruled her in France, and Moray when she first came to Scotland. Bothwell had not forgotten how he had been overboarded when Arran went mad. He did not mean to allow that to happen again.

At Dunbar he had his way. The method he employed is another disputed question. Some launch a charge of rape. The issue is obscured by the ambiguity of language. When contemporary writers say that Bothwell "ravished" Mary, they usually mean that he carried her off on her way from Linlithgow. "Abducted" is the modern equivalent. But Melville, present at first at Dunbar, goes further. "The Queen could not but marry him, seeing that he had ravished her and lain with her against her will." Melville was an enemy, but his categorical statement cannot be dismissed without examination. Other members of the anti-Bothwell party expand the charge. An English envoy was told later "how shamefully the Queen was led captive, and by fear, force and (as by many conjectures may be well suspected) other extraordinary and more unlawful means, compelled to become bedfellow to another wife's husband."

Gore-Browne, Lord Bothwell, 350–1.

There was another possible reason for Mary's connivance at her own abduction, namely, her hurry to marry the man with whom she was so madly in love. In the hearing of James Melville at Dunbar Bothwell boasted that he would marry the Queen, 'who would or who would not; yea, whether she would herself or not'; and, as Melville adds, 'the Queen could not but marry him, seeing that he had ravished her and lain with her against her will.' It is probable that this latter statement may have been to some extent true, though the act must presumably have been committed some time before the abduction to Dunbar, apparently even before Darnley's death. Whenever it took place, and however far Mary may have resisted at the time, it was soon condoned by her. Contemporary public opinion was probably not far wrong when it ascribed the abduction to a desire on the part of Mary to avoid personal responsibility for past transgressions, and for the subsequent hasty marriage which she desired, or her condition rendered necessary.

Hume, Love Affairs of Mary Queen of Scots, 382.

He took violent possession of her person, carried her off into the Castle of Dunbar where he detained her for nearly a week. At the end of that time can we wonder that she was aware that the only escape which was left from a ruined reputation was by a marriage with the man who had made her the victim of his brutal violence? This is the conclusion to which we are unavoidably led by the way in which Nau tells his tale. Considering the circumstances under which it was written, and the hearers for whose information it was primarily intended, it was impossible for him to have been more explicit. But the history is given with sufficient precision to make us sympathise with the condition in which this poor injured woman found herself, and to understand how she consented to patch up a marriage on any terms with the man who might become the father of her children.

Stevenson, *History of Mary Stewart*, clvi.

Thus the comfortles Princes seeing her selff captivated, and none of her nobilitie to come for her deliwerie and restitution agane to her former libertie, and on all sides assailed and importuned by the praiers and solicitations of some of the greatest and most mightie of the realme, and otherwise affrighted with the remembrance of her husbandis murder, and her secretarie, and howe then shee was threatened with the danger of her liffe, then being bigge with childe, as it wer shaking and trembling at the memoriall thereof, not being able to resist, nor knowing whom to trust, nor whether to turne her selff, seeing her selff destitute of her nobilitie, and that they had by ther wretinges and signes conspired to bring this mariage to an end, gaiwe place, though much against her stomake, to the present danger and necessitie, assuring her selff no thing could be imputed unto her for faulte, if anie thinge did fall out otherwise then weele, upon ther heades who wer the onlie authouris and constrainers of her to yeelde to the mariage, which shee never dreamed nor thought of.

Blackwood, *History of Mary Queen of Scots*, 36–37.

The Queen, possessed with gratitude for this Nobleman's services, might never have felt the smallest emotion of love for him. It was surely no easy matter for Mary to believe him guilty of the crime attributed to him, without proof, which she never received. It was

no wonder she listened to every testimony in favour of his innocence. His trial, and acquittal, in which it does not appear she had
any hand, confirmed by Parliament, with the association of the
Nobility in his favour, must have therefore rendered him altogether guiltless in her eyes.

It is here to be remarked too, that, with many excellent qualities,
Mary was amazingly credulous, even to the degree of simplicity
and folly. Open, honest, and unsuspicious herself, she believed
others equally so, and trusted to the fair speech and profession of
those whom she thought her friends.

Tytler, *Historical and Critical Enquiry*, ii, 162–3.

Though no excuse can be found for conduct that put the Queen
in a position where at the mildest she was gravely compromised,
Mary may not have suffered the agony of mind that some of her
panegyrists have painted. Some women, it is said, like to be
coerced. She may have felt a thrill that was not unpleasurable to
find herself at the mercy of a strong man, determined to have his
way. After the immature Francis and the imbecile Darnley, the
virile Hepburn might seem a husband worth submitting to. She
was very weary and in his arms she may have hoped to find
security and peace.

Gore-Brown, *Lord Bothwell*, 354.

There was no national party to gratify, no end to gain, no family
alliance to support or strengthen the Crown. Such a marriage
under such circumstances would be simply a disgrace. It would be
at once the consummation of an enormous crime, and a public
defiant confession of it in the face of all men. The murder itself
might have been got over, and the private adultery, even if it had
been discovered, might have been concealed or condoned. But to
follow up the assassination of her husband by an open marriage
with the man whom all the world knew by this time to have been
the murderer, was entirely intolerable.

Froude, *History of England*, ix, 31–32.

Not the less of this opposition the marriage went on, and was celebrated the fifteenth of May by Adam, bishop of Orkney, in the palace of Halyrudhouse, after the manner of the Reformed Church. Few of the nobility were present (for the greater part did retire themselves to their houses in the country), and such as remained were noted to carry heavy countenances. Monsieur le Crock, the French ambassador, being desired to the feast, excused himself, thinking it did not sort with the dignity of his legation to approve the marriage by his presence which he heard was so universally hated. His master the French king, as likewise the queen of England, had seriously dissuaded the queen from the same by their letters; but she, led by the violence of passion, and abused by the treacherous counsels of some about her, who sought only their own ends, would hearken to no advice given her to the contrary.

Spottiswoode, *History*, ii, 54.

The Queen was . . . forced into the arms of Bothwell. Everything co-operated to force her. That dreadful deed of degradation to the honest pride of woman, first reduced her to a level with him. Her total inability to rescue herself from the toils, in which she had been so wretchedly entangled; her repeated proofs, of the general indifference of her subjects to her fate; and the horrible perfidiousness, of the only part of her nobles who spoke to her upon the subject, who urged and urged her to the fatal precipice, "who smiled, and smiled, and yet were villains;" impelled her forwards with him, beyond her power to struggle effectively against it. And all the while she had a principle of wounded delicacy in her breast, that was perpetually betraying her from within; while she was thus assaulted from without. To such an humiliation indeed was she reduced by all, that she was not even married to Bothwell in the only form, which could be agreeable to her conscience or her prejudices. She had been married in the POPISH manner to Darnly; though Darnly was equally a Protestant with Bothwell, though Darnly was of the blood royal of England and Scotland; and though Darnly was the very choice of her heart. Yet she was married in the PROTESTANT manner to Bothwell. . . . Her prejudices, her pride, and her conscience, must all have revolted at

this. But her ravisher and her tyrant insisted upon it. And she was
obliged to comply. He insisted upon it, to please those whom he
knew to be considered, as the leaders and protectors of the Protestants; by whom principally his bond had been signed, and by
whom peculiarly his marriage was to be fortified.

Whitaker, *Mary, queen of Scots Vindicated*, iii, 126–9.

There is one point on which all her censors agree, though they
regard it from different points of view. They clearly state that
Mary's marriage with Bothwell admits of no defence, that it was
a shame and disgrace. We cannot suppose that the Pope and his
informants—predisposed as they were to favour her, actively employed at the time in trying to ascertain the truth, and drawing
their information from friendly sources—would under such circumstances arrive at the very reverse of the truth. We are therefore on firm ground when we draw from our documents the conclusion that Mary should be unequivocally condemned for her
marriage with Bothwell.

Pollen, *Papal Negotiations*, cxxxi–cxxxii.

Mary lost no time in endeavouring to repair some of the injury
which her marriage had done to her prospects. Chisholm, Bishop
of Dunblane, was sent to France and Robert Melville to England
with a similar story. It was necessary, said Mary, for her to marry;
the state of the country demanded it, and her nobility had urged
her to do so, specially mentioning Bothwell as a fit match for her.
She was young, and desired more offspring, and had consented.
Bothwell, it is true, had used her roughly, but had afterwards
purged his offence by submission. He had been legally divorced,
and had been acquitted of the murder of Darnley, and Mary had
acted for the best, and begged their friendship for her husband.
The defence was a weak one, and was received both by Elizabeth
and Catharine with contemptuous coolness, the great effort of
each of the queens being, by special envoys and trimming messages to Mary, to prevent the influence of the other from be-

coming paramount in Scotland. From Spain Mary heard nothing direct, the action of the ambassadors in London and Paris being confined to throwing obstacles in the way of French intrigue in Scotland. But Mary was a diplomatist too experienced not to see that the all-powerful support of Philip, for which she had intrigued so long to aid her in obtaining the English throne, would never be at the command of a woman married in a heretic Church to a divorced Protestant. Connivance at murder would have been in Philip's sight a very venial offence in comparison with this; and it was only long afterwards, when the persecution of Mary had assumed an essentially Protestant character, and she was driven again to look exclusively to Catholics for support, that Philip once more slowly and cautiously pledged the power of Spain to aid her at the critical moment of a Catholic rebellion in England and Scotland.

Hume, *Love Affairs of Mary Queen of Scots*, 392–4.

As this unfortunate Princess might in a very particular manner be noted to have been born unto trouble, the same having remarkably attended her from her cradle, so this bad and ill advised action, her marrying the very person who was but reputed (though he had not really been) the murderer of her former husband, may truly be said to have involved her in endless and remediless misfortunes— an action for which her well-wishers were sorry and grieved at the heart, seeing by it she mightily increased the aversion already instilled into the people, and deprived her friends of all just apology in her behalf; but an action which her enemies rejoiced to see accomplished, since by it she laid the foundation, as it were, of her own ruin, and advanced their wicked designs faster than they themselves could have looked for.

Keith, *History*, ii, 582–5.

Mary and Bothwell may have fondly hoped that once the ceremonies of the Church had hallowed their escapades, the majority of the nation would be disposed to make the best of what they could not help; and there was just a possibility that Bothwell, had he been given a chance, might have turned over, as he said he would, a new leaf, and have proved after all to be the masterful husband, the Queen needed to cure her of her Catholicism, and the strong ruler that would bind the various factions of the nation into unity. He had will and daring, and did not lack talents, if his moral obliquities had hitherto prevented him from turning them to a proper account: his letters announcing his good fortune to Charles IX and Queen Elizabeth are characterised by dignity and diplomatic tact. But murder and rape do not form a promising beginning for a new career of usefulness; and, at any rate, it was soon seen that Scotland had no intention of risking its destinies in his hands.

Henderson, *Mary Queen of Scots*, ii, 463-4.

Bothwell had attained the end for which he had so desperately gambled, but he was now to learn that there were moral forces in the world which he had left out of his reckoning. The religious revolution that had taken place in Scotland had not left men's minds as it had found them; and there now existed a force of intelligent opinion in the country such as was unknown in previous periods of the national history. In the public indignation aroused by the late events, which had reached their climax in the Bothwell marriage, a group of the leading nobles found the momentum requisite to stay the headlong career of the infatuated pair. From Borthwick Castle, where they were constrained to seek refuge, they were driven to the safer stronghold of Dunbar during the second week of June. But neither Mary nor Bothwell was the person to yield without a struggle, and having collected a considerable force they marched towards the capital. With an army of nearly equal strength the confederates met them (June 15) at Carbery Hill, close by the field of Pinkie. Mary was eager for fight; but, while the armies were facing each other, her ranks were thinned by desertion, and there was evident wavering among those who still stood by her. In these circumstances she had no choice but to place herself in the hands of the insurgent lords—Bothwell being permitted to retire from the field. As she rode into Edinburgh that evening, she was received with insulting cries from the populace which must have painfully reminded her how her actions of the last few months had been interpreted by all ranks of her people. It was but one month since she had married Bothwell in the old chapel of Holyrood.

Brown, *History of Scotland*, ii, 112–13.

13

ABDICATION AND EXILE

After her defeat at Carberry and the flight of Bothwell, Mary was taken first to Edinburgh and then to the castle of Lochleven where on 24 July 1567 she was forced to abdicate in favour of her son, on whose behalf the earl of Moray was to act as regent.

The cause of Mary's downfall has frequently been debated. Some have chosen to explain her failure in religious terms, while others have favoured passion, but it is doubtful, even admitting that both these viewpoints have something to commend them, as to whether either of these opinions can be accepted. Mary in all her actions as queen of Scots appears to have been guided to a far greater extent by politics than by either religion or passion. Certainly, neither of her marriages was quite so precipitate as they are often portrayed and premeditation as well as passion played its part. In both her marriages, however, Mary calculated wrongly and, as her mistakes were politically irretrievable, she inevitably fell from power. In the long run this may well be the final judgement on Mary Stuart. Judged by contemporary standards she had tried to rule not by personal beliefs or commitment to religion, but as a politician. Her greatest rival Elizabeth showed this could be accomplished for she too showed little religious zeal and her morality was at times questioned, but she succeeded as a politician because she could compromise and temporise. Mary too succeeded as long as she was prepared to compromise, but when that policy was abandoned and her direct authority asserted, Mary had not the measure of her task.

Even at this juncture, Mary's career in Scotland had not run its course. The regent's position was not assured, and when Mary escaped from captivity on 2 May 1568 she was able to command sufficient support to raise a considerable army. Yet it is doubtful, even if success had attended her efforts, whether she personally would have been able to effect a successful comeback as she was now totally dependent upon the house of Hamilton. The experiment was not to be put to the test as Mary's army was defeated at Langside near Glasgow on 13 May. Mary's courage appears to have collapsed completely, and apparently in fear of her life she fled to the south-west where three days later, she made the fateful decision to cross the Solway into England and throw herself upon her cousin Elizabeth's mercy.

The queen of Scots was now thoroughly alone. And her entry into the camp of the rebels immediately and rudely jolted her confidence in the love which she still believed her subjects bore for her. Here was no enthusiastic reception, no cheers, no protestations of devotion. On the contrary, the soldiers shouted crude insults at her. The queen's spirit still held. She said loudly and openly to Morton: 'How is this, my lord Morton? I am told that all this is done in order to get justice against the king's murderers. I am told also that you are one of the chief of them.' Morton slunk away. But Mary Stuart needed all her courage to endure the ordeal before her, for which she seems to have been ill-prepared. She, who all her life had been greeted publicly with adulation and enthusiasm, now heard the soldiers shout: 'Burn her, burn the whore, she is not worthy to live,' as they conveyed her along the road into Edinburgh. 'Kill her, drown her!' they cried. Close to Mary's side rode Drumlanrig and Cessford, two notorious young thugs, who joined their insults to the soldiers' as they rode. Amazed, almost stunned, the queen allowed tears of shock and humiliation to pour down her cheeks, as she rode forward in the clothes she had acquired at Dunbar—now 'all spoiled with clay and dirt'. For the first time she began to realize what the effect had been on the ordinary people of Scotland—the people who had once loved her— of her reckless action in marrying her husband's assassin, and of those weeks of propaganda by the enemies of Bothwell. To them she was now no longer their young and beautiful queen, but an adulteress—and an adulteress who had subsequently become the willing bride of a murderer.

Fraser, Mary Queen of Scots, 331–2.

Her enemies could prove that she was infatuated with Bothwell, whom they and practically every one believed to be the chief murderer; and they saw, more clearly even than most modern historians could hope to understand, that Mary's love for Bothwell condemned her in the judgment of ordinary people with far more devastating certainty than could any nebulous evidence of her participation in the murder. Sexual morality was a strong element in the new reformed religions. It has always been of supreme significance in the moral judgments of ordinary people. Anyone who flouted the moral sanctions as far as Mary was believed to have done could only meet with hostility. It was logical and inevitable that the Queen's opponents should seize upon this aspect of her situation and exploit it to the full.

Gatherer, *The Tyrannous Reign of Mary Stewart*, 35–6.

Her deliverance from thraldom was one of the objects which the Confederate Lords professed to have in view when they marched to Carberry Hill. For now imprisoning her, they assigned the reason that, instead of agreeing as they proposed to punish Darnley's murderers, she rather 'apperit to fortefie and mantene' Bothwell and his accomplices in their wicked crimes; and as the realm would therefore be utterly ruined, if she were left 'to follow hir awin inordinat passioun,' it was 'thocht convenient, concludit and decernit that hir Majesties persoun be sequestrat fra all societie of the said Erll Boithuile, and fra all having of intelligence with him, or ony utheris quhairby he may have ony comfort to eschaip dew punisment for his demeritis.'

Mary's ambitious projects were now hopeless, her reputation blasted, her freedom gone; meanwhile, at least, all had been wrecked by what seemed to be an infatuated love for Bothwell.

Fleming, *Mary Queen of Scots*, 165–6.

It is difficult indeed to read the proclamations of the Lords with patience. They were written by the men who had plotted against the Queen. They were written by the men who were the accomplices of Bothwell. The declaration that they had risen to release

Mary was ridiculous pretence; the declaration that they had risen to revenge Darnley was odious hypocrisy.

Skelton, *Maitland of Lethington*, ii, 235.

Never, indeed, had Knox's course been clearer to him than now. At length, the woman who had been the sole obstacle in the way of national salvation had been delivered into their hands. By the people's will, he held, the true religion had been established in the country, and surrounded with every legal sanction. From the moment of her return Mary had set herself to undo this work, and to restore an idolatrous system which involved the eternal ruin of all who bowed the knee to it. To Knox, moreover, it was easy to believe, and it was, in truth, his immovable conviction, that Mary was at once the murderer of her husband and the paramour of her partner in crime. As a common criminal and the betrayer of her people, but one judgment could be meted to her. To spare her would be a mistaken mercy which must call down the wrath of Heaven on the nation that suffered crime and idolatry to pass unpunished in its midst.

Brown, *John Knox*, ii, 243–4.

The detention of a Queen by her subjects was an extraordinary circumstance, even in that age of civil wars and religious revolutions. Insurrection against authority had rarely been carried so far as the imprisonment of those who were considered its sacred depositaries. But notwithstanding its enormity, this bold deed aroused no strong disapprobation, or serious resistance, in Scotland. The unwise, passionate, and blameworthy conduct of Mary Stuart had deprived her of all devoted adherents. The murder of Darnley, and her marriage to Bothwell, had destroyed her reputation; and the unshaken attachment which she displayed to this proscribed murderer precluded the possibility of a reconciliation with the confederate lords. Crushed by her victorious adversaries, her intimidated partisans took no vigorous steps for her defence.

Mignet, *Mary, Queen of Scots*, i, 330–1.

The revolution which consigned Mary Stewart to a prison had been brought about by a section only of the Protestant nobility of Scotland. . . . The position of the men who had imprisoned their queen and usurped her authority was therefore full of peril; but the abilities of their leaders were equal to their ambition. Having once embarked in the path of rebellion, they allowed nothing to turn them from their purpose; and while the friends of the queen, numerous though they were, remained irresolute and inactive, the dominant faction made the most strenuous efforts to consolidate its power. In the towns, where its strength chiefly lay, and especially in Edinburgh, the Protestant preachers rendered the most valuable aid. By indulging in furious invectives against the queen, and charging her directly with the murder, they prepared their hearers for the prospect of her speedy deposition, and the establishment of a regency in the name of the infant prince.

Hossack, Mary Queen of Scots, i, 342–3.

Mary was to be persuaded or forced to resign the crown; the young prince was to be proclaimed King, and the earl of Murray was to be appointed to govern the Kingdom, during his minority, with the name and authority of regent. With regard to the queen's own person, nothing was determined. It seems to have been the intention of the confederates to keep her in perpetual imprisonment; but, in order to intimidate herself, and to overawe her partisans, they still reserved to themselves the power of proceeding to more violent extremes.

It was obvious to foresee difficulties in the execution of this plan. Mary was young, ambitious, high-spirited, and accustomed to command. To induce her to acknowledge her own incapacity for governing, to renounce the dignity and power which she was born to enjoy, to become dependent on her own subjects, to consent to her own bondage, and to invest those persons whom she considered as the authors of all her calamities with that honour and authority of which she herself was stripped, were points hard to be gained. These, however, the confederates attempted, and they did not want means to insure success. Mary had endured, for several weeks, all the hardships and terror of a prison; no prospect of liberty appeared; none of her subjects had either taken arms, or so much as solicited her relief, no person, in whom she could confide, was admitted into her presence; even the ambassadors of the French King, and queen of England, were refused access to her. In this solitary state, without a counsellor or friend, under the pressure of distress and the apprehension of danger, it was natural for a woman to hearken almost to any overtures. The confederates took advantage of her condition and of her fears. They employed Lord Lindsay, the fiercest zealot in the party, to communicate their scheme to the queen, and to obtain her subscription to those papers which were necessary for rendering it effectual. He executed his commission with harshness and brutality. Certain death was before Mary's eyes if she refused to comply with his demands. At the same time she was informed by Sir Robert Melvil, in the name of Athol, Maitland and Kirkcaldy, the persons among the confederates who were most attentive to her interest, that a resignation extorted by fear, and granted during her imprisonment, was void in law; and might be revoked as soon as she recovered liberty. Throkmorton, by a note which he found means of conveying to her, suggested the same thing. Deference to their opinion, as well as concern for her own safety, obliged her to yield to everything which was required, and to sign all the papers which Lindsay presented to her.

W. Robertson, *History of Scotland*, ii, 238–9.

Mary was one of those characters, which we meet with very seldom in the world; and which, whenever they appear, are applauded for their generosity by a few, and condemned for their simplicity by the many. They have an easy affiance of soul, which loves to repose confidence, even when confidence is weakness. They thus go on, still confiding and still confounded; unable to check the current of affiance that runs strong in their bosoms, and suffering themselves to be driven before it in their actions. And all the first half of their lives forms one continued tissue of confidences improperly placed, and of perfidies natural to be expected. Such a person was Mary! She once had her bastard brother and his adherents under her feet; but too easily forgave them. She once had all her other rebels under the harrows of the law; but too readily released them. The former rose in rebellion, and were defeated. The latter murdered her foreign secretary in her presence, and even imprisoned her own person in her palace; and yet were overpowered by the management of the Queen, and the fidelity of her peers. And she not only allowed them to return home from their banishment; but restored them to their estates, restored them to their honours, and even restored them to their posts about her court. She thus enabled them to repeat their rebellions with equal power and improved experience. In so doing, she was certainly guilty of great folly. Yet she did even more than this. She afterwards took the *verbal assurances* of the very same men in rebellion, who to be rebels at first, must have previously broken through the strongest assurances that man can give, even their very oaths; and who, to be rebels again, must have violated every additional obligation of gratitude and honour. But she took their words, notwithstanding. She relied upon them so implicitly, as to put her person into their hands. Then they behaved, just as such ungrateful, dishonourable, and perjured wretches were sure to behave. They thrust her into a prison. They forced her to resign her crown.

Whitaker, *Mary queen of Scots Vindicated*, i, 38–39.

Mary's position, which for long had been one of difficulty and danger, might now be regarded as all but hopeless. Everywhere enemies, friends nowhere. Probably she was not fully aware of the gravity of the dangers by which she was surrounded. She did not realise the fact that her enforced marriage with Bothwell had induced many of her former adherents, both at home and abroad, to believe that to a certain extent she was implicated in the murder of Darnley. She still had some lingering faith in the honesty and affection of Moray, who at this very time was busily employed in ruining her cause on the Continent. She deluded herself with the belief that in the King and Queen Dowager of France she had allies whom she could trust in every emergency. When Elizabeth lavished on her professions of friendship and promises of assistance, Mary was credulous enough to think her sincere. She outlived all these hopes, and awoke from all these visions, but at the time when she entered Lochleven they had not ceased to be vivid and influential. They gave her strength and comfort and patience; and thus supported by them, she endured with the constancy of an honest heart and a strong will, the dangers, the insults and the trials to which she was exposed during the eleven months of her imprisonment.

Stevenson, *History of Mary Stuart*, clxxvi–clxxvii.

While the Queen was confined in Lochlevin, although the constant unremitting practices of Elizabeth, in stirring up her seditious subjects against her, had brought her to that prison; although she took no step for effecting her relief; yet, on that occasion, affecting much commiseration for her distress, she had amused her with promises of interposing between her and her rebellious subjects; and by her letters had solicited Mary to take refuge in England, where she offered her a princely reception and a safe asylum. The weakness of Queen Mary now inclined her to trust to these promises; and in opposition to the earnest entreaties of her faithful friends the Lords Herries, Maxwell, and Fleming, who never forsook her, she took the fatal step to complete all her misfortunes by throwing herself into the hands of her steady and determined foe; who, for a course of years, and by a series of schemes, had been contriving to bring this important event about.

W. Tytler, *Historical and Critical Enquiry*, ii, 195–6.

The indignation of Elizabeth on hearing of the harsh treatment of the Queen of Scots had been extreme. At no period of her history, indeed, does she appear to more advantage, either as a woman or a queen. She abandoned for a time that studied ambiguity of language under which it was her custom to cloak her real sentiments, and spoke in tones that all could understand. She forgot that Mary Stewart had once worn the arms and aspired to the crown of England. She only saw her sister queen and nearest kinswoman a helpless captive in the hands of men whose characters and aims she knew too well, and she would at any cost obtain her deliverance ... right or wrong, she would not stand tamely by and see her

cousin murdered. She would remonstrate with these rebellious
Scots, and if remonstrances proved ineffectual, she would send an
army to chastise and reduce them to obedience. Elizabeth, like her
tyrant father, was capable at times of generous emotions; and
there can be no doubt that her conduct at this time, and more
especially the many loving messages which she caused to be
delivered to the Queen of Scots at Lochleven, induced the latter in
the following year to seek a refuge from her enemies in England.

Hossack, *Mary Queen of Scots*, i, 355–7.

Nothing proves more strongly the extraordinary personal fascina-
tion of Mary Stuart than the events that followed her incarceration
at Lochleven. She went there surrounded by Douglases and
enemies, warded by Murray's mother and his half-brother, a close
kinsman of Morton. She was broken-hearted and desperate, in
delicate health, and her condition was aggravated by the frequent
agues and low fevers induced by a damp residence. Most women
in such circumstances, in hourly fear of death, outraged and betrayed as she had been, would have pined and lost heart. Not so
Mary Stuart. After her nearly successful attempt at flight in July
she was for a time shut up in the strictest seclusion; and yet on the
5th August, only three weeks later, Throckmorton reported that
the lords were desperate, and at their wits' end to know what to do
with her. 'The occasion is that she has won the favour and good-
will of the house, men as well as women, and thereby she means
to have great intelligence, and was in towardness to have escaped.'

Hume, *Love Affairs of Mary Queen of Scots*, 413.

The hope that sche had to get frendis and favourers anew, causet
her mak hir moyen to eschaip outt of Lochleven over hastely, or
ever the tym was ryp anough to restore again the hartis of the
subiectis that wer yet allianit; for albeit my L. Regent was rygorous,
he was facill, and mycht have bene won with proces of tym be hir
wisdome, and the moyen of hir frendis that wer in his company.

Melville, *Memoirs*, 194–5.

Hir Maieste was not myndit to feicht, nor hazard battaille, bot to pass unto the castell of Dombertan, and draw hame again to hir obedience, be litle and litle, the haill subiectis. Bot the bischop of St Androwes and the house of Hammiltoun, with the rest of the lordis that wer ther convenit, finding themselves in nomber far beyond the other party, wald nedis hazard the battaill, whereby they mycht overcom the Regent ther gret ennemy, and be also maister of the Quen, to command and reull all at ther plesour. Some allegit that the bischop was myndit to cause the Quen mary my L. Hammiltoun, incaice ther syd wan the victory, and . . . the Quen hir self fearit the same.

Melville, *Memoirs*, 200.

So soone as the Queen saw the day lost, she was carried from the field by the Lords Herreis, Fleming, and Livistoune. . . . She rode all night, and did not halt untill she came to the Sanquhir. From thence she went to Terregles, the Lord Herreis hous, wher she rested some few dayes, and then against her friends advyce, she resolved to goe to England, and commit herselfe to the protection of Queen Elizabeth; in hopes by her assistance, to be repossessed in her Kingdome. So she imbarked at a creek neer Dundrennen, in Galloway, and carried the Lord Herreis to attend her with his counsel; and landed at Cockermouth, in Cumberland. Heer she stayed, and sent the Lord Herreis to Londone, in hopes to be receaved with honor. . . . But before his returne, the Lord Scroop, whoe was Warden upon the English syd, and lived at Carleill castle, was commanded to carrie her to the castle of Carleill, where, with a shaddow of honor, she was kept under strict guard.

Lord Herries, *Memoirs*, 103–4.

14

ENGLAND—TRIAL AND IMPRISONMENT

Mary's wisdom in fleeing to England in May 1568 has often been debated, but with her life in danger if she stayed in Scotland and unprepared for the longer voyage to France where her presence would not necessarily have been welcome, her choice of refuge was not an unreasonable one. Elizabeth's views on sovereignty and the duty of subjects was well known to Mary, and all things being equal, she might confidently have expected English assistance in regaining her throne. All things were not equal, however, for Mary was not only Elizabeth's heir, but had been proclaimed as queen of England. In such circumstances, Mary could not be allowed to go to France in which her claims to the English throne had first been pressed. On the other hand return to Scotland seemed equally impracticable as to repatriate Mary without military assistance would be to commit her to close captivity and probable execution, and to restore her by force would require the defeat of the pro-English party in that kingdom. If, however, Mary remained in England it seemed equally certain that her presence would provide a catalyst for all Elizabeth's disaffected subjects. Faced with such a dilemma, the English government took refuge in the idea of an enquiry at which Mary and Moray should both be represented.

This enquiry, or trial as it has sometimes been described, which took place before a board of English commissioners assisted by others representing the queen and the regent, was held in 1568–69 first at York, then at Westminster and finally at Hampton Court. Its function was to discover by what authority Mary's enemies had deprived her of her crown and inevitably the principal point at issue was to be that of the queen's alleged complicity in the murder of Darnley. It was not the murder, however, but Mary's subsequent marriage to Bothwell which had precipitated her deposition and consequently her relationship with Bothwell was to figure prominently in the charges laid against her.

In theory a vindication of Mary's actions could have brought about

her restoration, but the self-interest of the English and Scottish com-
missioners was such that, in spite of a spirited defence by Mary's
representatives, her detention in England was almost inevitable from
the outset. Nevertheless, not until the withdrawal of Mary's com-
missioners, following a refusal to allow the queen to attend the enquiry
in person, was the main indictment against Mary, the Book of Articles
and supporting evidence in the shape of the Casket Letters produced
and the case against her clinched. At Hampton Court, the principal
evidence was reiterated before an augmented commission which in-
cluded six earls, and this was followed by Elizabeth's final pro-
nouncement which while refusing to condemn either Mary or Moray,
allowed the latter to depart for Scotland while intentions as to Mary's
future were deliberately left obscure. In practice, however, the de-
cision had already been made, and ahead lay the many years of de-
tention which led eventually to the final scene at Fotheringhay.

The danger of returning Mary to Scotland was that the English
party there would be 'abased' and the Marian party exalted, and
England exposed once more to the old danger of an enemy at her
postern gate.

Yet Cecil foresaw grave danger also in keeping Mary in England.
She would, he believed, campaign with her friends in England for
the Crown and he pointed out these friends were numerous, 'some
for religion, some for affection to her title, others from discon-
tentation and love of change'. He believed also that even in England Mary would be able to recapture the support of Scotland—
'for no man can think but such a sweet bait would make concord
betwixt them all'.

Cecil in short proposed that Mary should be held incommuni-
cado that the charges against her should be investigated and that
her subsequent treatment should be determined by the result of
that investigation. He evidently assumed Mary's guilt, but he
could not decide about her eventual fate. He rejected at once the
idea of allowing her to go to France, but he saw grave dangers
either in restoring her to Scotland or in keeping her in England.

Whether the Privy Council at large was in substantial accord

6

with Cecil's views does not appear. Probably it was. Elizabeth herself was certainly more kindly disposed to Mary, and Cecil's main problem at the time was to prevent his mistress from any ill-considered magnanimity.

Read, *Mr. Secretary Cecil*, 399.

During the residence of the Queen of Scots at Bolton was played that strange judicial farce known as the Conference of York. Ostensibly its object was to compel the Earl of Murray, and his colleagues in the government of Scotland, to answer for their conduct in deposing the Queen; but its real purpose was to supply Elizabeth with a much needed pretext for Mary's continued detention. The interest of the enquiry centred about the question of Mary's complicity in Darnley's murder, and there for the first time were produced the famous casket letters, upon the question of whose genuineness so much in this controversy turns. Around the York conference, and all its circumstances, the Marian champions have fought with the Marian assailants. Every inch of ground has been hotly contested, and yet nothing has been settled.

Leader, *Mary Queen of Scots in Captivity*, 9–10.

The regent being urged to declare the causes moving the nobilitie to take armes, to committ to prisoun and depose the queene, and to purge himself of calumneis, declared the whole maner: produced the depositions of suche as were executed for the murther of the king; the decreet and Act of Parliament, whereunto manie of his accusers and calumniators did subscrive; and the silver caskett which the queene gave to Bothwell, wherin were conteaned her missives to Bothwell, writtin in Frenche, with her owne hand, and some love sonnets in Frenche, some secreets concerning the king's slaughter, the rapt after the murther, and three contracts of mariage; one before the murther, writtin with her owne hand; the secund before the divorcement of Bothwell, writtin with Huntlie's hand; the third, a little before the mariage, which was not concealed in the meane time. Buchanan could not be ignorant of these proceedings ather at home or in feild, when he was with the regent. As he was ingenuous and upright, not givin to avarice or bribes, so did he never repent afterward of anie thing he had writtin, in his booke intituled *The Detectioun,* but insert afterward the substance of it in his *Historie,* which was printed when he was neere his death.

When these things were produced, and read before the English counsellers and commissioners, the whole mater was made so evident, that there remained no doubt. And, indeid, we can find nothing in the Bishop of Rosse his owne memorialls after this, but fretting and fooming, and suche frivolous defences and impertinent harangs, as can give no satisfactioun to anie reader of anie meane judgement.

Calderwood, *History,* ii, 466–7.

For the nobles of *England,* that were appointed to heare and examine al suche Matters as the Rebels should lay against the Queene, have not onely found the said Queene innocent and guiltlesse of the Death of her Husband, but do withal fully understand that her Accusers were the very Contrivers, Devisers, Practitioners and Workers of the said Murther, and have further also so much encreased, and in such wise renued the good Estimation and greate Hope they alwaies had of her, now perfectly knowing her Innocency, and therto moved through other princely Qualities resplendent in her, with many wherof she is much adorned and singularly endued, that they have in most earnest wise solicited and entreated, that she might be restored againe to her Honour and Croune. They have moved the said Queene of *Scotland* also, that it may please her to accept and like of the most noblest Man of all *England,* betwene whome and her ther might be a Mariage concluded, to the Quieting and Comforte of both the Realmes of *England* and *Scotland.*

Finally the noblemen of this our Realme acknowledge and accept her for the very true and right Heire apparent of this Realme of *England,* being fully minded and alwaies ready (when God shal so dispose) to receave and serve her as their undoubted Queene, Maistresse and Sovereigne.

Leslie, *Defence,* 80–81.

If the reader shall desire to know, as it is likely he will, how Queen
Mary's Commissioners could be employed all this time, that they
did not either refute these letters, or at least, give in their objections against them, as they certainly always esteemed them forgeries;... But to refute the letters was altogether impossible for them,
because they could never obtain either a sight of the pretended
originals, or copies of them, although they often demanded them,
at the Queen of England's hands. Nay, Elizabeth declared that she
would receive proof of Murray's accusation of the Queen, his
sovereign, before she were heard for herself; and really did so. But
as the particulars of that accusation were kept a profound secret
from Queen Mary and her Commissioners, there was no remedy
left them but simply to deny. This indeed was done; both the
Queen herself, and her Commissioners in her name, did absolutely
deny that she ever wrote to any creature for such purposes; and
affirmed, that if there were any such writings, they were false,
feigned, forged and invented by Murray, Morton and their accomplices themselves: and this they undertook to prove, providing
they might be permitted to take a view of the pretended originals,
and get copies of them; but neither the one nor the other could
ever be obtained; without which nothing could be done.

Goodall, *Examination of the Letters*, i, 5–6.

Had she been *guilty*, had she *in the slightest degree* been accessary
to the crime charged upon her, had there been even a fair probability of proving her guilty of the charge, in spite of her innocence;
her enemies would have acted in a very different manner. No
ambuscade would they have laid for her. They would never have
skulked behind the bushes, and wounded her with invisible shafts.
They would have come forward into view. They would have
engaged in open fight with her. They would have produced the
originals, with pretended regret and with real triumph. They
would have lodged them with the commissioners at York. They
would have lodged them with the commissioners at Westminster.
They would have compelled both to collate them carefully with
private and with public, with foreign and with domestic, writings
of Mary's. Her commissioners would also have *been called upon* to

inspect them, would have been *urged* to compare them, would have been *challenged* to disprove them. Mary herself would have been brought up from her confinement in the country, as she frequently requested to be; have been suffered to enjoy *the freest access* to them; have been allowed to make every objection to them, and have been heard with all the patience of candour, for days and for weeks, in her attempts to invalidate their authority. Such *must* have been the demeanour of Murray the producer, and of Elizabeth the receiver, of the letters; if they had thought her *guilty*, if they had thought her *probably* so, if they had thought her so *in appearance only*. And a conduct, totally the reverse of all this, proves what they never reflected it would prove, the falsehood of their own pretences, the profligacy of their own conduct, and the purity of hers.

Whitaker, Mary, queen of Scots Vindicated, i, 119–20.

As regards Elizabeth, the question of the genuineness of the letters necessarily greatly affects the judgment to be passed upon her treatment of the Queen of Scots. Elizabeth's position—whether she believed the letters to be genuine or not—was one of enormous perplexity. She was placed in a cruel dilemma. It was dangerous to be severe, and yet the temptation to use severity was peculiarly strong. Mary was perhaps the most deadly enemy she possessed. She had awakened Elizabeth's ill-will not merely by laying claim to the English throne, but by the fame of her remarkable personal charms. As the only great Protestant sovereign in Europe, Elizabeth's position was specially perilous. Though Elizabeth had known the letters to be forgeries, she might have been excused for declining to aid her rival or to set her free; but indelible infamy would attach to the promulgation of such a vile calumny against her if it were baseless. On the other hand, if they were genuine, or if Elizabeth believed them to be so, it is difficult to discover any fault of a heinous kind in her treatment of Mary. Elizabeth's conduct was, perhaps, not consistent with strict rules of law or equity,—superficially it was marked by hesitation, uncertainty, and fickleness,—but nevertheless, if the letters were genuine, not only was it characterized by a regard to broad principles of justice, but by

considerable long-suffering towards her unhappy captive, and by
some merciful consideration for her, if not as a woman, at least as a
deposed fellow-sovereign.

Henderson, *Casket Letters*, 109–10.

It may be doubted if any even of the principals really wanted the
enquiry to be pushed to a decisive conclusion. Mary, indeed, may
well have hoped for a vindication and her unconditional restoration, but, if she realised that to be unlikely, she was bound to prefer
an equivocal outcome to an unqualified condemnation as a criminal.
Besides, she must have wondered how she might fare if she went
back to Scotland, necessarily to rely on some faction, and she can
hardly have believed that she had many supporters who were
altruistic enough to put her welfare before their own. She may
even have reflected that it might on the whole be more to her
advantage to remain in England—provided it was on terms which
gave her some freedom of action—and exploit her claims to the
English throne in order to build up a party which might in the end
win two kingdoms for her. Elizabeth, even without Cecil's patient
analysis of the 'dangers' inherent in various possibilities, and even
apart from her constitutional irresolution, had most to gain from
an outcome which neither restored a rival nor justified a sentence
on a sister queen. She probably aimed at some kind of compromise
which would save Mary from condemnation but at the same time
maintain Moray's government in Scotland, preferably with Mary
restored to nominal sovereignty. Moray, the third of the principals, remained uneasy about the future of his person, property
and authority should he publicly accuse Mary of murder and then
find the charge not sustained and Mary restored. Apart from his
apprehension on this score, he wanted his government to continue, which it could do with indubitable legality only if Mary
would accept a settlement involving its recognition. It was reported
that, just before the conference at York opened, Moray sent an
agent to Mary to seek her agreement to a compromise whereby she
would have a large allowance and remain in England, while Moray
continued in office as regent. One of the English commissioners at
York—the Earl of Sussex—thought that if only Mary would

agree to surrender the crown voluntarily and continue to live in England, Moray's party would 'forbear to touch her honour' and perhaps even publicly absolve her. So far were they from any interest in justice for its own sake.

Donaldson, *First Trial of Mary, Queen of Scots*, 93–94.

So terminated in impotence and self-contradiction the long and shapeless enquiry. Murray was able to say that he was allowed to return to the Regency. The friends of the Queen of Scots could say that Elizabeth still refused to recognise him as Regent, and had confessed in the sentence that the Queen of Scot's guilt had not been proved. The world at large, the continental courts, who had hitherto believed her to be indisputably a party to the murder, the English Catholics, whose interest in her succession disposed them to believe in her innocence, interpreted by their wishes the inconsecutiveness and insincerity of the conclusion. Elizabeth had desired to leave the Queen of Scots unconvicted yet with a blemished reputation; the truth had been forced upon the Peers, and so far she had gained her object; but beyond the circle of those who had seen the letters, she had created an impression that the Queen of Scots might, after all, have been false accused; that Elizabeth could not condemn her, yet for her own sinister objects refused to acquit her, and had aggravated the injustice of the imprisonment by hypocrisy and perfidy.

Froude, *History of England,* ix, 389.

For the moment Elizabeth had seemingly won a victory over her defenceless rival; but she was soon to realize that it was a Pyrrhic victory. By imprisoning Mary in England she all unwittingly lost her own freedom, and for the next nineteen years lived in ceaseless anxiety lest her prisoner might escape. While the two queens lived, there could be no quiet in the realm. Far better would it have been —such is the irony of history—had Elizabeth allowed her defeated and discredited enemy to go whither she pleased. The Catholic world, influenced by her recent behaviour, would have treated her

with cold contempt; she would have sunk into comparative insignificance, suffered, it may be complete political eclipse; and her
name would have left no mark on history. But the incarceration
saved her from this. As the victim of an unjust fate she became
invested with a halo of martyrdom, recovered her position in the
eyes of her co-religionists, and lived to plague the inventor of her
misery, with even greater misery than she herself endured.

Black, *The Reign of Elizabeth*, 118.

15

THE CASKET LETTERS

The Casket Letters and other documents, including the so-called sonnets, were first officially produced as evidence against Mary at Westminster in December 1568, although they had been unofficially shown to the English commissioners at York in October. If genuine they prove Mary's passion for Bothwell before Darnley's death and her part in encompassing his murder by her lover. As a result their authenticity, or lack of it, has often been seen as cardinal in establishing her guilt or innocence. In this respect, however, Mary's accusers are at marked advantage for while the queen's guilt can be established beyond question if the letters are genuine, their spuriousness does not necessarily prove her innocence, only that her accusers in 1568 manipulated the evidence to make assurance doubly sure. In this respect, the violent arguments which have taken place over the contents of the casket allegedly found on 20 June 1567 in possession of Bothwell's servant George Dalgleish can never be conclusive. Moreover, the original documents have long since disappeared, and this likewise must cast strong doubts on the reliability of the letters as evidence. This, and many other arguments from the philological to the circumstantial have been used to prove the falsity or authenticity of these documents while a compromise solution has been found in the suggestion that genuine documents, either from Mary or other paramours to Bothwell were manipulated and possibly partially forged with the connivance of both English and Scottish commissioners to meet a desired end. Mary herself was to deny authorship of these letters, which she was not allowed to see, but this was only to have been expected, and while her own commissioners had already withdrawn before the production of the letters, their belief in Mary's innocence, in the matters of which these documents purported to prove her guilty, was not overwhelming. In short the importance of the Casket Letters is not finally in their authenticity or spuriousness, but that in the critical days of Mary's

6*

'trial', they proved beyond doubt what everyone firmly believed to be true.

THE LETTERS

Is there in the Scottish history of the sixteenth century, a much more momentous event than that lucky, or unlucky, find in the squalid garret of the Potterrow? The artificial mists of dubiety that, in the course of centuries, gradually gathered round the authenticity of the Letters, have prevented many from realizing the enormous political effect produced not in Scotland merely, but in Europe, by their discovery. Whatever the doubts of the pamphleteers, who were not behind the scenes, we may be sure in the sixteenth century, no doubt of their authenticity was entertained by the chief European politicians—including even the Pope himself. The Guises evidently had none, nor the French Sovereign and ministers, nor Elizabeth and Cecil, nor Mary's accusers, nor her defenders, nor herself. The discovery broke for a time Mary's own spirit; it paralysed the efforts of her friends both in Scotland and abroad; it was a very Godsend to her enemies; it tied the political hands of France; it immensely strengthened the hands of Elizabeth; it foiled the policy of Rome; it gave a new impetus to the Scottish Reformation; it remained a suspended sword over Mary's own head; it induced her to consent to her own deposition, it practically sealed her fate both in Scotland and England.

Henderson, Mr Lang and the Casket Letters in *SHR*, v, 173.

The Long Casket Letter

Excuse it, yf I write yll, you must gesse the one halfe. I cannot doo with all, for I am yll at ease, and glad to write unto you when other folkes be asleepe, seeing that I cannot doo as they doo, according to my desyre, that is betwene your armes, my deere lyfe whom I besech God to preserve from all yll, and send you good rest as I go to seeke myne till tomorrow in the morning that will end my bible. But it greevith me that it shuld lett me from wryting unto you of newes of myself so much I have to write. Send me word what you have determinid heerupon, that we may know the one the others mynde for marryng of any thing. I am weary and am asleepe, and yet I cannot forbeare scribbling so long as ther is any paper. Cursed be this pocky fellow that troublith me thus muche, for I had a pleasanter matter to discourse unto you but for him. He is not muche the worse, but he is yll arrayed. I thought I shuld have bene kylled with his breth, for it is worse than your uncle's breth, and yet I was sett no nearer to him than in a chayr by his bolster, and he lyeth at the furdre syde of the bed.

Extracted from the text published in Lang,
Mystery of Mary Stuart, 403–4.

If the guilt of Mary supplies the necessary harmonising circumstances to render the existence of such letters conceivable or probable, there also remain sufficiently strong motives and harmonizing circumstances to render the forgery conceivable. A forgery in such circumstances would undoubtedly have been specially dangerous —dangerous to the Regent Moray in Scotland should it by any possibility have been discovered, probably still more dangerous to him should Elizabeth or her advisers have detected it, and dangerous to Elizabeth's reputation should she wittingly or unwittingly have permitted herself to be influenced by forged documents. Nevertheless, the position of the Regent Moray would undoubtedly have been more dangerous had he been destitute of the peculiarly direct and unanswerable evidence which the Casket Documents supplied. Thus, if antecedent probabilities are rather in favour of the genuineness of the letters, there is nevertheless a considerable amount of presumptive evidence to favour the conclusion that they are forgeries.

Henderson, *Casket Letters*, 10–11.

There are two theories on which the guilty conclusion to which the casket documents point has been resisted with great perseverance and gallantry; the one is that, as we now see them, they have been tampered with; the other, that they are forgeries from the beginning.

All questions raised on the prior theory are at once settled by the fact that those to whom the letters were first shown drew conclusions from them as damnatory as any they can now suggest. Little more than a month after the documents were in possession of the confederates—on the 25th of July—Throckmorton, the English ambassador, got sufficient information to write home that "they mean to charge her with the murder of her husband, whereof, they say, they have as apparent proof against her as may be, as well by the testimony of her own handwriting, which they have recovered, as also by sufficient witnesses." Farther still, Sir Ralph Sadler made what may be called a précis of the significant portions of the documents. According to the natural practice on such occasions, he briefly sweeps over the trivial or indistinct passages, and dwells on those which convey significant conclusions, translating them at full length; and these translations echo the corresponding passages in the letters, as we now possess them, with decisive precision.

The theory of an entire forgery seems not to have occurred to any of those friends or foes of the queen who saw the documents. In the Parliament held in December there were several of her partisans present, such as Huntly, Athole, Errol, Herries, and others; but we have no hint anywhere that they stood up for her fame, or had anything to say, when in the very body of an Act of Parliament, the nature of the documents and the guilty conclusion drawn from them were set forth in the plainest and severest terms. The theory of forgery, indeed, seems to have become prevalent only after any appeal to the original writings, and to the recollection of the persons referred to in them, had ceased to be practicable. And it is impossible not to connect the absence of contemporary impugnment with a notable peculiarity in the documents. They are so affluent in petty details about matters personally known to those who could have contradicted them if false, that the forger of them could only have scattered around him, in superfluous profusion, allusions that must have been traps for his own detection.

Burton, *History of Scotland*, iv, 263–5.

As to forgery or genuineness of the letters who can now pronounce? For they have long disappeared, and it may be questioned whether anyone ever saw them. It seems to me that, guesswork for guesswork, it is simpler to think that no originals ever existed in ane caskit, except the murder band of Craigmillar, and that the rest was a made up thing between Moray, Morton, and very possibly Maitland for the satisfaction of the English commissioners; so that nothing but purported copies which were not literal forgeries but an imagination ever existed.

Wilkinson, 'Mystery of Maitland' in *SHR*, xxiv, 25.

Another argument against the genuineness of these letters is founded on the style and composition, which are said to be altogether unworthy of the queen, and unlike her real productions. It is plain, both from the great accuracy of composition in most of Mary's letters, and even from her solicitude to write them in a fair hand, that she valued herself on these accomplishments, and was desirous of being esteemed an elegant writer. But when she wrote at any time in a hurry, then many marks of inaccuracy appear. . . . Mary's letters to Bothwell were written in the utmost hurry; and yet under all the disadvantages of a translation, they are not destitute either of spirit or of energy. The manner in which she expresses her love to Bothwell has been pronounced indecent and even shocking. But Mary's temper led her to warm expressions of her regard; those refinements of delicacy, which now appear in all the commerce between the sexes, were, in that age, but little known, even among persons of the highest rank.

W. Robertson, *History of Scotland*, iii, 263.

Though it is extremely unlikely that the letters were written by Mary, yet it cannot be asserted with absolute certainty of conviction that she did not write them. The historian, however, is not required to address himself to the solution of problems which the lapse of time, or the animosity of the partisans, may have rendered insoluble. He has to consider only whether certain documents, to which, ever since they were first produced, acute suspicion has been held to attach, can be accepted by him as material on which it is safe to build. For my own part, I am slow to believe that any entirely candid and cautious inquirer will be willing to accept the responsibility. He will hold, on the contrary, that the contents of Morton's casket have been insufficiently authenticated and that Mary must be condemned, if condemned at all, upon other evidence.

Skelton, *Maitland of Lethington,* ii, 342.

One of the circumstances that has been regarded as most strongly corroborative of the genuineness of the Casket Documents is the almost unbroken silence in reference to them maintained by Mary and her friends. When the silence was broken by Mary, it was under the compulsion of stern necessity, and the language made use of was indecisive and ambiguous. All that she instructed her Commissioners to say was: 'I never writ anything concerning that matter to any creature; and gif ony sic writings be they are false and feinzeit forgit and invent be thamselfis, onlye to my dishonour and sclander; And thair ar divers in Scotland baith men and women, that can counterfeit my handwriting, and write the like maner of writing quilk I use, as weill as myself, and principallie sic as ar in companie with thameselfis'. This denial, such as it is, is deprived of all validity by the fact that Mary denied much more emphatically her authorship of the letters to Babington, the genuineness of which has now been conclusively established.

Henderson, *Casket Letters,* 105.

Without granting to Mary's correspondence with Bothwell, be it real or apocryphal, more historical authority than it deserves, it is evident that a correspondence of that nature did exist between the Queen and her seducer, and if she did not write what is contained within those letters (which are not written by her own hand, and the authenticity of which is consequently suspected), still she acted in all the preliminaries of the tragedy in such a manner as to leave no doubt of her participation in the snare by which the unfortunate and amorous Darnley was inveigled.

The letters written at Glasgow by the Queen to Bothwell breathe insensate love for her favourite, and implacable aversion for her husband. They inform Bothwell day by day of the state of Darnley's health, of his supplications to be received by the Queen as a King and a husband; of the progress which her blandishments make in the confidence of the young King whose hopes she now nursed; of his resolution to return with her and to go with her wherever she might wish, even to death, provided she would restore to him her heart and his connubial rights. Although these letters, we repeat, may possess no material textual authenticity in our eyes; though they even bear the traces of falsehood and impossibility in the very excess of their wickedness and cynicism, it is yet certain that they very nearly approach the truth; for a grave and confidential witness of the conversations between Darnley and the Queen at Glasgow gives a narrative in perfect conformity with this correspondence.

Lamartine, *Mary Stuart*, 58–59.

When you have taken your best Advantage you can of them, such kinde of Letters missive and Epistles, especially not conteining any expresse Commaundment of any unlawful Acte or Deede to be committed and perpetrated, not ratifying or specifying the Accomplishment of any such Facte already past, but by unsure and uncerteine Ghesses, Aymes and conjecturall Supposinges, are not able in any wise to make a lawful Presumption, much lesse any good and substantial Proufe, not only against your Soveraigne and Prince, but not so muche as against the poorest Woman, or simplest wretched Creature in al *Scotland*.

Leslie, *Defence*, 17–18.

We shall not enter into a long discussion concerning the authenticity of these letters: we shall only remark in general, that the chief objections against them are, that they are supposed to have passed through the earl of Morton's hands, the least scrupulous of all

Mary's enemies; and that they are to the last degree indecent, and even somewhat inelegant, such as it is not likely she would write. But to these presumptions we may oppose the following considerations. (1) Though it be not difficult to counterfeit a subscription, it is very difficult, and almost impossible, to counterfeit several pages, so as to resemble exactly the hand-writing of any person. These letters were examined and compared with Mary's handwriting, by the English privy council, and by a great many of the nobility, among whom were several partizans of that princess. They might have been examined by the bishop of Ross, Herries, and others of Mary's commissioners. The regent must have expected that they would be very critically examined by them; and had they not been able to stand that test, he was only preparing a scene of confusion to himself. Bishop Lesly expressly declines the comparing of the hands, which he calls no legal proof. . . . (2) The letters are very long, much longer than they needed to have been, in order to serve the purposes of Mary's enemies; a circumstance which increased the difficulty, and exposed any forgery the more to the risk of a detection. (3) They are not so gross and palpable as forgeries commonly are, for they still left a pretext for Mary's friends to assert that their meaning was strained to make them appear criminal.

Hume, *History of England*, 888–9.

We shall, therefore, begin with examining the heaviest weight in the scale against the Queen, that is, her Letters to Bothwell: and, to avoid all imputation of partiality, let us try them according to the rules of equity, as in a court of justice, by hearing both sides. We begin with the accusers.

1. The Earl of Morton at first produced those Letters, and affirmed, *on his word of honour*, that his servants seized them in the custody of George Dalgleish, one of Bothwell's servants, who had brought them out of the castle of Edinburgh.

2. The earls of Murray and Morton affirm, *on their honour*, that they are the handwriting of the Queen, both in their own Secret Council, and in the Regent's Parliament in Scotland, and before Queen Elizabeth and her Council in England.

3. They are produced at York and Westminster to the English Council, and compared with other letters of Mary's handwriting and appear to be similar to them.

4. and lastly, Several of the incidents mentioned in the Letters themselves, such as the conversations between the King and Queen at Glasgow, are, by Crawford, one of the Earl of Lennox's vassals, affirmed, upon oath, to be true.

Such are the proofs brought in support of the Letters. Let us now turn to the other side, and hear what are the answers, and the objections made to them on the part of Queen Mary,

1. Queen Mary denies the Letters to be her hand-writing, and asserts them to be forged by her accusers, Murray, Morton, and Lethington, and offers to prove this.

2. Morton's bare affirmation of the way in which the Letters came into his hands, as he is a party, can never in equity be regarded. Nay, the Letters appearing first in his hands, was of itself suspicious. Besides, his stifling the evidence of *Dalgleish*, or forbearing to interrogate him judicially, how he came by these Letters, which would have put this affair in a true light; and his neglecting to examine his *own servants* publicly who seized Dalgleish with the Box, as to what they knew of the affair; and in place of the legal declaration of those who were the only proper witnesses to prove this fact, obtruding his own affirmation only: these omissions, I say, double the suspicion, that he himself, and his faction, were the contrivers of the Letters.

3. The affirmation of Murray and Morton on the authenticity of the Letters, both in Scotland and England, can bear no greater degree of credit, than Queen Mary's denial, and the affirmation of herself, and most of the *nobility of Scotland*, that these Letters were forged.

4. The similarity of one hand-writing to another, is such a proof as no man can be certain of; far less in the case of these Letters, appearing in so clandestine a way, in the hands of Morton, the Queen's inveterate enemy and accuser. Add to this, what is affirmed by Mary, that her enemies had often counterfeited letters in her name; which is corroborated by a contemporary author, who relates it as a well-known fact, that Lethington her Secretary had often practised this vile fraud.

5. That several of the incidents mentioned in the Letters might be

very true, is not denied. The plan of the forgers was surely to intersperse truth with falsehood. Crawford's testimony on the truth of several of the incidents mentioned in the Letters might therefore be true, and yet the Letters themselves might be forged.

But the objections to the Letters on the part of the Queen, are of a different nature.

1. The Letters, as exhibited by Murray and Morton, wanted the dates, place from which they were written, the subscriptions, seals and addresses. Could any judge or jury, then, have admitted these Letters as authentic, and as written by Queen Mary to the Earl of Bothwell, upon the bare word of her accuser?

2. The only proof they could have brought to support their affirmation, was by the oath of Hubert, that he got the Letters from the Queen's own hand, and delivered them to Bothwell; and by Dalgleish, that he got them from Sir James Balfour, in the castle of Edinburgh, and was carrying them to Bothwell, and lastly by Morton's servants, who seized Dalgleish with the Box and Letters. It is impossible, therefore, to frame any plausible reason, why these several persons were not called upon to prove these facts, but this only, that there was not a word of truth in the story.

3. The Letters are produced in public under different dresses. Before the Secret Council, they bear to be *subscribed by* the Queen's hand; in their second appearance, before Regent Murray's Parliament, they *want the subscription* altogether. This is proved by the acts of Council, and of Parliament, in the registers.

4. While the conferences were going on at York, the Letters were privately, and in secret conference, shown by Lethington and Buchanan to the English commissioners, but carefully concealed from Queen Mary and her commissioners.

5. The Queen, on the first hearing of these Letters, earnestly supplicates to have inspection of the originals, and to be allowed copies: from which she offers to prove them to be forged and spurious. Both requests are refused to her, the Letters are delivered back to her accusers, and to her dying day she never could get a sight of these originals, or attested copies of them.

6. The Letters, of which copies only are now extant, are, to demonstration proved, and forced to be acknowledged, even by the writers against the Queen, to be palpable translations from the Scotch and Latin of George Buchanan.

And lastly, Murray and Morton, the Queen's accusers, in order to make good their charge or accusation against the Queen have produced false and forged evidence, *viz.* Hubert's confession . . .; from whence the same presumption, had we no other proof against the Letters, must arise, that they are forged likewise.

Such are the proofs on both sides for and against the authenticity of the Letters. Let us now put the question to any impartial person who understands the nature of evidence. Would those Letters, found in the custody of Morton, destitute of subscription, seal and address, and in the face of so many other surmountable objections, have been sustained as genuine authentic writings, in any court of law or justice, upon the bare appearance of similarity of the Queen's hand-writing, and the naked word of Murray and Morton, the accusers? I am not afraid of the imputation of rashness, when I venture to say, that at this day, I am convinced that no impartial jury or judge, could, upon conscience, have given judgment for these letters as genuine, and returned a verdict and sentence in their favour as such.

W. Tytler, *Historical and Critical Enquiry*, i, 330–8.

Suppose it to have been settled in conclave that such a set of letters were to be forged, who was there with the genius to accomplish the feat? Nowhere else, perhaps, has the conflict of the three passions, love, jealousy, and hatred, been so powerfully stamped in utterance. Somewhat impoverished though it may be in the echo of a foreign medium, we have here the reality of that which the masters of fiction have tried in all ages, with more or less success, to imitate. They have striven to strip great events of broad, vulgar, offensive qualities, and to excite sensations which approach to sympathy with human imperfections. And, indeed, these letters stir from their very foundation the sensations which tragic genius endeavours to arouse. We cannot, in reaching them, help a touch of sympathy, or it may be compassion, towards the gifted being driven in upon the torrent of relentless passions, even though the end to which she drifts is the breaking of the highest laws, human and divine. A touch of tenderness towards those illustrious persons who show their participation in the frailty of our common nature by imperfections as transcendent as their capacities, is one of the mysterious qualities of the human heart, and here it has room for indulgence. In fact, it is the shade that gives impressiveness to the picture. With all her beauty and wit, her political ability and her countless fascinations, Mary, Queen of Scots, would not have occupied nearly the half of her present place in the interest of mankind had the episode of Bothwell not belonged to her story.

Burton, *History of Scotland*, iv, 272–3.

It was Cardinal Richelieu who remarked with the emphasis of experience, "Give me two lines of a man's handwriting and I will hang him!" Unfortunately for those who would base any conclusion on the Casket Letters, the Queen's handwriting is conspicuously absent. Three hundred and fifty years ago, as soon as their purpose was served, the alleged originals disappeared. All that exists to-day is a collection of copies and translations which do not agree with the descriptions of contemporaries who claimed acquaintance with the originals.

It is true that before they conveniently vanished, an investigation was held into their charges against the Queen; but the procedure followed would satisfy no modern court. Every shift was adopted to avoid producing the originals. At last they were read in the absence of any representative of the Queen. On another occasion they were laid on a table to be hastily compared with admitted specimens of her hand. They were hurriedly withdrawn and neither the Queen nor any partisan of hers was ever allowed to see them. No witness was examined to confirm any of the statements contained in the letters.

But though the conduct of the case reeks with fraud, it is difficult to believe that in the time available to the captors of the Casket, such a bulk of evidence could be manufactured. The supposed forger must be credited with abnormal energy and ability if he sat down before a blank sheet of paper to produce in an imitation of the Queen's hand a document as circumstantial as the "Long Glasgow Letter". At the same time he must be convicted of excessive flippancy if he wasted his time inventing anything as futile as the "Margaret Carwood Letter".

A far simpler method could be trusted to give better results. After Mary's capture, her enemies had access to her papers; Bothwell's private correspondence no doubt also fell into their hands. Those rugged consciences made no difficulty of inserting into a chance love-letter received by the gallant Earl, an extract from one of Mary's papers that would attribute the concoction to her. In other cases into one of Mary's genuine memoranda could be imported some lurid patch from the Bothwell collection. The services of an expert forger could then be called in—and at that date plenty of amateurs or professionals were easily found—to copy the compound into a reasonable imitation of Mary's large Italian hand. The result would not stand up to careful examination, as the reluctance to exhibit the Casket Letters, their brief appearances and their final disappearance indicate.

Gore-Browne, *Lord Bothwell*, 102–3.

To forge letters for Queen Mary was no easy matter. To her natural parts, which were great, she had added more learning than the half of her enemies put together could pretend to. She spoke almost all the *European* languages, and possest a great taste in the fine arts. The *French* was as it were her mother-tongue, which she spoke and wrote in all the perfection that was to be found at the court of *France*. Her hand-writing was formed after what is commonly called *Italick* print, which it much resembled both in beauty and regularity, and not to be easily imitated but by a fine writer. When such a writer was found he must write *French* too, and that as well as the Queen, to which few, even of the natives of *France*, could pretend: And not only so, but he must be acquainted with persons and transactions about her court, so as to make proper allusions, lest her Majesty should appear to write quite out of character, which would have spoiled all.

To compass all these ends, and to surmount all these difficulties, these assassines of their Queen's fame took the following method. Some one or other of them drew up, in the *Scottish* language, such letters, as being disperst under her name, they thought might be sufficient to blacken her. And now there was nothing wanting but to get them put into *French*: but it would seem that the person

THE ENIGMA OF MARY STUART

destined for that office did not sufficiently understand the *Scottish* language. In these straits *George Buchanan*, who had that year been chosen, for his piety, moderator of the General Assembly, found out a remedy by translating the letters out of the *Scottish* language into *Latin*, a language with which the *Frenchman* was acquainted. Thus the forgery was accomplished: At least this is certain, that the *French* letters which *Murray* and his accomplices produced, and swore to be written wholly by the Queen's hand, are only a translation from *George Buchanan's Latin*, and his *Latin* a translation from the *Scottish* original forgery, even that very original, of which *Murray* sent a copy to be considered by the *English* judges before-hand, calling it a translation. Why a translation? as if the court of *England* had not understood *French*!

Goodall, Examination of the Letters, i, 79–80.

Either Mary wrote the Letter or a forger wished to give the impression that this occurred. He wanted the world to believe that the Queen, her conscience tortured and her passion overmastering her conscience, could not cease to converse with her lover while paper served her turn. Her moods alternate: now she is resolved and cruel, now sick with horror, but still, sleepless as she is, she must be writing. Assuredly, if this Letter be, in part at least, a forgery, it is a forgery by a master in the science of human nature.

Lang, Mystery of Mary Stuart, 313.

It is weele knowen, that the letters of Marie Betun, one of her Maiesties ladies of honour, resembled so nearlie those of her mistres, that it is not possible to discerne the one hand wreting from the other: yee hawe also at this daie by your juglinge, . . . wheroff you knowe some that can so naturallie and cunninglie imitate the hand wretinge of an other, that you wold mistake your owen hand writinge, and approwe and allowe that for yours which hath beene falsifeed by them, and you never did see with your eyes before. We saie then, that the Queene never wrete those letters, and albeit shee had writtin them, they could make no proofe against

her, nor be receiwed in judgment; for . . . we know not what time
they wer written, nor by whom, nor where, neither superscribed
nor endorsed with the name or person of anie person, nor signed,
nor sealed, nor the wretinge knowen or challenged of anie, and yeet
will you hawe her Maiestie condemned of so greate and heinous a
crime?

> Blackwood, *History of Mary Queen of Scots*, 82–3.

There is, of course, no reason to believe that any of the Casket
Documents was a forgery in the usually accepted sense of that
word: indeed, all the evidence is to the contrary. The discussion
concerning the manipulation of the letters must have taken some
time. . . . Casket Letter II certainly passed through two separate
stages, being first prepared as two separate letters, each receiving
some additional matter from the letters of the 'other woman', and,
later, being condensed into one epistle. The work of reading and
assimilating the contents of the letters alone would take some time;
in the few days at their disposal there was no time for much forgery;
nor was much required. A few words had to be inserted, such as
the date of Casket Letter I and the alteration of the address of the
Bothwell part of Casket Letter II: the supreme simplicity and
effectiveness of these touches guarantees the authorship of
Maitland. . . .

The re-shuffling of the sheets of Mary's letters with those of
the 'other woman' and the alteration and addition of a few phrases
were not, however, all that was necessary. In at least one place,
part of one letter had to be copied on to the blank verso of another,
and it may be that other sheets had to be copied out to omit irre-
levant material such as addresses, signatures, dates or unacceptable
phrases. It is possible that a professional forger was pressed to this
service, or even that Maitland undertook it himself, but another,
and less pleasing solution presents itself: it is that the copying was
done by someone whose own handwriting was so similar to Mary's
that it is difficult to tell them apart, and who was devotedly
attached to Maitland and wholly at his bidding; that person was
Maitland's wife, Mary Fleming, one of the Queen's four Maries.

> Armstrong Davison, *The Casket Letters*, 244–5.

THE SONNETS

Certane *Frenche* Sonettis writtin by ye Quene of *Scottis* to *Bothwel*
befoir hir Mariage with him and (as it is said) quhile hir Husband
levit, but certanely befoir his Divorce from his wyfe, as ye Wordis
thameselfis schaw, befoir quhome scho heir preferris hirself in
deserving to be belovit of *Bothwell*.

Buchanan, Detectioun, 115.

> O Goddis, have of me compassioun,
> And schew quhat certaine profe
> I may geif, which shall nat seem to him vaine
> Of my love and servant affectioun.
> Helas! is he nat alredy in possessioun
> Of my bodie, of hart, that refusis no payne,
> Nor dishonour in the life uncertaine,
> Offence of frendes, nor worse afflictioun,
> For him I esteme al my frends les then nathing,
> And I will have gude hope of my enemies.
> I have put in hasard for him both fame and conscience,
> I will for his sake renounce the world,
> I will die to set him forwart.
> Quhat remayneth to gief proofe of my constancie?

Laing, History of Scotland, ii, 247.

The sonnets too seem to have been first written in the *Scottish*
language as well as the letters. Each sonnet is known to consist of
fourteen verses; but, unhappily, two of ours, to wit, the third and
eighth in the original *French*, have only thirteen verses; and yet we
have the full fourteen verses always in the alledged *Scots* translation; which would rather argue that it was the original. *George
Buchanan* tells us that they are written with tolerable elegancy:
Indeed it was necessary that they should have been so, to make
them pass for Q. Mary's composition. But every man's eyes and
ears will tell him, that this is not so; the versification is stark

naught, the thoughts altogether mean and incoherent; and in a word, the whole composition, and every part of it, quite destitute of the elegance and accuracy required in a sonnet.

Goodall, *Examination of the Letters*, i, 127.

Their authenticity is still disputed, on the authority of Brantome, who asserts, that they were too gross and unpolished to be the composition of Mary; and the forgery is ascribed to Buchanan, because there was no one in Scotland capable of writing French verse, except himself or the queen. The sonnets, therefore, were originally forged in French, by Buchanan, who was unable, however, to give a French version of the letters which he translated, as it seems, into Latin, for the supposed Camus to convert into French. That the sonnets were first written in French might have taught those disputants to suspect that the letters were originally composed in the same language. But the grossness of the sonnets is a prevailing argument with those who either are ignorant of the grossness of the age, or are persuaded with Goodall, that Mary never once betrayed a single foible from the cradle to the grave.

Laing, *History of Scotland*, i, 346–7.

16

THE YEARS OF CAPTIVITY

Mary's imprisonment in England was only to be terminated by her execution, but this outcome could not have been foreseen on Mary's arrival in 1568. Nor were Mary's hopes of release centred solely on foreign invasion or a successful coup d'état. Elizabeth's attitude to Mary was ambivalent from the onset and while she refused to meet her, or judge her case personally, the assurance given to Mary by Elizabeth that she would protect her interests and proceed against her enemies if her cause was just, was not necessarily hypocritical. If, however, Elizabeth ever believed that unconditional restoration was a possibility, she was persuaded by Cecil that terms would have to be insisted upon, and that Mary herself was not unwilling to fulfil certain conditions can be seen in her move towards Anglicanism at this time. Unfortunately, for Mary, the requisite conditions to satisfy all interests could never be found, although many such schemes were formulated, and this failure must have gone far to dictate the inconclusive nature of the 'sentence' of 1569 which allowed the retention of Mary in honourable captivity. Even then plans to secure her restoration were mooted at intervals and not until 1584 was all hope finally extinguished. The proposed marriage to Norfolk suggested in 1568, and revived the following year had Mary's restoration firmly in mind, as had further negotiations initiated by Elizabeth in 1571. These, however, were ended by the Ridolfi plot, and when further proposals were made to return Mary to Scotland in 1572 they were not designed to further Mary's interests as she was to be handed over without any personal safeguards. In such circumstances, Mary would have been very reluctant to leave the safety of England, and there is little doubt that throughout the regency of Morton (1572–78), Mary's chances of survival had she returned to Scotland would have been very slim indeed. Not until 1580 when Morton's eclipse was complete could negotiations be revived in the form of schemes of association whereby James and Mary would have ruled jointly, but while Elizabeth for a

while favoured the idea, a satisfactory formula could not be found to
meet the various interests at stake. By late 1584, Mary's hopes of
restoration were at an end, and she thus entered the last phase of her
captivity devoid of all hope of regaining her throne by peaceful means,
a fact which almost certainly coloured her reaction to the schemes of
Babington.

Mary Stuart never resented direct speaking. After a fortnight's experience Knollys wrote to Cecil:—'This lady and princess is a notable woman. She seemeth to regard no ceremonious honour besides the acknowledgement of her estate royal. She showeth a disposition to speak much, to be bold, to be pleasant, to be very familiar. She showeth a great desire to be revenged of her enemies. She shows a readiness to expose herself to all perils in hope of victory. She desires much to hear of hardiness and valiancy, commending by name all approved hardy men of her country, although they be her enemies; and she concealeth no cowardice even in her friends. The thing she most thirsteth after is victory; and it seemeth to be indifferent to her to have her enemies diminished either by the sword of her friends, or by the liberal promises and rewards of her purse, or by divisions and quarrels among themselves. So that for victory's sake pain and peril seem pleasant unto her; and in respect of victory wealth and all things seem to her contemptuous and vile.'

Froude, *History of England*, ix, 242–3.

When Mary Queen of Scots went to Tutbury in Shrewsbury's care and Elizabeth recognized the regency of Murray in Scotland, Anglo-Scottish relations assumed a pattern which they followed in the main for the rest of Elizabeth's reign. Probably few people either in Scotland or in England imagined at the end of the year 1568 that the pattern was any more than a temporary expedient. Elizabeth herself certainly did not think so. But so it was. For the next eighteen years Mary remained an unwilling guest in England, virtually a prisoner, and Scottish affairs, though they were turbulent enough, never again took the form of a serious effort to restore to her Scottish throne. She herself thought less of that and more of her aspirations to the English throne. She never at heart relinquished her hopes of the English throne. And she became the focus of a succession of plots to depose Elizabeth with the help of the Roman Catholics in England and one or both of the two great Catholic powers France and Spain on the continent.

Increasingly her cause was identified with the cause of the old Church. Her Scottish connections gradually paled into insignificance in comparison with this more splendid objective, and her struggle for freedom became part of the greater struggle on the one side to wipe away the great stronghold of heresy and restore the unity of the faith, on the other to preserve the Tudor dynasty and the Protestant establishment. The Marian problem henceforth gets inextricably entangled in Elizabeth's relations with France, with Spain and with her own discontented Roman Catholic subjects.

Read, *Mr. Secretary Cecil*, 416.

The Satanic malice of her enemies assailed her in the tenderest point, that of religion; and they sedulously strove to prejudice her in the opinion of the other Catholic sovereigns, by asserting that she was indifferent to the faith, for which she eventually, by her martyrdom, demonstrated her sincerity. In a beautiful letter, written from Bolton, 30th November 1568, to Philip II, condolatory on the death of his queen, she expresses her pain at learning that, operated upon by the poison of the malignants, he had entertained some suspicion of her religious fealty. She thus protests to him: 'If I do not exercise my religion, they ought not to believe for that I waver between the two. Besides, since my arrival in this Kingdom, I have demanded that they permit me at least the power of exercising it, as they grant it to the ambassador of a foreign prince; but they replied to me that I was a relation of the Queen, and that I should never obtain it. They afterwards introduced to my house an English minister, who simply recited some prayers in the vulgar tongue; which I was unable to prevent, because I was and still am deprived of liberty, and closely surrounded with guards. But if it is thought that I erred in participating at these prayers, at which I assisted because no other exercise of my religion was allowed me, I am ready to make such satisfaction as may be deemed necessary, so that all the Catholic princes of the world may be convinced that I am an obedient, submissive, and devoted daughter of the holy Roman Catholic Church, in the faith of which I wish to live and die, without having ever had any other desire than that, a desire which with God's assistance I shall never alter in any manner'.

Turnbull, *Letters of Mary Stuart*, xi–xii.

As Mary had nothing now to gain from coquetting with Protestantism, she declined to attend the Protestant services of the household, and demanded facilities for the exercise of her own religion. But, on account of her previous pretences of a half conformity to Protestantism, her English guardians professed to regard her anxieties about the consolations of her old religion with some degree of ridicule: and even many Catholics had come to have doubts as to her real attachment to their faith. She therefore had to assure Le Mothe that she made the demand seriously and not for her own mere amusement, 'I do not,' she affirmed, 'joke at all in regard to so serious a matter.' She was resolute, she said, to remain, as she had always been, faithful to the Church she 'recognised as alone approved of God, the Church Catholic, Apostolic and Roman.' She had given no testimony as to the merits of the other religion, that could properly be termed faith. She had refused communion after the Protestant fashion; and Knollys and others could bear witness that she had never pretended to be in any sense a Protestant, but had often disputed with them on the points of their faith. Her sole aim in attending Protestant services was, she said, to help Elizabeth to recognise that she was not possessed by such hatred or rancour towards Protestantism, as to make it necessary for her to despair of having peace with her. This was all very clever and ingenious, but her aim had not been to gain Elizabeth's confidence, but to delude the Protestant friends of

Norfolk. She was much nearer the truth when she went on to say that the late proceedings of the Protestants had made it needless for her to carry her pretences in regard to Protestantism further.

Henderson, *Mary Queen of Scots,* ii, 543–4.

With no supporters at home and hopeless of assistance from abroad, she changed her tone and conduct, and endeavoured to pacify Elizabeth by submission. The liberty which she had been unable to obtain by force, she now strove to gain by fair means. Her high spirit had at first been offended by the silence of Queen Elizabeth, who returned no answer to the numerous letters which she had written to her. She now, however, subdued her feelings of irritation and pride, and assumed a tone of patient resignation; and the Queen, who had been so haughty in her bearing, so eloquent in her complaints, so bold and daring in her projects, became a gentle, calm and humble prisoner. She avoided everything likely to give umbrage to Elizabeth; and limited her correspondence, which had reference chiefly to matters connected with her dowry in France. In return, she obtained permission to walk in the park and gardens of Sheffield. The dampness of her prison walls had brought on an attack of rheumatism in the arms, which frequently prevented her from writing, and added greatly to the unpleasantness of a liver-complaint, from which she had long suffered, and which had been greatly aggravated by her misfortunes. She therefore requested and obtained permission to go, from time to time, to the baths at Buxton, in the vicinity of Sheffield.

In order to lessen the *ennui* of her tedious captivity, which was no longer occupied on the formation of plots in England, Scotland, and the Continent, in the construction and renewal of the ciphers necessary for her secret correspondence, in the dictation of letters to her Scottish secretary, Curle, or her French secretary, Raullet, or in procuring and employing skilful and trusty agents, she spent her time in needlework, and in attending to her dogs and birds. 'My lord of Glasgow,' she wrote to her ambassador in France, 'I beg you to obtain for me some turtle-doves and Barbary fowls, that I may try to bring them up in this country. I should take pleasure in feeding them in their cages, as I do all the little birds I can find. These are the only pastimes of a prisoner.'

Mignet, *Mary Queen of Scots*, ii, 189–90.

While she occupied herself with needlework, the results of which she sometimes sent to the English queen as an earnest of her good-will, or amused herself with pet birds and small dogs, or listened to court scandal purveyed to her by 'Bess of Hardwick', Shrews-bury's terrible spouse, she kept an eye constantly lifting for the propitious moment when, as the Cardinal of Lorraine assured her, her 'patient dissimulation' would be rewarded. Her indefatigable ambassadors, the bishop of Ross and the archbishop of Glasgow, advocated her cause in Rome and Paris. She corresponded with the pope, the kings of France and Spain, the emperor, and a number of potentates great and small. Indeed her intrigues rami-fied through the length and breadth of Europe. Always professing the most amicable intentions, she constantly plotted to bring the whole fabric of society in ruin about Elizabeth's ears. When brought to book—for sometimes her correspondence miscarried into Walsingham's hands—she lied volubly but unconvincingly. She was a credulous and impulsive conspirator, full of exaggerated optimism, unburdened by a conscience, but void of a sense of reality, which is the basis of success in plotting as in all other things. It was a wearing and tearing existence. Disappointment rendered her irritable and frantic: she grew prematurely old: her hair whitened; and her health suffered from the prolonged con-finement. The surprising thing is not that she failed, but that Elizabeth persisted so long in the attempt to seek a *modus vivendi* with her.

Black, *The Reign of Elizabeth*, 374–5.

It was her duty to be particularly careful lest she should give her adversaries any reason to suspect her fidelity. She was closely watched; her acts were spied, and she had scarcely freedom of speech. 'I am so observed,' she wrote, 'and all those who are near

me, that what I write or cause to be written must be done by
stealth; and, for fear of surprise, hourly expecting a visit or a
searching of my coffers, I instantly cause the minutes of the
cyphers to be burned, and, as a general rule, I should be unable to
have duplicates of them drawn out.' That supervision, however
close, did not debar the captive from finding means to correspond
with her partisans, and to communicate her councils to them. Her
hope lay in France. With men and money, one might gain in Scotland great advantages—one might muster in a body the friends
whom fear or poverty had dispersed, and throw strong garrisons
into Edinburgh and Inchkeith Castle; thence rule the country and
pacify it, by rushing unexpectedly on the enemy, retire within
the walls, if they were in too great a number, and wait and choose
an opportunity to sally forth again with a bold front. While the
Queen liked to busy herself with those strategic calculations, time
seemed to pass more quickly, and her captivity to be more bearable.

Petit, *Mary Stuart*, i, 252–3.

Mary was the most generous and most grateful of mistresses; the
letters of her long years of captivity are full of proofs that she forgot
no loyal retainer and never wearied in securing their welfare. On
their part they never wished, or very seldom wished, to leave her.

Lang, The Household of Mary Queen of Scots in 1573
in *SHR*, ii, 346.

During her long and miserable captivity in England, extending to
no less than eighteen years, every thing that can disappoint, or can
distress the human mind, befel the Queen of Scots. From time to
time, and even so late, as a few years before her death, the English
Queen continued deceitfully to amuse her with hopes and treaties
for being restored to her Crown. All plots against Elizabeth and
the reformed religion were ascribed to Mary. Letters were forged
in her name to prove this. Numberless insults were committed
against her. She soon lost her best friends. The Duke of Norfolk
early suffered death in her cause. About the same time, the faithful

Lesly, Bishop of Ross, was imprisoned, and afterward banished. Charles IX, King of France, her friend and admirer died soon after. She was successively carried from castle to castle; shut up in closer and closer confinement, while labouring under disease, no mitigation of her hardships could be extorted, but with the utmost difficulty.

T. Robertson, *Mary Queen of Scots*, 135.

17

PLOTS AGAINST ELIZABETH

As had been anticipated, Mary's continued presence in England after the enquiry of 1568–69 made her the central figure in any subsequent political unrest. Some of this was occasioned by no more than transient dissatisfaction, or more commendably in an effort to settle the question of succession. More dangerous and more persistent, however, were the plots based on the misapprehension that the Catholic princes of Europe were prepared to restore Catholicism in England by force, and supplant Elizabeth in favour of Mary.

Nevertheless, the first of the many plots in which Mary was so involved had not this direct aim as the intention of marrying Mary to the Protestant duke of Norfolk in 1569 had probably no deeper design than restoring the queen to her Scottish throne and gaining recognition of her right to succeed Elizabeth. Nevertheless, the interest of the northern earls of Northumberland and Westmorland extended beyond this to the deposition of Elizabeth and the restoration of Catholicism, and when Norfolk was committed to the Tower, they rose in arms and attempted to free Mary with whom they had been in communication. All, however, was to no avail. The rising collapsed without achieving anything except, for the time being, the stricter detention of Mary.

The possibility of further Catholic plots was strengthened by the excommunication of Elizabeth in February 1570, and that these fears were not merely fantasies was proved by the Ridolfi plot of the following year. The actual scheme as envisaged by the Florentine Ridolfi had little chance of success, as a Spanish army was required for its implementation, but Norfolk, Mary and her representative John Leslie, bishop of Ross, were all involved to a greater or lesser degree, and the only upshot of the plot was the execution of the duke, the imprisonment of the bishop and a heightening of the feeling that Mary herself must be brought to justice. Closely questioned by English commissioners, Mary admitted to having dealings with Ridolfi, but

*denied that these in any way included a conspiracy against Elizabeth.
It was not these denials, however, which saved her, but the personal
intervention of Elizabeth who in spite of the fears expressed in her
own sonnet in which she dubbed Mary 'the daughter of debate' refused
in 1572 to allow parliament to pass an act of attainder.*

*After four years of intrigue, the following eight years saw some
respite from such plots, for, while hopes continued to be centred on
foreign intervention on Mary's behalf, the continental political situation became so complex that not even the most optimistic conspirator
could have envisaged success. Not until 1580, when the forces of the
counter-Reformation became more aggressive in England, did it appear
propitious to make further efforts on Mary's behalf. Once again a
Spanish invasion was the prerequisite of most such plots, which on one
occasion in 1582 would also have involved the invasion of Scotland,
but England was normally regarded as the base of such operations.
Not unnaturally the English government viewed all these developments
with the gravest concern and when Mary's part in the negotiations
with Spain were revealed after the arrest of Francis Throgmorton in
November 1583, the outcry against her became even more intense.
This culminated in the Bond of Association, which as adopted by
Parliament in November 1584 prescribed the death penalty for all
who plotted against Elizabeth and also for those in whose favour the
conspiracy had been devised. If, however, Mary should be this person,
and clearly that was the intention of the Bond, Elizabeth insisted on a
trial and proof of complicity in the plot, whereas the Bond as originally framed would have allowed for the execution of Mary whether she
knew of the plot or not. It was this condition which made it necessary
when the inevitable plot did emerge, to prove Mary's foreknowledge
of its existence.*

*The prevention of further plots was beyond the ability of Mary, or
of the English government, but after January 1585 when the queen
was placed in even more rigorous confinement under the guardianship
of Sir Amias Paulet, her correspondence could have been, and for
almost a year was, completely stopped. In allowing the resumption
of her 'secret' mail, Walsingham deliberately set a trap for the queen,
which with the emergence of the Babington plot in early 1586, was
sprung when Mary welcomed Anthony Babington's schemes for the
assassination of Elizabeth. Of this wish she was undeniably guilty,
and Mary's protestations of innocence, which some have affected to*

believe, were manifestly false, a point not without bearing on her
similar pleas on the question of the Casket Letters. Walsingham, how-
ever, can clearly be reproached for allowing Mary to incriminate her-
self in this manner, but with eighteen years of plotting behind her, the
opportunity to prove her complicity beyond all doubt and rid England
of this dangerous political menace, might in itself be held to justify
the means. To many at that time, Mary was not simply a poor helpless
captive. This theme, nevertheless, has been adopted by many sub-
sequent writers, who in reluctantly admitting her guilty ill-will to-
wards Elizabeth, have taken refuge in the theory that Mary only
wanted to be free. It can be argued, however, that they have failed to
judge her by the standards by which alone she can be assessed, not
merely as a woman or a pious Catholic, but as a politician who at the
end of the day in England failed as completely in her policies as she
had done at an earlier stage in her own kingdom of Scotland.

From the epoch of Mary's arrival, at Carlisle . . . there was,
scarcely, a moment, in which there was not some plot, either
feigned, or real, for the freedom of the one Queen, and the dis-
turbance of the other. And it is equally clear that Elizabeth constantly thought that she had every power over Mary's person;
while Mary had no power over Elizabeth: And, Elizabeth seems to
have completely forgotten, that there was not a conspiracy against
the Queen of Scots, from the demise of Francis II to her expulsion,
from Scotland, in which Elizabeth was not concerned against
Mary: Neither were there a murderer, a traitor, a rebel, who fled,
from Scotland, to England, that Elizabeth did not protect. Add to
these intimations, that when the wise Lord Burghley, sat down to
write formal reasons, to justify the Scottish Queen's imprisonment, he found it too hard a task, for his wisdom, and experience:
so that he cast the responsibility of the violence offered her upon
inferior agents, who felt the injustice done to themselves, without
questioning the rights of their mistress. At this time, Elizabeth,
had her envoy Randolph, in Scotland, attempting to raise a rebellion, in order to protect her agent, Morton, one of the most guilty

miscreants, on earth. From all these facts, it is apparent, that Elizabeth, and her ministers, considered every thing convenient to themselves, to be consistent with law, and agreeable to morals, without regarding the wrongs of the Queen of Scots.

Chalmers, *Mary Queen of Scots,* i, 382.

Adhering tenaciously to her rights, Mary declined to purchase indulgence by renouncing her claims to the English crown, though she professed to believe that liberty might any day be hers if she would take such a step. Mary was, however, far from contemplating any renunciation of that kind. The English succession was the dream of her life, and nothing was neglected to smooth the way to that splendid prize.

Leader, *Mary Queen of Scots in Captivity,* 411.

Mortimer: Soon after this, summon'd to France, he sent me
            To Rheims, where the holy company of Jesus
            Piously labour'd, training English priests.
            Here did I find that noble Scotchman, Morgan,
            And your faithful Lesley, the learn'd bishop of Ross,
            Dragging their joyless days of banishment
            Out on the soil of France. . . .

            With words that thrill'd my heart then did he paint
            Your dreary martyrdom and your foes' bloody hate.
            Your royal lineage he laid before me,
            And your descent from the high house of Tudor;
            Convinced me you alone should reign in England,
            And not this after-thought of queen—brought forth
            From an adulterous bed—by her own father
            Henry cast off for cause of bastardy.

Schiller, *Maria Stuart,* 230–1.

During the two years and a half which she had been a prisoner in England, she had sought to obtain her deliverance and restoration by the exertions of her party in Scotland, by her marriage with the head of the English nobility, by the insurrection of Elizabeth's Catholic subjects, by the union of the Scottish lords, sustained by the Court of France, and finally, by an accommodation with her fortunate and powerful rival. All attempts had, however, failed. The Scotch who were faithful to her cause had been overcome by Murray in 1569, and weakened by Elizabeth in 1570; her marriage with the Duke of Norfolk had met with but little favour in Scotland, and had been positively prohibited in England; the English Catholics had twice revolted, and had been twice defeated, the accommodation negotiated at Chatsworth, with so many concessions on her part, had been rejected; and France had not only failed to support her, but seemed likely to renounce her ancient league with Scotland, to form a new alliance with England.

Mignet, Mary Queen of Scots, ii, 128–9.

'THE DAUGHTER OF DEBATE'
A Sonnet by Queen Elizabeth

The dread of future foes exiles my present joy,
And wit me warns to shun such snares as threaten mine annoy.
For falsehood now doth flow, and subject's faith doth ebb;
Which would not be if Reason ruled, or Wisdom weaved the Web.
But clouds of toys untried do cloak aspiring minds,
Which turn to rain of late repent by course of changed winds.
The top of hope supposed the root of ruth will be,
And fruitless all their graffed guiles, as shortly ye shall see.
Those dazzled eyes with pride, which great ambition blinds,
Shall be unsealed by worthy wights whose foresight falsehood finds.
The Daughter of Debate, that eke discord doth sow,
Shall reap no gain where former rule hath taught still peace to grow.
No foreign banished wight shall anchor in this port;
Our realm it brooks no stranger's force, let them elsewhere resort.
Our rusty sword with rest shall first his edge employ,
To poll their tops that seek such change and gape for joy.

Creighton, Queen Elizabeth, 158.

Elizabeth was extremely anxious to implicate Mary in Norfolk's guilt, and, for this purpose, sent commissioners to her to reproach her with her offences. Mary heard all they had to say with the utmost calmness; and when they called upon her for her answer, she replied, that, though she was a free Queen, and did not consider herself accountable, either to them or their mistress, she had, nevertheless, no hesitation to assure them of the injustice of their accusations. She protested that she had never imagined any detriment to Elizabeth by her marriage with Norfolk; that she had never encouraged him to raise rebellion, or been privy to it, but was, on the contrary, most ready to reveal any conspiracy against the Queen of England which might come to her ears; that though Rodolphi had been of use to her in the transmission of letters abroad, she had never received any from him; that, as to attempting an escape, she willingly gave ear to all who offered to assist her, and, in hope of effecting her deliverance, had corresponded with several in cipher; that, so far from having any hand in the bull of excommunication, when a copy of it was sent her, she burned it after she had read it; and that she held no communication with any foreign state, upon matters unconnected with her restoration to her own Kingdom. Satisfied with this reply, the commissioners returned to London.

Bell, *Mary Queen of Scots,* ii, 198.

Considering that she was acting at this time entirely without advice, no one will deny the ability, and even the forensic skill, with which Mary defended herself against the charges of Elizabeth's commissioners. It is to be observed that she evaded the most serious point urged against her—namely, that she had invited the King of Spain to invade the realm. But the broad question for the decision of posterity is not whether she was justified in returning an evasive answer to Elizabeth's commissioners, but whether she was justified in authorising Ridolphi, which she unquestionably did, to seek at this time the active assistance of the Spanish King to relieve her from captivity. Upon this point there can be but one impartial opinion. When Richard I was detained a prisoner in Germany, it is well known that he appealed for aid to the Pope as well as to other princes; and who ever questioned his right to seek his deliverance by means of foreign aid? Yet the detention of Richard was a much more justifiable act than the imprisonment of the Scottish queen. He was made a prisoner while travelling in disguise, and without a safe-conduct, through the dominions of a prince with whom he was on most unfriendly terms. Mary was induced to come to England in consequence of the warm and repeated invitations of her sister queen, and her detention as a prisoner was a breach, not only of the law of nations, but of the still more sacred laws of hospitality.

Hossack, *Mary Queen of Scots*, ii, 123–4.

It was only by a supreme exercise of will-power that Elizabeth saved Mary from the scaffold on which Norfolk perished, and vetoed the retaliatory measures against her title to the English crown which both houses had formally approved. . . . There were moments, of course, when she wavered in her attitude. After the massacre of St. Bartholomew, when 'all men cried out' against the Scottish queen and her Guise relations, she would only too willingly have handed her over to Regent Mar to be executed in Edinburgh for her share in the Darnley murder. But the regent stood upon conditions; and rather than be held in any way responsible for the deed, Elizabeth allowed the matter to drop. She reverted to it in 1574, during Morton's regency, but again was unsuccessful; and Mary remained for the next twelve years the great 'untouchable' in English politics—rebellious, defiant, incorrigible in her hope of ultimate victory. The tragedy of her position lay in the fact that, while there was a chance of elevation to power by way of conspiracy, war, and revolution, she would not honestly accept the *pis aller* of a settlement by treaty. The hope of the English succession, always the dominant ambition of her life, was far too precious a thing to be bartered away for personal security or even freedom. With amazing effrontery she said she would not leave her prison save as queen of England.

Black, *The Reign of Elizabeth*, 373–4.

That she was engaged in more than one plot need not be doubted;
but we cannot blame her any more than we blame the bird that
beats its wings against the bars of its cage. For liberty she was ready
to venture much. She made no secret, indeed, that she was willing
to embark on any plot that would facilitate her escape. 'She says she
will use what means she can to help herself, meaning certainly
among other things to escape if she can, saying she had rather lose
her life than lead this life.' If her freedom could only be obtained
through Philip of Spain or Henry of France, Philip or Henry let it
be. If it could not be obtained so long as Elizabeth was on the
throne, let Elizabeth look to herself. Her rival, a powerful sovereign, had schemed for her disgrace, for her death; why should she,
a prisoner, be restrained by any nicer scruples?

Skelton, *Mary Stuart*, 162.

It might have been a tolerable life for anyone of a placid nature,
but not for Mary. She had, as she said, a great heart; her passion
was unassuageable. After so many disappointments and so many
years of captivity, she could still declare that she would not leave
her prison save as Queen of England; and despite the danger into
which plotting had led her, she persisted in the habit, intriguing
everywhere and with everyone who could serve her interests,
pledging herself to the Pope, to Philip II, to the King of France, to
Elizabeth, and all simultaneously, with complete lack of scruple.
According to the practice of the age, she was no doubt entitled, as
a Queen, to do this. Morals need not enter into the question, but
simply prudence. She wrote far too much and too impetuously,
committing her fate to the risks of secret correspondence, though
spies were everywhere, she herself handicapped by captivity, and
the English government's intelligence service the subtlest and
most efficient in existence. Her flagrant lies and her malice con-
fronted Elizabeth in letter after letter, intercepted, or copied by
spies. They afforded the most damning answer to all her pleas for
better treatment.

Neale, *Queen Elizabeth*, 258.

No one can blame the Scottish Queen for encouraging every plot formed for her release from the miserable life she was compelled to lead for the long period of nineteen years. Not one of these plots, to her knowledge, had anything to do with Elizabeth, and up to the day of her death she repudiated the charge that she ever did anything against Elizabeth's life. When this denial was so repeatedly given, Elizabeth's duty was to produce proof in support of the charge, or, failing that, to release the Queen. She neither did the one nor the other. Nothing was ever produced but these notable 'interpolations'. Notwithstanding these, she kept nagging and torturing the Scottish Queen to confess her guilt; and when that failed she executed her. During the captivity of Mary many plots were formulated for her release, principally by the Catholic party or individual members of that party, all of which are not recorded. It is natural to suppose that the patience of the Catholics was exhausted at the conduct of Elizabeth. Who could blame them if they got up a rebellion or an invasion of England by the aid of France and Spain to compel Queen Mary's release? And who could blame Savage and Ballard, two noted Catholics, if they said they would themselves assassinate Elizabeth, in order to release Mary? There might be reasons for assassinating Elizabeth; there were none for assassinating Mary.

Cowan, Last Days of Mary Stuart, 132–3.

Walsingham's technique, however, was more subtle, more far-sighted, and more perfidious. Of course, if he wished, he could nip the conspiracy in the bud. It would not suit his purposes, however, merely to send a few noblemen to the block or to have some of the lesser conspirators hanged, drawn, and quartered. What would be the use of cutting off five or six heads of the hydra of this unceasing conspiracy, if, next morning, two new heads would have taken the place of each? 'Carthage must be destroyed' was Cecil's and Walsingham's motto; they were determined to make an end of Mary Stuart; and for this purpose no minor conspiracy would suffice. They would need to prove the existence of widespread activities in favour of the imprisoned Queen of Scots. Instead, therefore, of stifling Babington's plot in the germ, Walsingham secretly encouraged it; manuring it with good wishes, supplying it with funds, furthering it by assumed indifference. Thanks to his skill as director of provocative agents, what had been no more than an amateurish conspiracy of a few country gentlefolk against Elizabeth, developed into the famous Walsingham plot for ridding the world of Mary Stuart.

Zweig, The Queen of Scots, 300–1.

Liberty and her rights were the objects for which Mary strove. She was ready to lose her life in that struggle. Why should she forbear lest Elizabeth should lose hers? She would accept Babington's offer, and do all in her power to make it a success.

Pollen, Queen Mary and the Babington Plot, cxlv.

Her Secretaries letters written to Babington, wer discowered and showen: but who did see them? wer they written or subscriwed with her hand, and signed with her seale of armes? Tell me that I praie you: You shall newer be able to prowe it; and althought yeet they be simple and poore meanes to effectuate the thinge you charge her with, and bringe to the full upshott such a weightie enterprise, sithence ther was no thinge but paper that could speake. What was writen in these letters you alledge? the deliwerie of the Queene of Scottes out of prison. I aske you againe, wer they all writen and signed with her hand? No, no. But giwing and grauntinge they had beene, was this a goode and conscionable cause to putt her to death, who had so often protested by her letters to Elizabeth, that shee wold never do anie thinge to the prejudice of her so longe as shee liwed? If the Catholiques of England did worke, plotte, or do anie othir thinge in fawour of her then her deliwerance, what coulde shee do withall? Shee knewe no thinge of it, much lesse consented to ther designes. . . . Last of all, I saie, albeit this renounned Queene had conspired against the liffe and state of Elizabeth, because she had used her so hardlie for the space of twintie yeares, against her othe and fidelitie promesed her, yeet hawinge in acte done no thinge, shee could not much be blamed in human sense and reason, she hawinge so tyrannouslie used her: the law of nature might excuse her, which is not onlie approved by the lawes grauntinge manie thinges, as saieth Seneca, which honestie, faith, pietie and religion do not permitte.

Blackwood, *History of Mary Queen of Scots,* 201–2.

A great deal of controversy has taken place over the Babington conspiracy. It was skilfully managed, and disgraced all who were connected with it. We cannot help identifying Elizabeth with its conception and development, for it is beyond doubt that Walsingham, her secretary, who had the sole direction of it, communicated to her all his negotiations, including the sending of a spy to Paris to Mary's friends to suggest Elizabeth's assassination. He, as the head of the spies, was admirably adapted for this work, but while his cunning practices served their purpose at the time, he cannot impose on posterity, for posterity will estimate him at his true value. His interpolations on Mary's letters provided for the assassination of Elizabeth, and on the strength of these Mary was condemned, and twelve men, including Babington, cruelly executed. There are those, and not an insignificant number, who condemn Mary because of this conspiracy; but what is their authority? Mary's letters to Babington, as she wrote them, never were produced. They were evidently destroyed by Walsingham because they had no reference to Elizabeth's assassination, Mary, on her solemn oath, emitted a declaration repudiating any connection with such a plot, and she demanded a sight of any letters of hers so as to verify her words. Her accusers were unable to produce any such letters. Notwithstanding this, Walsingham accused her of the assassination, an accusation he knew to be false. The Babington plot was for her release and nothing more, and she was quite entitled to encourage any such scheme. The assassination of Elizabeth formed no part of the plot of Anthony Babington. But to accomplish her condemnation it became an integral part of the Walsingham scheme, which embraced the most skilful interpolation of letters that is to be found in history.

Cowan, *Mary Queen of Scots,* ii, 327–9.

If the assassination was a crime, Mary was not free from guilt. If it was not a crime, but an inevitable incident in the struggle for liberty, Mary was free from blame. That was the reason uppermost in her mind. She considered herself an independent sovereign: with every right to recover her liberty, if necessary by an act of war; and not bound to interfere between the English Queen and her subjects. This, without doubt, was for her the determining factor in the situation.

Pollen, *Queen Mary and the Babington Plot*, cxliv.

18

TRIAL AND EXECUTION

Mary's trial, which followed the execution of Babington and his fellow conspirators, began in October 1586 at Fotheringhay to which she had been moved in preference to the Tower of London. The manner of the trial has been attacked on the grounds that the prosecution depended entirely upon written statements, especially upon those of Mary's secretaries, Nau and Curle, neither of whom were called in person. Mary, moreover, who pleaded ignorance of English law, was allowed no counsel and had her notes and papers taken from her. However, such objections are only valid by modern standards, and by sixteenth century rules the proceedings were quite in order. A more serious question can be raised; the competence of the court to try a foreign queen for treason against a monarch to whom she was not subject. This objection was quashed at the trial itself, but has frequently been advanced by her subsequent champions. On the other hand, it can be argued that as Mary was no longer accepted as queen in Scotland, her immunity on that score was open to doubt. In addition, Mary had been resident in England for some eighteen years, and her trial before an English court for crimes committed in that country was not unjust. If either, or both, these arguments lack conviction, refuge can be found in the Act of Association which made no distinction on grounds of sovereignty or nationality. In challenging the competence of the court Mary was, nevertheless, making her best possible defence. The overruling of this objection seriously weakened her case, and her own admissions of having attempted to gain her freedom by means of foreign intervention were sufficient to secure her conviction even without the statements which were held to disprove Mary's rather unconvincing denials of having corresponded with Babington and agreeing to Elizabeth's death. The verdict of guilty was probably as just, as it was expedient, as Mary's execution alone could give Elizabeth security. Of this all English Protestants, but their queen, were convinced. Irresolution and indecision by Elizabeth delayed the final act, which in her heart she must have known was inevitable and necessary. Finally on 1 February 1587, Elizabeth was induced to sign the death warrant, and as she had probably hoped her secretary and the Privy Council thereupon acted upon their own initiative. Mary was executed seven days later. The enigma of Mary in life was at an end, the enigma of Mary in the pages of history was just about to begin. Not for nothing did she have as her motto: in my end is my beginning.

Mary at her trial tacitly admitted that she had written a letter to Babington and that her letter contained a complete ratification of his plans for rebellion and for her own liberation. She could not very well deny this much. In letters to Thomas Morgan, to Charles Paget, to Sir Francis Englefield, and to Mendoza, the Spanish ambassador at Paris, of which the drafts were found among her papers at Chartley, she had practically confessed it. But she did deny vehemently that she had ever mentioned or in any way ratified a plot for the murder of Elizabeth. It is worth while to consider how much reliance is to be placed upon her mere denial. At the beginning of her trial she had denied that she ever had had any dealings with Babington at all. It was not until she was faced with the overwhelming evidence against her upon that point that she changed her pleading. This ought to be sufficient to show that Mary meant to admit no more than was actually proved against her. She was fighting for her life and she knew it. She knew also that her fate practically hung upon the question of her implication in the murder plot. Of course she denied it. To have admitted it would have been for her little short of suicide. Her pleading in itself is worth nothing, and will prove nothing either as to her guilt or her innocence. Mary did what every person accused of crime who had the shadow of a case would do. She pleaded innocent and challenged proof.

Read, *Mr. Secretary Walsingham*, iii, 35.

Thus terminated a trial which in legal history has probably no counterpart, and regarding which the following points especially strike us: the incompetence of the English tribunals, as then constituted, to judge an independent sovereign; the refusal of counsel to the prisoner, in violation of the laws of England, and in especial of the statutes of Mary Tudor and Elizabeth; the absence of the witnesses, whose presence in face of the accused was essential to all just procedure; the forced position of Mary, not before independent and trustworthy judges, but before Commissioners carefully chosen beforehand, and who, combining the offices of judge and jury, united in endeavouring to nullify the defence.

At Fotheringay we find the prisoner standing alone before her judges. At Westminster the witnesses appear in the absence of the accused, while at neither is a single original document produced; copies, not of written letters, but pretended copies from ciphers were admitted and believed on the faith of men whose confessions were drawn from them by fear of torture or documents forged by Philipps. Such was the evidence by which Mary was tried and condemned.

Maxwell-Scott, *The Tragedy of Fotheringay*, 82.

Mary was probably right in asserting that the commission had already made up its mind about her guilt before the trial began. The trial itself followed the usual pattern of English trials for treason in the sixteenth century. Obviously it does not conform to modern ideas of justice. Its object was not to establish Mary's guilt, but to display the evidence upon which the judgment was based. On the evidence presented she was, without much doubt, guilty. Her letter to Babington, confirmed by Babington's confession and by the confession of Mary's secretaries and by the implications of other letters which she wrote at the time, leaves little doubt about the matter. Mary's demand that her guilt must be determined by her own words or her own writing could not be met. She dictated what she would have written to Nau in French and Curle wrote out the letter in English and then put it into cipher. The best that could be hoped for was Nau's notes and many of them were recovered when his papers were seized,

though not, unfortunately, his notes on her fatal letter to Babington.
Read, *Lord Burghley*, 357.

If shee had confessed that to sett her selff at libertie, shee had
conspired against Elizabethes liffe, or attempted anie mater preju-
diciall to her estate, they had some apparance of reason for ther
proceedinges so summarlie. But shee hath ewer sworne upon her
honour and conscience the contrarie, yea at the werie point of
death, yeelding her soule in the handes of her Savioure, shee protested thus upon her salvatioun, shee onlie sought libertie, but not
to shedde anie blood for the attaininge theroff. But yeet to giwe
cullour to ther proceedinges, that they had werie honourablie dealte
in this mater, they signe the cruell sentence with ther handes, they
send it to the Christian King of Fraunce, to excuse them and ther
mistres; they write unto him thus, That the Queene of Scottes was
so contrarie to her in all her actiouns, that ther liwes could not be
compatible and subsist together, and that it was necessarie for one
of them should be assured of liffe and estate by the death of the
other. It is woorthe the notinge to showe the falsnes of the pretended accusatiounes, that they alledge they could find no other
meanes to saiwe Elizabeth aliwe, but by the death of the nearest
kinniswoman she had in the world. Fie, shameles mouthes, speake
plainlie the truth! Had you not longe before premeditated and
suborned, yea dewised a plotte to trap this ladie in? Your consciences and your God knoweth you did it, and that you longe before
imagined amongst your selwes to putt her to death, accusinge her,
and pronuncinge your sentence so cruellie against her, most
iniustlie condemninge her of these thinges which she newer
dreamed of.
Blackwood, *History of Mary Queen of Scots*, 217.

Of this sentence which depended wholly on the credit of the
Secretaries, was very much speech and different amongst men,
some judging them unworthy of credit, and others againe thought
them worthy to be beleeved. I have seene the Apologie of Nauus
written unto King *James,* in the yeere 1605 in which hee doth

laboriously excuse himselfe, in protesting that hee was neither the
Author, nor perswader, nor first discoverer of that plot or device,
neither that hee failed at all in his dutie through negligence or
incircumspection, but rather that he did impugne the heads of the
accusations against his Ladie this day. Which thing yet doth not
appeare by the publike records. But the same day it was declared
by the Commissioners, and by the Judges of the Realme, *That that
Sentence did derogate nothing from JAMES King of Scotland in his
right or honour, but him to be in the same place, estate and right,* as if
that Sentence had not beene given at all.

Stranguage, *Life and Death of Marie Stuart,* 204.

Meanwhile, Mary was at Fotheringhay—according to Paulet,
'utterly void of all fear of harm', and plaguing him with 'superfluous and idle speeches'. On November 16th, Elizabeth sent to
warn her of the sentence against her, of Parliament's petition, and
the possibility of death. She did not flinch. No repentance, no
submission, no acknowledgment of her fault, no craving for pardon
could be drawn from her. She sat down to make her appeal to the
world and posterity in eloquent and impassioned letters. She was
playing her last act, still with a great heart, still without scruple.
Her declarations to the Pope, though written in the solemn, con-
fessional mood of death, are, some of them, sorry lies. And yet
there was a sound instinct in the presentation of herself as a martyr
for the Catholic faith. The Catholic struggle in England had been
personified in her. She wished to die in that role. When Paulet
took down her cloth of state, she now being a woman dead to the
law and incapable of all dignities, she set in its place pictures of
Christ's Passion, and a Cross.

Neale, *Queen Elizabeth,* 277.

On the scaffold Mary is reported to have protested—

'As for the death of the Queen your sovereign, I call God to
witness that I never imagined it, never sought it, nor ever
consented to it.'

None of these protests are inconsistent with Mary's extant letter to Babington, in which Elizabeth's death is nowhere suggested, counselled, or commanded. Some disclaimers, like that to Archbishop Beaton, 'Je ne souffrirois que, pour mon particulier, une chiquenaud luy fust donnée,' 'I would not suffer her to receive a fillip for my particular interests,' are overstated. This may well have represented her normal attitude towards the Queen, but on the day when the hope of escape was dangled before her, other feelings passed through her mind. Still on the whole, considering her very trying circumstances and the secrets she still had to keep, the exaggeration is very slight. Taken together, her declarations of innocence do not overshoot the mark. She did not plead falsely.

Pollen, Queen Mary and the Babington Plot, cxcviii.

Finally on the 8th of February came the execution, the glorious day of Mary's everchanging fortunes. Never did she show greater courage, greater love, greater humanity. On this occasion her foils were Henry Grey, Earl of Kent, and Fletcher, Dean of Peterborough; fanatics indeed, both rude and inhuman, but just the men to stimulate her to her highest flights. They worried themselves little with the arguments about her complicity, but exulted openly in the hope of washing their hands in her blood. 'Your life would be the death of our religion,' said the Earl on the evening of his arrival, 'your death will be its life.'

These words gave Mary a keen satisfaction, and she returned to them that evening frequently and with smiles. 'Oh, how happy Lord Kent's words have made me! Here at last is the truth. They told me I was to die because I had plotted against the Queen, and here is Lord Kent sent to convert me, and he says I am to die on account of my religion.'

Yet this woman was no milk-and-water saint. That evening she had spoken bitterly of her son as having betrayed her. 'You should die at peace with all men,' cried the carping puritans. 'I forgive every one, and accuse no one,' was Mary's ready answer; 'yet I may follow David's example and pray God to confound and punish His enemies, and those of His divinity and religion; and to pardon my own enemies.' That same night she sent a long message to King Philip bidding him remember, if the Armada were successful, that Walsingham, Burghley, and their party had been his worst enemies as well as hers.

The last night was passed in arranging little presents for her servants, in writing her last letters, and in prayer, for she had been cruelly refused the services of her chaplain, de Préau. When Shrewsbury and Kent came to lead her out next morning, it was before the little altar that they found her. At first they wished to separate her at once from all her servants; but at her prayers and tears, she was allowed the service of four men-servants and two maids for her last unrobing.

After the sentence had been read by Beale, Fletcher came forward, and despite Mary's objections, began a long denunciation of popery, during which the Queen read her book of Hours. When quiet had been restored, she prayed for some time in English for the peace of Christendom, for the conversion of England, for her son, for Elizabeth, for all her enemies. Then came the disrobing, Mary bravely controlling her tearful ladies, while the brutal hangman Bull of Tyburn, stepping in, wrested from them the cross from Mary's neck, which he claimed and kept as his perquisite. Amid breathless silence Mary's gentle prayer, 'In manus tuas, Domine, commendo spiritum meum,' was heard throughout the hall; Shrewsbury by a sign gave the signal to Bull, and then turned away. Two blows and the neck was severed; a third and the head rolled upon the scaffold. Picking it up, Bull cried, 'God save Queen Elizabeth'; while Kent standing over the corpse with his white wand, and supported by the Dean, called out, 'So perish all her enemies. Amen.'

> Pollen, *Queen Mary and the Babington Plot*, cxcviii–cc.

Alive a Queene, now dead I am a Sainte;
  Once Mary calld, my name nowe Martyr is;
From earthly raigne debarred by restraint,
  In liew whereof I raigne in heavenly blisse.

My life my greife, my death hath wrought my joye,
  My frendes my foyle, my foes my weale procur'd;

My speedy death hath shortned longe annoye,
And losse of life an endles life assur'd.

Southwell, Poetical Works, 155–6.

Barbara: Now
That priest lifts up his voice against her prayer,
Praying: and a voice all round goes up with his:
But hers is lift up higher than climbs their cry,
In the great psalms of penitence: and now
She prays aloud in English; for the Pope
Our father, and his church; and for her son,
And for the queen her murderess; and that God
May turn from England yet his wrath away;
And so forgives her enemies; . . .

Swinburne, Mary Stuart, 200–1.

Never did any human creature meet death more bravely; yet, in the midst of the admiration and pity which cannot be refused her, it is not to be forgotten that she was leaving the world with a lie upon her lips. She was a bad woman, disguised in the livery of a martyr, and, if in any sense at all she was suffering for her religion, it was because she had shewn herself capable of those detestable crimes which in the sixteenth century appeared to be the proper fruits of it.

To assume and to carry through the character of a victim of religious intolerance, to exhibit herself as an example of saintliness, suffering for devotion to the truth, would be to win the victory over Elizabeth, even in defeat and death to fasten upon her the reputation of a persecutor which she had most endeavoured to avoid, to stamp her name with infamy, and possibly drag her down to destruction.

Nor can it be said she failed. She could not indeed, stay the progress of the Reformation, make England a province of Spain, or arrest the dissolution of an exploded creed; but she became a fitting tutelary saint for the sentimental Romanism of the modern world. She has had her revenge, if not on Elizabeth living, yet on her memory in the annals of her country, and English history will continue, probably to the end of time, to represent the treatment of Mary Stuart, which, if it erred at all, erred from the beginning on the side of weakness, as the one indelible stain on the reputation of a great Queen.

Froude, *History of England*, xii, 341–2.

Plots and intrigues were the familiar weapons of the Queen of Scots. One who could conspire . . . with France and Spain, to levy war upon the Queen of England, at the time when she was making the fairest professions of amity and good faith, was not the person to hesitate, when the indiscretion of Babington, and the ardour of Gilbert Giffard, placed within her reach the attractions of a great and encouraging plot. That she was an accomplice with Babington and his companions cannot be doubted, and it was for the welfare of England that she should be restrained from further mischief. It does not concern us to justify the devices by which her evil practices were counteracted, or to commend the manners of the age that brought her to the block. Rough justice was done. A most dangerous person was removed from the realm; and by way of compensation for the sternness of Mary Stuart's treatment, her memory has been handed down to posterity surrounded with a fictitious halo arising from misfortune. The recollection of her evil deeds, and evil designs, is obscured by her sad fate, and long as the page of history remains, Mary Stuart will enjoy an advantage over her successful rival in the sentimental regard of kindhearted people.

Leader, *Mary Queen of Scots in Captivity*, 620–1.

BIBLIOGRAPHY

BIBLIOGRAPHY

Hundreds of books in many different languages have been written about Mary, queen of Scots. For those published before 1700, John Scott, *Bibliography of Works relating to Mary, queen of Scots, 1544-1700* (Edinburgh Bibliographical Society No. 2, 1896) should be consulted, while a list of the more important sources and writings published before and after that date is to be found in S. A. and D. R. Tannenbaum, *Marie Stuart, Queen of Scots* (Elizabethan Bibliographies, no. 30-32, New York, 1944-46) and Conyers Read, *Bibliography of British History, Tudor Period 1485-1603* (2nd ed., Oxford, 1959). Details of the more important works cited in both these bibliographies will be found in the introduction to this volume, and consequently the following list of works has been restricted to those from which extracts have been taken. Where the source in question is literary or an article this may not have been mentioned in the introduction. It should likewise be noted that the edition cited below from which the extracts have been selected may not necessarily be the first to which reference was invariably made in the introduction.

Anderson, James, *Collections relating to the history of Mary Queen of Scotland,* 4 vols. (Edinburgh, 1727-8)

Bell, H. Glasford, *Life of Mary, queen of Scots,* 2 vols. (Edinburgh, 1831)

Black, J. B., *The Reign of Elizabeth* (Oxford History of England, 2nd ed., 1959)

Blackwood, Adam, *History of Mary Queen of Scots, a fragment* (Maitland Club, 1834)

Brown, P. Hume, *John Knox: a biography,* 2 vols. (London, 1895)

Brown, P. Hume, *History of Scotland,* 3 vols. (Cambridge, 1912)

Buchanan, George, *Ane detectioun of the doinges of Marie quene of Scottes* in Anderson, *Collections,* ii, 1–163

Buchanan, George, *History of Scotland,* ed. John Watkins (London, 1827)

Burton, J. Hill, *The History of Scotland,* 8 vols. (Edinburgh, 1873–4)

Calderwood, David, *The true history of the church of Scotland from the beginning of the reformation unto the end of the reign of King James VI* . . . ed. T. Thomson and D. Laing, 8 vols. (Wodrow Society, 1842–9)

Chalmers, George, *Life of Mary Queen of Scots,* 2 vols. (London, 1818)

Conn, G., *Vitae Mariae Stuartae* in S. Jebb, *De Vita et Rebus Gestis Mariae,* 2 vols. (London, 1725)

Cowan, Samuel, *Mary Queen of Scots and Who wrote the Casket Letters?,* 2 vols. (London, 1901)

Cowan, Samuel, *The Last Days of Mary Stuart and the Journal of Bourgoyne her physician* (London, 1907)

Crawford, David, *Memoirs of the Affairs of Scotland* (Edinburgh, 1753)

Creighton, Mandell, *Queen Elizabeth* (London, 1899)

Cust, Lionel, *Notes on the Authentic Portraits of Mary, queen of Scots* (London, 1903)

Davison, M. H. Armstrong, *The Casket Letters* (London, 1965)

Donaldson, Gordon, *Scottish Kings* (London, 1967)

Donaldson, Gordon, *The First Trial of Mary Queen of Scots* (London, 1969)

Duncan, Thomas, Mary Stuart and the House of Huntly in *Scottish Historical Review,* iv, 365–73

Duncan, Thomas, The Relations of the Earl of Murray with Mary Stuart in *Scottish Historical Review,* vi, 49–57

Fleming, D. Hay, *Mary Queen of Scots from her birth till her flight into England* (London, 1898).

Fraser, Antonia, *Mary Queen of Scots* (London 1969)

Froude, J. A., *History of England from the fall of Wolsey to the death of Elizabeth,* 12 vols. (London, 1856–70)

Gatherer, W., *The Tyrannous Reign of Mary Stewart* (Edinburgh, 1958)

Goodall, Walter, *An examination of the letters said to be written by*

Mary, queen of Scots to James, earl of Bothwell, 2 vols. (Edinburgh, 1754)

Gore-Brown, R., *Lord Bothwell* (London, 1937)

Henderson, T. F., *Mary Queen of Scots*, 2 vols. (London, 1905)

Henderson, T. F., Mr. Lang and the Casket Letters in *Scottish Historical Review*, v, 161–74.

Henderson, T. F., *The Casket Letters* (Edinburgh, 1889)

Herries, Lord, *Historical Memoirs of the reign of Mary, queen of Scots* (Abbotsford Club, 1836)

Hossack, John, *Mary Queen of Scots and her Accusers*, 2 vols. (Edinburgh, 1870–74)

Hume, David, *History of England*, with continuation by T. Smollett, 3 vols. (London, 1824)

Hume, Martin, *The Love Affairs of Mary, queen of Scots* (London, 1903)

Keith, Robert, *History of the Affairs of Church and State in Scotland down to 1567*, ed. J. P. Lawson, 3 vols. (Spottiswoode Society, 1844–50)

Jancy, Thomas, Master Randolphes Phantasy in *Satirical Poems of the Time of the Reformation*, ed. J. Cranstoun, 2 vols. (Scottish Text Society, 1891–3), 1–29

Jebb, Samuel, *De Vita et Rebus Gestis Serenissima Principis Mariae Scotorum Reginae*, 2 vols. (London, 1725)

Knox, John, *Works*, ed. D. Laing, 6 vols. (Edinburgh, 1846–64)

Laing, Malcolm, *History of Scotland with a preliminary dissertation on the participation of Mary, Queen of Scots, in the Murder of Darnley*, 4 vols. (London, 1819)

Lamartine, Alphonse de, *Mary Stuart* (Edinburgh, 1859)

Lang, Andrew, *Portraits and Jewels of Mary Stuart* (Glasgow, 1906)

Lang, Andrew, The Household of Mary Queen of Scots in 1573 in *Scottish Historical Review*, ii, 345–55

Lang, Andrew, *The Mystery of Mary Stuart* (London, 1901)

Leader, J. D., *Mary Queen of Scots in Captivity 1569–1584* (London, 1880)

Lee, Maurice, *James Stewart, earl of Moray* (London, 1953)

Leslie, John, *A Defence of the honour of the right highe, mightye and noble Princesse Marie Quene of Scotland* in Anderson, *Collections*, i, 1–150.

McCrie, Thomas, *Life of John Knox*, 2 vols. (Edinburgh, 1831)

Mahon, R. H., *Mary Queen of Scots: a study of the Lennox Narrative* (Cambridge, 1924)

Mahon, R. H., *The Tragedy of Kirk o' Field* (Cambridge, 1930)

Maitland, Sir Richard, *Poems* (Maitland Club, 1830)

Mathieson, W. L., *Politics and Religion. A Study in Scottish history from the Reformation to the Revolution*, 2 vols. (Glasgow, 1902)

Maxwell-Scott, Mrs., *The Tragedy of Fotheringay* (London, 1905)

Melville, Sir James, *Memoirs of his own Life,* ed. T. Thomson (Bannatyne Club, 1827)

Mignet, François, *The History of Mary, Queen of Scots,* 2 vols. (London, 1851)

Nau, Claude, *Memorials of Mary Stewart*, ed. J. Stevenson (Edinburgh, 1883)

Neale, J. E., *Queen Elizabeth* (London, 1934)

Petit, J. A., *History of Mary Stuart, queen of Scots*, translated by Charles de Flandre, 2 vols. (Edinburgh, 1873)

Pollen, J. H., *Mary Queen of Scots and the Babington Plot* (Scottish History Society, 1922)

Pollen, J. H., *Papal Negotiations with Mary Queen of Scots* (Scottish History Society, 1901)

Pollen, J. H., *Queen Mary's Letter to the Duke of Guise* (Scottish History Society, 1904)

Pollen, J. H., The Dispensation for the Marriage of Mary Stuart with Darnley and its Date in *Scottish Historical Review*, iv, 241–8

Read, Conyers, *Mr. Secretary Cecil and Queen Elizabeth* (London, 1955)

Read, Conyers, *Mr. Secretary Walsingham and Queen Elizabeth*, 3 vols. (Oxford, 1925)

Read, Conyers, *Lord Burghley and Queen Elizabeth* (London, 1960)

Ridley, Jasper, *John Knox* (Oxford, 1969)

Robertson, Thomas, *The History of Mary Queen of Scots* (Edinburgh, 1793)

Robertson, William, *History of Scotland*, 3 vols. (London, 1809)

Ruthven, Patrick lord, *A relation of the death of David Rizzi* in Keith, *History*, iii, 260–78.

Schiller, Johann Friedrich, *Maria Stuart*, translated by F. A. Kemble (London, 1863)

Scott, Alexander, Ane New Yeir Gift to Quene Mary in *The Poems of Alexander Scott* ed. James Cranstoun (Scottish Text Society, 1896), 1–8

Scott, Sir Walter, *The Abbot*, Border edition, 2 vols. (London, 1893)

Sempill, Robert, Ballads in *Satirical Poems of the Time of the Reformation*, ed. J. Cranstoun, 2 vols. (Scottish Text Society, 1891–3)

Skelton, Sir John, *Maitland of Lethington and the Scotland of Mary Queen of Scots*, 2 vols. (Edinburgh, 1887–8)

Skelton, Sir John, *Mary Stuart* (London, 1893)

Southwell, Robert, *The Poetical Works of the Rev. Robert Southwell*, ed. William Turnbull (London, 1856)

Spenser, Edmund, *The Faerie Queene* (Routledge, London, n.d.)

Spottiswoode, John, *History of the church of Scotland . . . to the end of the reign of James the VI*, 3 vols. (Spottiswoode Society, 1847–51)

Stevenson, Joseph, *Mary Stuart* (Edinburgh, 1886)

Stevenson, Joseph, ed., *The History of Mary Stuart* (Edinburgh, 1883)

Stoddart, Jane, *The Girlhood of Mary Queen of Scots* (London, 1908)

Stranguage, W., *The historie of the life and death of Marie Stuart, Queene of Scotland* (London, 1624)

Strickland, Agnes, *Letters of Mary, Queen of Scots*, 3 vols. (London, 1872–3)

Strickland, Agnes, *Life of Mary Queen of Scots*, 2 vols. (London, 1888)

Swinburne, Algernon, *Bothwell* (London, 1874)

Swinburne, Algernon, *Chastelard* (London, 1865)

Swinburne, Algernon, *Mary Stuart* (London, 1881)

Terry, Charles S., *A History of Scotland* (Cambridge, 1920)

Turnbull, William B., *Letters of Mary Stuart* (London, 1845)

Tytler, Patrick F., *The History of Scotland*, 4 vols. (London, 1877)

Tytler, William, *An historical and critical enquiry into the evidence against Mary, queen of Scots*, 2 vols. (Edinburgh, 1790)

Whitaker, John, *Mary, queen of Scots Vindicated*, 3 vols. (London, 1787)

Wilkinson, M., 'Mystery of Maitland' in *Scottish Historical Review*, xxiv, 19–29.

Zweig, Stefan, *The Queen of Scots* (London, 1935)